SUMMER LEARNING AND THE EFFECTS OF SCHOOLING

SUMMER LEARNING AND THE EFFECTS OF SCHOOLING

BARBARA HEYNS

Department of Sociology
University of California, Berkeley
Berkeley, California

With a Foreword by Christopher S. Jencks

ACADEMIC PRESS New York San Francisco London
A Subsidiary of Harcourt Brace Jovanovich, Publishers

ACADEMIC PRESS, INC.
111 Fifth Avenue, New York, New York 10003

United Kingdom Edition published by
ACADEMIC PRESS, INC. (LONDON) LTD.
24/28 Oval Road, London NW1 7DX

Library of Congress Cataloging in Publication Data

Heyns, Barbara.
Summer learning and the effects of schooling.

Bibliography: p.
1. Summer schools. 2. Educational equalization.
I. Title.
LC5715.H49 370.19'34 78-3339
ISBN 0-12-346550-8

PRINTED IN THE UNITED STATES OF AMERICA

To my parents

FRANCES CARPENTER HEYNS

ROBERT ERNEST HEYNS

Contents

Foreword

Why study what students learn during the summer? The answer is deceptively simple. Summer is the only time when Ivan Illich's (1970) vision of a "deschooled" society comes true. Thus, if we want to know what might happen to children in such a society, we can gain invaluable clues by studying what happens during the summer. Conversely, if we want to know what has happened during the past century as a result of compulsory schooling, comparing the lives of children during the academic year to their lives during the summer provides some of the best available evidence.

This landmark study is the first thorough investigation of summer learning. By following sixth and seventh graders in the Atlanta public schools through 2 academic years and an intervening summer, Barbara Heyns is able to show that compulsory schooling really *does* make a difference, just as educators have always claimed. This difference is especially dramatic for poor children. Affluent children learn more than poor children both during the school year and during the summer, but the difference is far smaller during the school year than during the summer. This same pattern holds when one compares whites to blacks. Heyns's data therefore suggest that if all schools were closed down, converting childhood into an endless summer, the eventual achievement gap between initially advantaged children and initially disadvantaged children would be even greater than it now is. While compulsory schooling does not suffice to equalize incentives or opportunities for learning, it seems to be a step in this direction.

This conclusion is at odds with the currently conventional wisdom about schooling. This view rests primarily on the findings of James Coleman and his colleagues, reported in *Equality of Educational Opportunity* (EEO) in 1966. The massive EEO survey showed that black students scored about one standard deviation below white students on standardized tests when they entered first grade, and that they still scored one standard deviation below whites in twelfth grade. If the black–white gap in first grade reflects differences in home environment, whereas the black–white gap in twelfth grade reflects differences in both home environment and school environment, the EEO results imply that racial differences in school environment are about as great as racial differences in home environment.

The EEO survey also collected considerable evidence about the impact of socioeconomic status (SES) on achievement. It found that the correlation between SES and achievement *increased* as students grew older. Most analysts assumed, however, that this "finding" was attributable to poor measurement of socioeconomic background among younger children, and that with accurate measurement the correlation between SES and achievement, like the correlation between race and achievement, would not vary with age. This implied that rich and poor children's incentives and opportunities to learn were about as unequal at school as at home. This inference, however, is clearly at odds with Heyns's findings.

In an effort to resolve this apparent contradiction, Heyns reexamined the evidence from the EEO and elsewhere regarding the correlation between SES and achievement. She found that when one obtains measures of parental status directly from the parents, or makes plausible corrections for errors in children's reports, the correlation between SES and academic achievement actually *falls* between sixth and twelfth grade. This is precisely what we would expect if SES had less effect on what students learn in school than on what they learn elsewhere. On close scrutiny, then, all the available evidence indicates that schools do more than other institutions to equalize incentives and opportunities for rich and poor children to learn.

The picture for blacks and whites is less clear-cut. Heyns's findings suggest that the learning differential between black and white children in Atlanta is smaller during the school year than during the summer. Another independent study, which I will discuss shortly, found the same pattern in New York City. But neither the EEO nor any other survey suggests that the achievement gap between blacks and whites falls as a result of prolonged schooling, even if this gap is measured in standardized terms. Perhaps this just means that the Atlanta and New York City schools are better for blacks than most other schools, but that seems unlikely. Rather, the most likely explanation is that the forces influencing summer learning during the elementary school years are not the same as those that influence learning prior to first grade. Test score differences among first graders are likely to reflect differences in native ability and home environment. By the time children reach fifth, sixth, and seventh grade, when Heyns studied them, differences in how much they learn during the summer are also likely to reflect differences in the neighborhood peer culture to which students are exposed at this age. It would not be astonishing if black urban "street corner society" differed more from its white counterpart than black urban homes do. Nor would it be surprising if street corner society exerted more influence on black elementary school children than on whites of the same age. This would explain the available evidence. The one standard deviation difference between entering black and white first graders would reflect the difference in their home environments—or conceivably differences in their genetic endowments, although I find that less likely. Exposure to school would reduce this difference. But exposure to street corner society during the summer would increase it again, at least after students reached the age at which peers became a major part of the environment. The equalizing influence of the schools would thus be offset by the unequalizing influence of the peer culture, leaving the overall gap between blacks and whites about the same as when they entered school. This explanation is, of course, completely speculative. Neither Heyns nor anyone else has collected the data needed to test it. But it strikes me as the most parsimonious explanation of her otherwise puzzling results.

If Heyns's findings are correct—and the evidence she presents strikes me as very persuasive—they have profound implications for public policy. Both the EEO survey and its many successors suggest that equalizing the *quality* of the schooling we give students from different backgrounds would only slightly reduce the present disparity in academic outcomes. In theory, of course, we could go beyond equalization to establish truly "compensatory" arrangements, in which initially disadvantaged students would receive *higher* quality instruction than initially advantaged children. But advantaged classmates are themselves a "resource" to disadvantaged children, so there are strong arguments for trying to keep advantaged and disadvantaged children in the same classrooms. A "compensatory" policy must therefore operate *within* classrooms, and there are clearly limits on how far most teachers will go in this direction. In light of this, it is hard to be optimistic about the chances of greatly reducing disparities in academic outcomes by changing the quality of the schooling we give different groups.

Heyns's findings suggest that we might do considerably better if we tried to equalize the *quantity* of schooling we provided to different children. At a minimum, we should not take it for granted that the right way to distribute educational opportunities is to encourage students with high test scores to stay in school and learn more, while encouraging students with low scores to drop out. This makes life easier for educators, but it exacerbates the very inequalities that egalitarian reforms seek to reduce. Open enrollment is obviously an attempt to reverse this pattern.

If we really want to equalize outcomes, however, we will have to get initially disadvantaged students to stay in school *longer* than their advantaged classmates. It is hard to imagine this really happening. Some high school graduates from poor backgrounds may take advantage of adult education to bring their academic skills up to the same level as their more privileged age-mates, but this is not likely to become widespread, much less compulsory. Nonetheless, Heyns's findings suggest that egalitarians should probably concentrate on changing the distribution of time spent in school, rather than concentrating primarily on what happens to different kinds of students while they attend school. At least at the elementary school level, family background exerts less effect on what children learn in school than on what they learn elsewhere.

Heyns carried out the research she describes in this book under the auspices of the Center for the Study of Public Policy, a nonprofit research group in Cambridge, Massachusetts. The research was conceived, however, at Harvard University's Center for Educational Policy Research (CEPR), of which I was briefly Executive Director, and where both Heyns and I were research associates from 1969 to 1973. CEPR is known mainly for research that reached much more "pessimistic" conclusions than those reached here. This was especially true of our book, *Inequality* (Jencks *et al.*, 1972), of which both Heyns and I were coauthors. It may therefore be of some historical interest to describe the relationship of this study to the work reported in *Inequality*.

The Center for Educational Policy Research was founded in 1968, as an outgrowth of a project that was reanalyzing the Coleman *et al.* EEO survey. During CEPR's early years, it was almost exclusively concerned with assessing the likely impact of changes in school quality on various students' achievement. Like Coleman and his colleagues, we reached relatively pessimistic conclusions about the likely effects of most commonly proposed school reforms. By 1971, however, our attention had begun to shift away from the effects of school quality to the effects of quantitative differences in exposure to schooling. This shift in interest reflected the fact that our research consistently showed that while improving school *quality* had little long-term impact on any tangible outcome, an extra *year* of schooling still raised men's occupational status and earnings, even after controlling family background and initial ability. Whereas *Inequality* emphasized the fact that even men with the same amount of schooling ended up with quite unequal incomes, it did not seriously question the conventional view that staying in school improved a man's chances of economic success.

What puzzled us was *why* schooling affected economic success. According to the traditional view, schools promoted economic success by teaching cognitive skills that employers valued. But Otis Dudley Duncan's (1968a) model of the factors affecting individual success suggested that only 3% of the occupational benefit of schooling and 10% of the earnings benefit was traceable to the fact that schooling raised scores on general aptitude tests like the Armed Forces Qualification Test. Our own models implied almost the same thing. Both Duncan's models and our own involved synthesizing data from disparate sources, which is a risky business. But longitudinal data from Malmö, Sweden, also suggested that only 15–20% of the effect of schooling on adult occupational status and earnings was attributable to the fact that schooling enhanced the skills measured by the Swedish military aptitude test.[1] Some of us concluded that schooling must improve life chances by inculcating noncognitive traits that employers valued.[2] Some of us speculated that schools might teach specialized cognitive skills (e.g., knowledge of law and medicine) that were valuable independent of general academic aptitude. Some concluded that employers must value educational credentials per se, independent of a worker's potential productivity. *Inequality* waffled.

Our interest in the effects of what we called the "exposure" question had been intensified by a paper that Donald P. Hayes and Judith Grether had presented at the 1969 convention of the Eastern Sociological Association. They examined changes in New York City elementary school students' mean achievement from fall to spring and from spring to the following fall. They found that students learned more during the academic year than during the summer, which came as no surprise.

[1] Estimated from data now most conveniently available in Fägerlind (1975).

[2] Herbert Gintis, who was then one of our colleagues at CEPR, was a forceful exponent of this view. See, for example, Gintis (1971) or Bowles and Gintis (1976).

More striking was the fact that students in black schools gained almost as much during the academic year as students in white schools. The difference between mean achievement levels in black and white schools was largely attributable to the fact that students in white schools learned more over the summer. As we noted in *Inequality*, this implied that universal schooling probably reduced cognitive inequality between advantaged and disadvantaged students, just as liberal social theorists had always assumed.

Unfortunately, Hayes and Grether's work was by no means definitive. To begin with, it was based on the mean achievement of schools, not on individual performance, and we knew that aggregation of this kind could sometimes distort results. Furthermore, New York was only one city, and hardly a representative one. We therefore decided to initiate several efforts to pinpoint who learned what during the summer, in the hope that this would throw light on the overall impact of exposure to schooling. One of these projects was Jane David's (1974) study of Philadelphia summer programs. The other was Heyns's work on Atlanta.

Heyns's findings are consistent with those of Hayes and Grether, but far more convincing and detailed. She was able to follow individual students rather than just looking at aggregate data for schools. Furthermore, she obtained data from each student's parents about their education, occupation, and income as well as their race, so she could analyze the effects of socioeconomic background in considerable detail. Then, too, she had students' scores on a wide range of tests, and was able to examine these tests from a number of different angles. (As she shows in this volume, what one finds depends to a significant extent on how one measures educational progress.) As a result, what previously seemed like an intriguing hypothesis about the equalizing impact of schooling on achievement can now be treated as a quite well established fact.

This book also explores many other aspects of summer learning: what students actually do during the summer, how their activities affect what they learn, and whether conventional achievement tests provide reliable evidence about how much students have learned. While most readers are likely to find the interaction between family background and summer learning the most intriguing aspect of Heyns's study, it is filled with other fruitful hypotheses and findings, and will repay extremely close reading.

Christopher S. Jencks

Acknowledgments

Research on the effects of education has burgeoned in recent years, with conclusions that have not always proved to be particularly constructive or favorable to public schools. With some justification, educators have come to regard social scientists as a cadre of hostile critics, conducting forays into the schoolyards of this country. The major debt incurred during the course of this study is to the numerous teachers, principals, and administrators of the Atlanta school system who cooperated so willingly and gave so generously of their time and expertise, despite their skepticism. Dr. John Letson, then superintendent of schools, was instrumental in securing support for the study from the school board; had he not intervened at a crucial juncture, biannual testing might not have been extended through the fall of 1972 and this study could not have taken place. Jarvis Barnes, director of research and development, was especially helpful in the early stages of planning. Tom McConnell, then director of the computer center, provided enormous assistance in assembling the data files. Richard Cole and Jackie Reynolds were responsible for retrieving and organizing the school records required for the study.

The parents of the sixth- and seventh-grade sample children were gracious and cooperative, despite misgivings about the usefulness of discussing summer activities in order to study schooling. The parental interviews were extensively modified, formatted, and conducted by

Response Analysis of Princeton, New Jersey; Marilyn Jackson and associates of Atlanta, Georgia fielded and supervised the survey with great skill.

Funds for the research were provided by the Office of Economic Opportunity, although the grant was later transferred to the National Institute of Education. During the course of the research, the project changed funding agencies, institutions, and project officers. Patricia Koshel of the National Institute of Education and John Case of the Center for the Study of Public Policy provided indispensible aid in sorting through the bureaucratic paperwork, pyramiding subcontracts, and other complications involved in these transitions. For a brief period of time, Ms. Koshel supervised, from Washington, D.C., a project funded in Cambridge, Massachusetts, and a principal investigator employed in Berkeley, California, who was completing fieldwork in Atlanta, Georgia, while the survey results were being coded and put on tapes in Princeton, New Jersey. Without enormous cooperation and several WATS lines, this research would never have reached fruition.

Intellectually, I am indebted to Christopher Jencks, David Cohen, and the staff of the Center for Educational Policy Research at Harvard University for advice, vigorous criticism, and sustained encouragement. Comments and criticism on part or all of the final manuscript were provided by Henry Acland, Margaret Cerullo, James S. Coleman, Judy Grether, Maureen Hallinan, Robert W. Hodge, Robert M. Jackson, Christopher Jencks, Nancy Karweit, David Kirp, Carl Milofsky, Richard Spieglman, Judy Stacey, Art Stinchcombe, Harry Summerfield, Kay Trimberger, Jeff Weintraub, Rhea Wilson, and Erik Olin Wright. Joyce Bird provided invaluable research assistance. Alex Lapidus helped enormously with the index. Kris Dymond, Norma Montgomery, and Diane Nuckles typed the results.

At this point, I am supposed to say that my spouse was invaluable; actually, my spouse *was* invaluable. I am indebted to Jeff Weintraub for badgering me into focusing on the central arguments and for being unalterably convinced of their importance. Jeff has served as critic and supporter; as orthographer, proofreader, and codirector of the domestic front; as an attentive audience for both good ideas and obsessive ravings; and as my best friend during the research and writing.

The final product is, of course, my responsibility. I can only hope that it lives up to the expectations of all the people who have participated in its completion.

A Parable

A sunlamp manufacturer wanted to test his new, improved product before marketing the item. He gathered a group of white subjects and divided them into two groups, equal in average social class, sex, and age. To the first group he gave samples of his sunlamp, and to the second, samples of a rival manufacturer's product. Although the experiment lasted only 2 weeks, it was another week before all participants were tested for suntan. In the intervening 7 days, the subjects put down their sunlamps to pursue other activities; some went to the beach, others to the local pool hall. Once the suntan test results were analyzed, they showed that social class was the chief determinant of suntanning. The brand of the lamp explained virtually none of the variation in skin color in an implied regression estimation of the form:

$$T = a + b_1(S) + b_2(L)$$

where T is the measure of tan, S is social class, and L is a variable indicating the manufacturer's brand of lamp.

When this study was published, some critics complained that the measure T was inappropriate. The effect of the lamp was supposed to be a change in skin color, yet no pretesting was done. Without measures taken before and after the treatment, one cannot assess change. Other critics argued that even though L ex-

plained little of the variance in tan, if the estimated effect of the lamp was large (b_2), *then the manufacturer's best unbiased estimate was that his lamp was effective. Yet other critics pointed out that skin color was genetically determined; the influence of even the most effective sunlamp would be temporary and relatively trivial.*

One day someone realized that the test was taken after 3 weeks, but exposure to the lamps was only 2 weeks long. The social class measure might be indicating differences in exposure to the sun during the third week. However, no one had asked the subjects what they did during the third week. The only reasonable conclusion was that the manufacturer just did not know the effect of his lamp.

PART I

Schooling, Socioeconomic Status, and Achievement

1
Introduction

It has become fashionable in social policy circles to view the 1960s as a period of unprecedented but largely unsuccessful attempts to intervene in the process generating inequality in American society. Commentators disagree as to whether the efforts were misguided from the outset or merely mismanaged; whether the programs were underbudgeted or oversold; in short, whether the War on Poverty represented a full-scale campaign or a minor skirmish. Curiously, the only matter about which a consensus exists is that despite the funds and the fanfare, little if any enduring social change occurred during the period that can be unequivocally attributed to social policy. Disillusionment has replaced optimism; analysts have turned from debating program objectives to speculating about the limits of social policy. The gloomy prognosis that little can be done to improve the lives of people has become the rationale for both retreat and retrenchment.

Insofar as such arguments are empirically grounded, education occupies a pivotal position in the debate. The reasons are threefold: First, educational programs were the salient political strategy throughout the period; second, the most convincing evidence of the failure of social policy emerged from evaluations of educational programs; and third, the consistently negative findings from such evaluations followed, or sometimes precipitated, rather global criticism of all educational institutions. The observation that specific programs were at best marginally effective was scarcely novel; taken alone, it would not have attracted very much attention or controversy. Yet such studies were quickly followed by the more baffling conclusion that schools in general played a modest role in altering either the achievement levels or lifetime opportunities of American students.

The current malaise afflicting educational research and policy stems in part from the grandiose and perhaps unwarranted expectations that surrounded certain programs, coupled with the insignificant gains in cognitive achievement found to result; however, it was the conclusions drawn from large-scale surveys of a broad range of schools that proved to be the most crippling indictment of education. Not only were new and innovative programs judged ineffective, but traditional programs as well. The most devastating results seemingly applied to all schools, even those that had been considered exemplary. The quality of education, as measured by differences observed among schools, was shown to have little independent relationship to achievement once socioeconomic status was controlled. The survey conducted for *Equality of Educational Opportunity* (Coleman *et al.*, 1966) challenged the notion that improving the schools would have very much impact on the achievement of children. Further analysis (Jencks *et al.*, 1972) confirmed this assessment but argued in addition that schools did not directly influence the distribution of adult outcomes; widening the traditional avenues of mobility or increasing educational opportunity would be unlikely to have much impact on the life chances of students.

These conclusions undermined the basic premises of educational policy. If one cannot identify any indisputably successful programs, the future of educational policy is bleak. Although this research has generated considerable controversy, the central findings have withstood attack. It has proved to be enormously difficult to demonstrate that particular schools or programs have an enduring impact on the educational performance of children. The goal of this book is to examine the effects of schooling and not to review policy alternatives; however, it is worthwhile to summarize the assumptions that led to the programs and policies of the 1960s.

Great Society programs embodied the assumptions of what has been termed the "human capital" approach to eradicating poverty. As Lyndon Johnson aptly phrased it, Americans were expected to "*learn* their way out of poverty [Norris, 1976, p. xvii]." Improved skills were equated with increased opportunity for mobility and higher income. This orientation involved retraining or retooling adults with obsolescent skills and inappropriate outlooks. Adolescents were admonished to stay in school and to be "upward bound," at least as far as college.

Compensatory education and remedial programs of all sorts flourished in the elementary schools. Very young children were judged to need a "head start" that would enable them to keep up with their more advantaged peers.

Educational programs were politically expedient and tended to be far less controversial than policies aimed at community organizing or redistributing income. Social welfare programs were intended to rehabilitate the poor, rather than to comprehend or remedy systemic inequalities. When the concern focused on the institutional fabric of this society, the public sector was viewed as the logical target for reform. Schools, welfare organizations, and other social services were singled out for both criticism and concrete proposals for change far more than were businesses or corporations. Public agencies were both highly visible and vulnerable to overt political pressure in a way that private enterprise was not. Reforming the social services is certainly a worthwhile goal, but it remains to be shown that they were or are either the major source of inequality or the primary obstacle to social change. I suspect the emphasis on educational programs was misplaced, for reasons having more to do with political expediency than with cogent analysis. Revamping public education seemed far less risky than tinkering with the economic system.

Educational programs, more than other policy interventions, were subjected to numerous quantitative evaluations. The objectives of most social action programs were vague, diffuse, and extremely difficult to operationalize in such a way as to permit rigorous evaluation. The goals specified for education were not an exception in this regard; however, unlike other policy arenas, the tools and techniques of educational evaluation were well established and widely accepted. Classrooms were a convenient laboratory for assessing the effects of programs and allowed far greater experimental control than was possible in other fields. Quasi-experimental designs, with clearly defined if not randomly chosen control groups, offered an elegant solution to the issue of the causal impact of intervention. Students were a captive clientele and could reasonably be assumed to constitute the universe of interest. The ethical dilemmas posed by experimentation were often intractable in other policy spheres, whereas schools provided a compliant and generally accessible institutional framework. Although most educational programs were probably never evaluated, the results for several stellar programs were distressing. The Westinghouse–Ohio evaluation of Head Start (Westinghouse Learning Corporation, 1969), for example, found little evidence that preschooling substantially influenced the cognitive skills of children much beyond their entry to formal education. Although certain programs reported some success, the bulk of evaluations offered precious little room for optimism concerning the likely impact of schooling on the achievement of children. Such results, in conjunction with the much cited conclusions of *Equality of Educational Opportunity* (Coleman *et al.*, 1966), contributed to the rising skepticism that schools or educational programs could substantially increase either individual opportunity or the equality of outcomes generally.

In sum, education is central to an assessment of the policies and programs of the 1960s because so much emphasis was placed on equality of opportunity and because educational programs tended to be the largest beneficiaries of congressional largesse. Education could be readily evaluated because of the nature of the services and the tools available for analysis. Education, in turn, became the symbol of both the failure and the frustrations of public policy and fell heir to the most virulent public criticism and attacks. Simultaneously, analysts began to question the assumptions that schools were a critical mechanism for attainment or that the patterns of individual achievement could be related to the educational process in any meaningful way. Differences among schools were found to contribute minimally to student achievement, once parental background status was controlled. Differences between schools were far more predictably related to the socioeconomic composition of the student body than to the prevailing patterns of educational expenditures or resources. Standardized achievement tests, by far the most widely used measure of educational outcomes, seemed immutable to the influence of schooling or other educational programs. Cognitive inequality, and perhaps inequality in general, appeared largely intractable.

This study is aimed at a clarification of such issues. I hope to provide more precise specification of how schooling is related to the achievement process. The research was undertaken in the context of the policies pursued and outcomes found in a single, quite ordinary urban school district. It is not, properly speaking, an evaluation of a particular educational program, nor was there an intervention to assess. Although a considerable amount of anecdotal information and supplementary material on the schools were gathered in the course of the field work, the analysis rests on the conventional measures of achievement and on the information provided by parents regarding their socioeconomic positions and their children's activities. The conclusions, however, lead to a far more optimistic view of public education than has been prevalent in the literature about schools.

To anticipate the major findings, I will argue that schooling has a substantial independent effect on the achievement of children and that the outcomes resulting from schooling are far more equal than those that would be expected based on the social class and racial origins of sample children. Differences between schools contribute little to the achievement process that is unrelated to student background, as other analysts have reported; however, this seems largely the product of a fairly uniform positive influence across all the schools studied. It is not the case that schools have no direct effects; rather, the general similarity among schools obscures the more dramatic impact of schooling generally. Schools systematically promote both racial and socioeconomic equality while enhancing the learning of all children. Although achievement differences persist, and schools cannot be regarded as equalizing in an absolute sense, the pattern of outcomes clearly implies that the achievement gaps between children of diverse backgrounds are attenuated by education.

Such propositions would not have seemed worthy of an extensive empirical study in the mid-1960s, but a decade later they were sufficiently at odds with the literature to warrant explanation. The results of this study flow directly from the analytic strategy employed and from the availability of longitudinal data on achievement. In the models to be presented, I assume that schooling is a temporal process; the effects of schooling are to be understood by contrasting patterns of cognitive growth when schools are open to those that prevail when schools are closed during the summer. I assume that schooling influences outcomes during specific time periods, and that education is not the only causal factor influencing achievement. Family background shapes learning continuously, during both the school year and the summer. Since children are simultaneously exposed to both environments, home and school, it is logically impossible to separate their impact. Analytically, one must attempt to hold constant the effects of either schooling or families. The models of the achievement process elaborated in this monograph are aimed at disentangling the complex and confounded determinants of learning and in particular, isolating the unique effects attributable to schools.

The central argument begins with the contention that educational research has tended to ignore two very basic tenets of causal inference, and that this has resulted in erroneous and misleading conclusions regarding the effects of schooling. The first proposition is that in order to examine the impact of a particular variable, such as schooling, one must collect observations over which the causal variable of interest can be said to vary. In a system of universal compulsory schooling, there is little variability in exposure to schooling; this is an almost insurmountable obstacle to an appropriate research design. Although the curriculum and the quality of particular schools differ, this is not an adequate basis for specifying the effects of schooling generally, particularly when cognitive outcomes are not measured over time. Since almost all American children between the ages of 6–16 attend schools, the effect of exposure to education is virtually constant for these age groups. Differences among individual children, due in part to the socioeconomic status of families, eclipse the more modest differences found between schools. This does not, however, prove that schooling is ineffective or even that it is less effective than families in promoting achievement.

The second proposition regarding causal inference is that when a set of outcomes are determined by more than one factor, their effects must be separated analytically in order to test their magnitude or relative importance. Schools are not the only determinant of achievement, nor can schools be assumed to operate in isolation. The central role of families in reinforcing, or perhaps subverting, the influence of education comes close to being a platitude for educational theorists; yet we expect education to reverse or overturn the patterns of socioeconomic inequality. The data suggest that this is both unrealistic and naive. Schools attenuate the effects of socioeconomic status by accelerating the rates of learning for all children and by augmenting achievement in a fairly uniform fashion during the school year, irrespective of race or family background. But schooling, operating in this manner, cannot and does not reduce cognitive inequality or the gaps in absolute achievement level between different children. Schooling appears to mitigate relative gaps; furthermore, I shall argue that schooling attenuates the cumulative impact of parental status over time. When the learning process during the school year is contrasted with the determinants of achievement during the summer, two consistent observations can be made. The first is that learning during school is determined by prior achievement; the impact of parental status is largely indirect, operating through prior test scores and exerting an insignificant direct effect. The second is that during the summer, parental status becomes substantially more important; irrespective of individual differences in ability or achievement, the direct effect of parental status roughly doubles, and the gaps in achievement between children from different socioeconomic strata widen perceptibly.

As these observations make clear, the notion of schooling developed in subsequent chapters is temporal. The effects of education are assumed to be intermittent, while the influence of families is continuous. The impact of schooling can be inferred by contrasting the achievement process during periods when schools are in session with periods when schools are closed. Longitudinal test scores, administered biannually, constitute the basic data for building a model of the achievement process and for assessing the role of schooling. Although the summer is not a completely adequate surrogate for "nonschooling" it is perhaps the only satisfactory time period that permits one to distinguish the effects of education from the effects of families. Short of conducting an impractical experiment, in which certain children would be systematically denied schooling, the summer allows one to describe both the level of achievement and the relative importance of determinants during specific intervals of time. Thus, schooling is considered a "treatment," which varies over a diverse sample of children during the course of a year.

The results of this study suggest that a substantial reassessment of many conclusions on the role of education is in order. The data do not imply, however, that schooling should be considered a sufficient solution for problems of unequal outcomes in either education or adult status. The image of education presented is considerably closer to that envisioned by classical theories of education and by liberal policy analysts, but the evidence also reveals the fairly substantial impact of socioeconomic background on achievement, irrespective of schooling. Although the results could be interpreted as a justification for increasing school expenditures or other social programs designed to raise achievement, such inferences are speculative. During the summer, numerous programs were available to the sample children on a voluntary basis. Summer schools as well as other summer programs had at best a modest impact on achievement and did not overcome the heightened impact of parental status. Although schooling seems to contribute to socioeconomic equality, it is difficult to isolate what aspects of formal education are most important in this process. This study offers few guidelines as to what reforms would be effective for American schools. Although education reduces socioeconomic inequality when compared to that which would exist in the absence of schooling, the data provide little insight as to how best to structure or organize schooling. It seems possible to sort out the mechanisms producing achievement in homes and schools, but as this study amply documents, the processes are exceedingly complex and difficult to capture using conventional measures of achievement.

The next section reviews in some detail previous studies specifically addressed to issues of summer learning or the effects of exposure to schooling on achievement. Although the results are somewhat peripheral to the concerns of this study, they provide supplementary information relevant to this study.

RESEARCH ON EXPOSURE TO SCHOOLING

The advantage of requiring children to attend school for longer periods of time has been the subject of a low-key administrative debate in education for sometime, particularly during periods in which American public education has been attacked as inferior to that of another country with higher standards of excellence. During the post–Sputnik era, several authors compared American schools unfavorably to those of Europe. The point was made that European children go to school 10 months per year, often for 6 days a week, and that European schools require punctuality, docility, and respectful behavior toward authority to a greater extent than do American schools (Rickover, 1962). Such schooling was presumed to produce character, as well as better educated and more productive adults. The causal linkage between exposure and education tends to be obscured, however, by the implicit connection of superior education with both rigorous discipline and attendance. In fact, American students spend a larger portion of their lives in school than do their European peers, and there is evidence that they spend more hours annually as well. A detailed comparison of schools in the United States with those in Switzerland found that the total hours per year, discounting recesses and lunch hour, "spent in school on nonreligious subjects is remarkably equal for children of the two countries [Whitfield & Egger, 1965, p. 256]."

Given the enormous variability of school systems in different countries, the effects of more time in school are difficult to isolate. Torsten Husén (1972) reported that the data from the International Association for the Evaluation of Educational Achievement supported the conclusion that school systems admitting children at the age of 6 produced slightly higher mathematics achievement at age 14 than those systems delaying admission for a year. A study of rural school systems in Norway was conducted, however, in which a group of students aged 12–14 were given half-time instruction combined with additional homework; when compared to a similar group experiencing full-time instruction, their test scores in basic skills were only slightly lower (Husén, 1972). The relationship between exposure and achievement was apparently not linear.

Within the United States, some variation exists in the length of the school day and the duration of the school year from state to state. South Dakota, for example, averages 184 days annually, whereas Arizona schools are open for 168 days (National Education Association, 1965). Several authors have suggested that the quantity of schooling, measured by the amount of time schools are in session, can be meaningfully compared to average achievement levels among students. In a series of papers, Wiley and his associates (Harnischfeger & Wiley, 1976; Wiley, 1976; Wiley & Harnischfeger, 1974) report that the average hours spent in school did affect the achievement levels in a sample of 40 Detroit schools once adjustments were made for family background. Karweit (1976a) has not been able to replicate these results on a larger sample, however. Jencks (1972b) found only insignificant relationships between the length of day and the days of schooling per year across school districts using the full Equality of Educational Opportunity Survey. Even if the results from aggregate comparisons indicated that exposure to schooling was consistently related to achievement, interpreting such differences would be difficult. The use of areal units, whether based on countries, states, or school districts, risks confounding many potentially important characteristics of schools and students with aggregate levels of exposure.

One obvious reason why one might expect the degree of exposure to schooling to influence learning is that the time spent on academic subjects would be likely to increase with additional instruction time. Experimental studies have provided support for this presumption (Carroll, 1963; Anderson, 1973; Block, 1971). Moreover, classroom observations suggest that learning is related to the amount of time individual children spend attending to instruction. Stallings (1976) reports that in 166 first- and third-grade Follow Through classrooms higher reading scores were associated with the amount of time spent in systematic instruction, with the amount of positive reinforcement, and with the degree of concentration observed among students during reading periods. The relationships are quite complex, however. Studies of classroom learning have tended to ignore social class differences among students or classrooms and have neglected to specify the determinants of attention or concentration at either the individual or classroom level. I suspect that middle-class children are both more likely to pay attention to the teacher during instruction periods and less likely to be taught in classrooms that are frequently disrupted. In order to specify how schooling interacts with socioeconomic background, one needs a model of the determinants of both the time allocated to instruction and the amount of time individual children spend attending to lessons.

A similar criticism applies to studies that have operationalized exposure to schooling in terms of differential absenteeism. Attendance levels tend to be negatively correlated to achievement, although this relationship is not large (Karweit, 1973; Schultz, 1958, Ziegler, 1928). Few studies have attempted to separate the determinants of missing school from the consequences for achievement. It seems reasonable to assume that either a serious illness or a serious dislike of school might influence achievement regardless of attendance. Although attendance tends to be related to social class, most studies have lacked the requisite background information on individuals to draw conclusions.

Many of the studies most relevant to issues of exposure to schooling have been undertaken during times of crisis, when the schools were closed for political reasons. DeGroot (1948,1951), for example, studied the patterning of IQ scores among applicants to an industrial training school in Eindhoven for 8 years. During the period 1944–1947, a substantial decline took place, followed by a recovery beginning in 1949. The decline, of nearly half of a standard deviation, was attributed to school conditions during the German occupation of Holland in 1941–1944. The available data were not longitudinal, and supporting evidence on the backgrounds of applicants was not collected. Although factors related to schooling may have been involved, the conditions of war and the resulting self-selection by low-achieving applicants are clearly rival hypotheses.

A second study was completed in Prince Edward County, Virginia, when the schools were closed for 4 years in order to avoid integration (Green *et al.*, 1964). Black children enrolled in privately organized free schools experienced less loss in IQ points and a more rapid recovery in achievement after reentering school than did children who were not exposed to any schooling during the period. Since no information was collected on the social class backgrounds of the children, however, it is likely that the children who received some formal schooling were more motivated and from higher status families than those who did not. Finally, the New York City teachers' strike caused the schools to open late in the fall of 1968, providing many children with an extended summer vacation. Spring test score data revealed consistent achievement losses perhaps caused by the reduced amount of schooling (Jencks *et al.*, 1972). Again, no one collected information on the experiences or environments of the children who lacked schooling.

The effects of exposure during such natural experiments are difficult to compare to the more mundane effects of schooling during normal times. None of the studies could control the effects of social class on differential learning, since no data were collected. Even had such data been available, other factors might have produced the achievement losses. The proposition that exposure to schooling has particular effects requires a comparison of the learning rates of children during a period in which nonattendance is the norm, such as during the summer.

There is an extensive literature in education on summer learning, although major problems afflict research in the field. The issue has typically been defined as one of sumner retention, not learning; the objective was assisting teachers in the development of an effective fall review curriculum (Parsley & Powell, 1962; Sterrett & Davis, 1954). Social class differences were ignored by the early researchers on summer learning. The studies were based on small and nonrepresentative samples and often lacked adequate information to justify comparisons. The results tended to differ by grade level in inconsistent and inexplicable ways and be contradictory. The most interesting studies from a sociological point of view are the least likely to be replicated. A comprehensive review of the literature is, therefore, not particularly useful.

Patterns of summer retention by subject level tend to be the most consistent across studies and grades, although the explanations for such differences are not always convincing. The majority of studies find that reading, vocabulary, and language skills show insignificant change during the summer, whereas skill in arithmetic, problem solving, and spelling generally declines (Beggs & Hieronymus, 1968; Brueckner & Distad, 1924; Irmina, 1928; Keys & Lawson, 1937; Morrison, 1924; North, 1955; Parsley & Powell, 1962; Patterson, 1925; Schrepel & Laslett, 1936; Soar & Soar, 1969). Scores on nature study (Bruene, 1928) and handwriting (Nelson, 1929) have been shown to improve during the summer more than during the school year perhaps due to practice. A variety of explanations are offered as to why skill in such subjects as arithmetic fundamentals, punctuation, or spelling show consistent loss during the summer. Such subjects are frequently taught through drill, which is a form of learning experience not generally encountered outside of schools, and thefore greater summer loss might be expected. Such subjects require specific factual information that is easily forgotten (Tiedeman, 1948); these subjects may also be intrinsically more difficult and less likely to be grasped independent of instruction. For many skills, maturation seems to be the key determinant (Kolberg, 1934).

Several authors have attempted to relate differential summer retention to styles of classroom teaching or student learning. The basic argument is that certain teachers are less authoritarian and thereby inspire independent, autonomous learning away from school, learning that carries over into the summer (Torrance, 1965). The alternative explanation is that student learning styles vary independent of teaching; certain students learn best through "self-discovery," or outside of a classroom context (Soar & Soar, 1969). An objective of several of the authors was to specify which subjects were best taught by direct instruction, and which were best taught indirectly, through self-discovery. The empirical results are inconclusive and unconvincing.

Several authors report higher levels of summer retention by more intelligent students (Breune, 1928; Cook, 1942; Schrepel & Laslett, 1936); although interesting, such a finding confounds social class differentials with those based on intelligence. Much of the research has been based on a single school, and the composition of the school has frequently not been documented; it is therefore difficult to assess the findings at face value. Elementary schools convenient to university researchers are typically somewhat advantaged by national standards. Educational research suggests that summer loss often occurs; the studies, however, provide inconclusive evidence as to the source.

Only four studies have attempted to assess differential learning by the socioeconomic status of children. Hayes and Grether (1969) conducted a study of the New York City schools with data on mean school achievement for students in predominantly black and Puerto Rican schools, compared to that of white children at different grade levels. The data were aggregated by school, and no information was available on individual social class or achievement scores; the results are striking, however, and clearly support differential summer learing. To quote Hayes and Grether (1969):

> In both reading and word knowledge, the differential progress made during the four summers between second and sixth grades accounts for upward of eighty per cent of the differences between the economically advantaged all-white schools and the all-black and Puerto Rican schools [p. 7].

A reanalysis of these data (Hayes & King, 1974) found essentially similar results for two consecutive summers in reading scores, over a number of grades. Although the test scores are only available for school aggregates, consistent results by socioeconomic status and ethnicity were found.

A second study begun in Cobb County, Georgia (Shapiro, Bresnahan, & Knopf, n.d.), attempted to replicate Hayes and Grether, while ensuring that longitudinal data would be collected for individual children. The sample was all-white, and unfortunately the only available socioeconomic information pertained to schools, not children. The report in large part supports the findings in New York, although Shapiro and his associates found that higher status children learned at a faster rate during the school year as well as during the summer. Without data on the distribution of socioeconomic status within schools, however, it is difficult to determine how disparate were the students examined, and it is not possible to make comparisons with other studies.

Murnane (1974) collected longitudinal achievement data on inner-city children in New Haven for a period of 2 years. He found dramatic summer losses in both reading and math for all children between the second and third grades; during the summer Anglo children consistently did better than Spanish-speaking children, and black children consistently lost the most.

David (1974) reported some empirical support for differential summer learning in a sample of Head Start–Follow Through children in Philadelphia. The largest differences were found between first- and second-grade children, in both reading and math. Exposure to schooling in these grades appeared to attenuate the relationship between social class background and achievement growth. Data for children in kindergarten, however, demonstrated far less support for the hypothesis that socioeconomic differentials were exacerbated during the summer. David's research was unique in that it included information on Follow Through summer programs at four sites, and in that she made an effort to assess which programs were most effective in narrowing the gap between poor and nonpoor children. Positive short-term effects of the summer intervention programs were observed; however, since the study was not experimental and included only a fairly restricted range of family backgrounds, conclusions regarding the effectiveness of such programs are tentative.

In sum, the research most relevant for testing socioeconomic differentials in summer learning tends to support the hypothesized effect. All of the studies have depended on Metropolitan Achievement Tests, except the Cobb Country, Georgia, project (Shapiro *et al.*, n.d.), which utilized Stanford Achievement Tests; the large differences between samples and the quality of socioeconomic information limit the possibility of making comparisons. The available data (*a*) have lacked longitudinal test scores for individuals (Hayes & Grether, 1969; Hayes & King, 1974); (*b*) have relied on estimates of the social class position of individuals, aggregated across schools (Hayes & Gether, 1969; Hayes & King, 1974; Shapiro *et al.*, n.d.); or (*c*) have based their samples primarily on disadvantaged minority children (David, 1974; Murnane, 1974). Although suggestive, the research on exposure to schooling has yet to address the central questions of this monograph: What are the effects of schooling on the cognitive growth of children and what role does schooling play in the creation or reduction of socioeconomic inequality in achievement?

A brief overview of the discussion to follow may be helpful and will perhaps alert the reader to the sections that spell out the relevant analyses and findings in greater detail. Chapter 2 reviews the study design, the sampling procedures, and the measures of standardized achievement utilized throughout. Chapter 3 examines the literature on school effects critically and presents initial tabulations of learning rates over time. This chapter is intended to be a nontechnical, largely descriptive introduction to the major findings. I will contrast the differences observed among the sample schools with the results from other studies and suggest a reformulation of ideas regarding equality of educational opportunity. Chapter 4 analyzes the effects of socioeconomic status and schooling in the context of an explicit model of the achievement process through time. The models presented are similar to those found in empirical studies of the effects of schooling on status attainment among adults; however, the results found in Chapter 4 differ from those common in this literature. Chapter 5 looks at one major source of differential exposure during the school year—level of attendance—and assesses the distribution and effects of missing school by socioeconomic status and race.

Part II of this monograph explores the determinants of learning when the schools are closed. The two central questions addressed are

1. How are summer activities patterned by social class and race?
2. What effects do such activities have on achievement?

Chapter 6 summarizes the findings regarding summer activities and sets the stage for the material to follow. Chapter 7 analyzes the effects of summer school programs on achievement. This chapter began as a conventional evaluation of the summer programs, in order to determine which schools were most successful in augmenting summer learning. Although attending summer school was associated with higher levels of achievement, the programs tended to benefit middle-class children more than the poor. Since the summer schools studied were in session for only 6 weeks, and since the students apparently attended for diverse and not wholly academic reasons, comparisons with formal schooling are hazardous. The data provide scant support for the effectiveness of year-round schooling, however. Chapter 8 explores the participation rates in other structured and unstructured activities and the effects of such experiences on summer learning. Although a number of programs tended to promote learning and to promote it at rates commensurate with those observed during the school year, the gains were not independent of the student's socioeconomic background. Voluntary summer activities are far more predictably related to social class than are the activities associated with formal schooling. Although the results do not suggest that particular programs have an effect independent of parental status, the findings reinforce the general conclusion that schooling is perhaps the most equal and homogeneous activity provided for children. Chapter 8 also examines sex differences in activities and learning and the allocation of time to various activities. Although the descriptive data enlarge our view of how children from various income strata spend their summertime, it is not until Chapter 9 that the findings have direct implications for social policy. This chapter presents numerous analyses of summer reading and library use among children. Both reading and libraries have a strong positive influence on summer learning that is quite consistent irrespective of parental background factors. Chapter 10 is devoted to summary impression and some conjectures regarding the impact of schooling on achievement in this society.

2

The Study Design: Students, Schools, and Standardized Testing

A unique data set was required to test the propositions on the effects of family and schooling outlined in the preceding chapter. First, longitudinal test scores, administered biannually for a large sample of children, were essential. To assess and compare rates of learning, at least three points in time were needed, encompassing a school year and a contiguous summer vacation. Ideally, such data should be collected on a series of grades and for a period of 2 or more years. Second, reliable information on the socioeconomic background of pupils had to be collected, preferably directly from parents. Finally, a fairly complete accounting of student activities outside of school would be necessary in order to examine the source and importance of extracurricular learning. The time children spend away from school is not devoid of activities and experiences that promote achievement. Insofar as such activities are shaped by families, one would expect them to operate to some extent as mechanisms through which parents might influence the educational performance of their children in school. Insofar as summer programs or activities contribute to learning, they may be viable alternatives for educational policy. Ideally, one would wish to design an experiment that included educational programs with different curricula and varying degrees of exposure to academic subjects, to test the effectiveness and potential of summer schools or extensions of formal schooling. The present goals were, however, more modest; it seemed most reasonable to document the patterning of summer activities as a natural experiment—as they occur without specific interventions—than to pursue the question of program effectiveness more rigorously.

This chapter is intended to provide a capsule view of the research strategy and the design, to summarize the characteristics of the schools and students sampled, and to alert the reader to the assumptions embodied in the analysis. Findings and substantive issues are postponed until Chapter 3. A more technical and detailed discussion of the sampling procedures can be found in Appendix B. The survey questionnaire is reproduced in Appendix C, and several tables concerning response rates and the choice of background variables are presented in Appendix F. In this chapter, I will present several preliminary analyses of the longitudinal test score data; however, these results are intended to justify the analytic procedures and assumptions utilized throughout this book, rather than to elucidate the general argument.

Despite widespread agreement that cross-sectional data on achievement are inadequate for many important theoretical questions, longitudinal test scores are surprisingly uncommon. Collecting the data required for this study would have been a costly and time-consuming venture. As a preliminary step, a large number of school systems, research and development centers, and other agencies engaged in educational evaluation were contacted for possible data resources. Although many schools administer tests biannually, few systems store or maintain the results for more than a single year. Careful evaluations are frequently restricted to special, federally funded programs, such as compensatory education classes; such programs seldom involve a very large number of children or a very diverse cross-section socioeconomically.

One school system, the Atlanta city public schools, had a data bank adequate for this study. For several years, an extensive fall and spring testing program had been conducted involving all students in Grades 1 through 7. In addition, the district was equipped with centrally stored computerized data files for every student; it was possible to locate and retrieve complete test histories, attendance records, and other information from the individual files through past years. Moreover, Atlanta sponsored one of the most extensive summer school programs for elementary school children in existence. The four-quarter schedule for high school students was in full operation (Anderson, 1972; Rice, 1970), and there was some sentiment among the school staff for extending this program into the elementary grades. Negotiations with the school board and other key administrators revealed substantial enthusiasm for a serious evaluation of the existing summer programs in the elementary schools, perhaps in the hope of augmenting financial support. At this point, planning for this study began in earnest.

THE SAMPLE

The sample was chosen by stratifying schools according to racial composition and the proportion of students receiving a free lunch, ordering schools within strata by enrollment, and then selecting schools systematically, beginning with a randomly chosen entry point. Forty-two schools were selected in this manner. The objective was to generate a sample with the following characteristics:

1. The total sample size should be roughly 4800 students with equal numbers of sixth and seventh graders.
2. The sample should be racially balanced, with approxiamately equal numbers of black and white students in each grade.
3. The sample should be heterogeneous with respect to socio-economic background, for both black and white students.

The design was not intended to yield a sample representative of either the schools or students within the district. Those schools that were characterized as both low-income and white or as both black and high-income were overrepresented relative to the district. The sampling design ensured that the students selected would be more diverse than the district in order to have sufficient numbers of cases at various income levels for analysis. This was accomplished.

The names, addresses, telephone numbers, and identification codes were compiled by the computer center for the 4866 students enrolled in a sample school in the fall of 1972. Interviews with the parents of these children were attempted in 4539 cases[1] and 86% responded to the survey, either by telephone or in person. Among the 3905 students with fall test scores and completed parental interviews, 76% also had test scores available for the entire preceding year, yielding three consecutive data points in time. This sample, which I will refer to as the matched sample, represents just over 60% of the original pool of students enrolled; these 2978 children, aggregated by school, constitute the primary sample for analysis.

[1] Between the time the student survey lists were compiled early in September and the time the fall tests were taken in October, 42 additional students had enrolled in the sample schools. These students were not surveyed. In addition, a random sample of 327 black children were withdrawn from the survey files when it appeared the black sample was excessively large.

During the summer of 1972, after the sample had been chosen, the composition of these schools changed markedly. For some time, the school system had been under pressure to integrate the all-white schools in the most affluent neighborhoods. This conflict reached a crisis point during the 1972–1973 school year, but an unprecedented number of white students had already withdrawn. Additionally, there were organized efforts by the black community to transfer inner-city youngsters to these schools on a voluntary basis. This political turmoil was eventually resolved in favor of greater racial balance throughout the system; however, the racial balance of the sample was seriously affected. Black students are overrepresented in the sample, relative to the original design for this reason.[2]

The Metropolitan Achievement Tests were administered in the sample schools in the fall of 1972 in the sixth and seventh grade classes. The sixth graders received the third form of the intermediate battery, while the seventh grade students took the initial form of the advanced battery. During the course of analysis, it became clear that it would not be possible to equate test forms across batteries for the purpose of comparisons. Within the intermediate battery, which encompasses the fifth and sixth grades, the test forms are essentially parallel. The items were assigned to forms so as to yield equivalent tests; derived measures, such as standard scores or grade equivalents, were constructed from a common national norming sample and had quite similar scales. Within a single battery, the relationship between pretest and posttest are linear and yield consistent estimates of cognitive growth. Comparisons across batteries do not share these properties and consequently often show anomalous results. Since it was essential to have meaningful comparisons across time, the only test scores included in the analysis were those drawn from the intermediate battery. This fact implied that the sequence of tests for the seventh-grade cohort were limited to the retrospective test history data based on the three tests taken in the spring and fall of 1971 and the spring of 1972. Since the survey questions were pertinent to the summer of 1972, only the sixth grade could be used for this analysis. For the purposes of comparing the patterns of growth by socioeconomic status, however, the seventh grade was used.

Throughout this monograph, three groups of students are central. Each group has at least three consecutive test scores on the intermediate battery of the Metropolitan Achievement Tests and a completed parental survey. These groups are schematized in Table 2.1 for convenience. The grade designation refers to the student's actual grade in the fall of

[2] Nearly two-thirds of the sample at both grades were black.

TABLE 2.1
Sample Students by Grade and Test Scores Available

	Test date					
Cohort	Fall 1970	Spring 1971	Fall 1971	Spring 1972	Fall 1972	*N*
Sixth grade			X	X	X	1493
Seventh grade		X	X	X		1485
Seventh grade[a]	X	X	X	X		739

[a] The seventh grade sample with 2 years of successive test score data available is analyzed separately in several sections.

1972, when the survey results were completed. For both the sixth and seventh grade students, the time interval analyzed as the summer is between May of the fifth grade and October of the sixth grade, the dates at which spring and fall tests were given. The school year for the sixth grade cohort is the fifth grade, between the fall of 1971 and the spring of 1972; for the seventh grade, the period of schooling is their sixth grade. Grade-specific results will be presented throughout. Although the difficulty with comparisons across batteries and grades was unanticipated, the ultimate result was two independent longitudinal samples of children that could be compared. As we shall see, the results are substantially strengthened by this comparison. The two grade cohorts yield quite similar patterns of growth, although the actual numeric estimates vary. The absolute amount of growth and the observed effects of socioeconomic background differ between groups, although for both the sixth and seventh graders learning rates are accelerated during the school year relative to the summer and the effects of parental status are magnified during the summer.

TEST SCORE METRICS

A recurring dilemma in educational research has been the utility of standardized achievement tests for the study of change (Bereiter, 1963; Cronbach & Furby, 1970). Since the evidence to be presented rests on such measures, it seems worthwhile to summarize the research strategy employed and the implicit assumptions. A more complete argument in support of these assumptions is found in Appendix A.

In order to infer patterns of learning from standardized achievement tests, many of the commonsense notions about what constitutes learning must be held in abeyance. Standardized tests measure relative position, not an absolute level of achievement. To compare rates of growth is to compare the scores of students relative to a comparison group, such as the norming sample used to scale values. The logic of norming ensures that the comparison group is a dynamic entity; test scores are not static measures relative to a fixed level of performance. Insofar as secular increases in average skills and knowledge occur, the expected values will also increase. Although it is tempting to contrast gains and losses, it is difficult to infer distinct processes producing either learning or inadequate retention. A decline in standard score might be due to either forgetting material or to learning, but at a slower rate than the norm group. Stability of relative position is compatible with either substantial cognitive growth or loss, provided the comparison group experienced similar change.

Three distinct scales of measurement are published with achievement tests and are commonly used in the educational literature. Raw scores consist of the absolute number of items correctly answered. Standard scores transform these values by normalizing the distribution and fitting intervals to standard units. Grade equivalent scores are constructed by plotting median raw scores or standard scores against the age or grade level of students in the norming sample, and imputing intervals based on the relationship observed over time. Although these derived scales tend to be highly correlated, they are not necessarily linear transformations of each other or of the raw scores. Test scores are ordinal measures; as such, any transformation of scale which preserves the order of students is permissible, even though the resulting intervals may differ considerably. On the Metropolitan Achievement Tests that I have investigated, the intervals implied by raw scores generate a distribution that is approximately normal, while the distribution of grade equivalent scores is log normal.

There is at present no agreement on which metric is most appropriate for the longitudinal study of change. A few authors recommend grade equivalents (Lindquist & Hieronymus, 1964), but the majority of analysts prefer standardized scores as a tool of analysis. The rationale given is statistical, rather than substantive. Grade equivalent scores are notoriously unreliable and have other undesirable statistical properties such as nonnormal distributions (Coleman & Karweit, 1972; Fennessey, 1973; Tallmadge & Horst, 1974). The chief advantage of grade equivalent scores is that they link achievement to a time-specific metric, defined by median scores at grade level. For descriptive purposes, this is the only test metric which can be used to infer relative change based on a scale that is independent of the distribution of students.

Since raw scores, standard scores, and grade equivalent scores imply different intervals, the means and variances calculated for particular samples are not equal. The choice of metric is, therefore, quite consequential. If the key research questions concern the amount of change observed during two different periods or the rates of change for students at different points on a scale, the scale of measurement assumed can substantially determine the answers in many cases. Raw scores tend to yield conservative estimates of change and to show the familiar regression to the mean for high-scoring children, while grade equivalents may not (cf. Appendix A). Since grade equivalent scales are positively skewed, a gain in raw score points is worth progressively more as one ascends the scale; thus high-scoring or high-status students gain more in grade-equivalent units than they do in raw scores.

The bulk of the analysis to follow will be devoted to explicating and elaborating a process model of achievement. The basic formulation of the hypotheses to be examined concerns not changes in level of cognitive achievement, but the determination of achievement at several points in time. The central questions will be how and to what extent do measurable attributes of students influence the learning process, and, how are the determinants of achievement influenced by the effect of being in school, rather than out of school? The investigation is thus oriented toward comparing the determinants of fall achievement with the determinants of spring achievement. The test of the hypothesis that certain factors, such as family background, have a larger impact during periods when school is not in session is equivalent to testing the differences between coefficients at two points in time, with prior achievement held constant. The basic model can be summarized by two structural equations,

$$A_{\mathrm{F72}} = b_1 A_{\mathrm{S72}} + b_2\mathrm{SES} + e,$$

$$A_{\mathrm{S72}} = c_1 A_{\mathrm{F71}} + c_2\mathrm{SES} + e,$$

where A_t represents the individual student's achievement score at a particular point in time, and SES is a measure of socioeconomic background. Estimates of the effects of summer activities will be presented as intervening variables, mediating or altering patterns of fall achievement net of spring achievement and socioeconomic background. The models to be presented will be summarized utilizing path analysis and structural equations (Duncan, 1966, 1975; Heise, 1969; Land 1969).

Measures of association, including correlations and path coefficients, are not, of course, insensitive to changes in the scaling or distribution of variables. It is possible to posit models of the achievement process involving ordinal transformations of the data to be presented that would alter the interpretations markedly. For the available metrics, however, the correlations between test scores are quite high at each point in time. The correlation between raw scores, which are normally distributed, and grade equivalent scores, which are log normal, is rarely less than .95 on the most reliable tests. As Labovitz (1970) has shown, correlational statistics and tests of significance are quite robust when subjected to ordinal transformations of scale similar to those that separate these two achievement metrics. Although the choice of metric can change conclusions about whether high or low-income children learned the most between any two periods, the correlations between income and achievement are substantially unaffected by changes in the metric of the order discussed.

In short, correlational techniques yield far more consistent models of the achievement process, irrespective of metric, than do other types of analyses. Estimates of the effects of background variables tend to be larger when grade equivalent scores are used, but the standard errors of estimate are correspondingly inflated. Raw scores will be used for all regression analyses because they are more conventional measures and hence permit comparisons to other studies and because they give more conservative estimates of the effects. Interpretations of the achievement process, when approached in this manner, are not influenced by choice of metric. For descriptive purposes, however, I will present grade equivalent gains as a more accurate assessment of the amount of cognitive growth occurring during a given period of time. I will also argue that theoretically important interactions between rates of growth and socioeconomic background occur in a number of contexts. For example, when the effects of particular summer programs on differential summer learning are compared, I argue that such activities are particularly beneficial to relatively advantaged children. Without strong metric assumptions, an interpretation of the presence and strength of such interactions is inherently speculative, since they occasionally do not persist across metrics (Wilson, 1971).

CONSISTENCY AND COMPARABILITY OF SUBJECT SUBTESTS

The Metropolitan Achievement Tests include nine subject subtests: word knowledge, reading, language, language study skills, arithmetic computation, arithmetic problem solving and concepts, social studies information, social studies study skills, and science. Although each of these subtests could be argued to assess a unique skill, the correlations between test scores on different subtests are quite high.[3] The tests are not equally reliable, however. An item analysis based on the test scores taken during the fall of 1972 was completed for each subtest. Table 2.2 presents a summary description of the nine subtests, their published reliabilities (Durost *et al.*, 1962) and the reliabilities or measures of internal consistency (KR-20) calculated from the sixth grade cohort for the intermediate battery by race.

Word knowledge was the most reliable subtest for both black and white students and the most highly correlated with the principal component extracted from a factor analysis of all nine subtests. The correlations between pretests and posttests for both the school year and the summer were larger for this test, and the relationships more nearly linear. This test also had the strongest correlation with IQ scores, and the highest relationship to measures of parental socioeconomic status. Virtually all students managed to complete this test, perhaps because it was the first test of the day. The raw scores based on word knowledge were most consistent when comparing derived measures, such as grade equivalent scores. Word knowledge was also the only test to yield significant gains during both the school year and the summer for both white and black sample children. For these reasons, and for simplicity of exposition, the detailed analysis to follow relies on this test as the measure of achievement.

The pattern of results is, however, quite similar irrespective of subject matter. Table 2.3 presents the mean raw scores for each subtest for the seventh grade cohort on the intermediate battery at four points in time. The modal pattern is for an increase of mean score at each test date, although losses in absolute terms occurred during the summer on three tests. Each form of the battery is constructed to be equivalent, yet the gains observed during the fifth grade tend to exceed those observed in the sixth. If one assumed that the progressive accumulation of raw score points between the fall of 1970 and the spring of 1972 could be described as a linear function of time, it is possible to estimate expected values for the test scores observed in both the spring and fall of 1971. Table 2.3 presents these estimates. Without exception, the test scores observed in the spring of 1971, at the end of the school year, exceed the expected values; moreover, the test scores are lower than expected for the subsequent fall, at the end of the summer. Although the magnitude of these differences varies by subject, and most are not significant, the

[3] The average correlation among all nine subtests was .72; the range was between .51 and .89.

TABLE 2.2
Summary of Metropolitan Achievement Test Subjects by Number of Items and Computed Reliability (KR-20) by Race, 1972, Intermediate Battery

Subtest	Number of items	Reliability			Published reliability (median)
		Black	White	Total	
Word knowledge	55	.9294	.9425	.9425	.94
Reading	44	.8288	.9123	.8781	.90
Language	81	.9025	.9391	.9208	.89
Language study skills	28	.8154	.9018	.8645	.79
Arithmetic computation	48	.8344	.8968	.8680	.88
Arithmetic problem solving and concepts	48	.8282	.9006	.8731	.92
Social studies information	60	.8236	.9046	.8707	.87
Social studies study skills	29	.7025	.8777	.8073	.73
Science	55	.8624	.9368	.8750	.89

TABLE 2.3
Mean Raw Scores by Test Date and Subject Subtest for the Seventh Grade Sample with Four Data Points, $N = 739$

	Date of test			
Subject subtest	Fall 1970	Spring 1971	Fall 1971	Spring 1972
1. Word knowledge	17.3	21.9 (20.7)[a]	22.8 (23.1)[a]	26.4
2. Reading	15.3	17.5 (16.9)	18.0 (18.1)	19.7
3. Language	35.6	39.7 (38.6)	41.3 (40.7)	43.7
4. Language study skills	9.4	11.6 (11.2)	12.2 (12.4)	14.2
5. Arithmetic computation	12.7	17.4 (15.7)	17.2 (17.8)	20.8
6. Arithmetic problem solving	15.6	18.8 (18.4)	19.5 (20.4)	23.2
7. Social studies information	17.7	20.4 (20.1)	21.3 (21.8)	24.2
8. Social studies study skills	9.6	11.7 (10.3)	9.8 (10.7)	11.3
9. Science	17.8	23.1 (20.9)	22.1 (23.2)	26.3

[a] Expected values based on a linear interpolation between Fall 1970 and Spring 1972 are shown in parentheses.

pattern is consistent. Learning rates, as a function of time, are systematically larger during the school year than during the summer, irrespective of skill.[4]

The subtests also consistently support the hypothesis that summer

[4] Various authors have argued that specific academic skills, such as spelling or arithmetic, are particularly dependent on instruction or practice and are therefore more prone to be forgotten during the summer months. The Atlanta test scores provide some weak support for this proposition, in that the three tests showing absolute declines across the summer required either specific knowledge (Social studies study skills, Science) or specific skills (Arithmetic computation). The other tests tended to require reading skills and hence to load on general verbal ability to a greater extent. The actual amount of gain or loss, however, is largely determined by the length or difficulty of the subtest; it does not seem to be a particularly sensitive indicator of the differential effects of schooling. Moreover, if one orders subtests by the degree of increase or decrease observed on raw scores and again on grade equivalents the patterns are quite different. Since the national norming sample also experienced differential retention and loss on certain skills, the expected summer gains were lower; despite a loss in average raw score points on arithmetic, for example, the sample gained on the average in grade equivalent terms.

learning is more highly related to parental socioeconomic status than is learning during the school year. Table 2.4 presents the partial correlations between family income and posttest, with prior achievement controlled, by grade and subtest. For both sixth and seventh grade students, the residual gains on eight out of the nine subject skills tested are more related to family income during the summer than during the school year. Although the differences are not significant in the majority of cases, the pattern of gains is unmistakable. For almost every subject tested, the influence of family socioeconomic status is attenuated during the school year relative to the summer. The degree of discrepancy seems to be a function of the reliability of the subtests, rather than the degree to which they reflect particular subject matter learned in schools. It would, therefore, be difficult to argue that certain skills were more or less sensitive to parental influences. In general, however, summer learning is systematically more dependent on family socioeconomic status than is school learning.

These results suggest that rates of learning measured by the specific subtests are temporally patterned in consistent ways and that this learning is influenced by common factors. The rates of gain observed during the school year are larger without exception than those observed

TABLE 2.4
Partial Correlations between Achievement and Income with Prior Achievement Controlled, by Grade and Subtest for Matched Sample Students[a]

	Sixth grade		Seventh grade	
Subtest	School[b]	Summer[c]	School[b]	Summer[c]
1. Word knowledge	.1524	.2601	.2146	.3058
2. Reading	.1798	.2503	.2216	.3100
3. Language	.2023	.2348	.2121	.2383
4. Language study skills	.2449	.2186	.2218	.2745
5. Arithmetic computation	.2403	.2992	.2010	.2481
6. Arithmetic problem solving	.2054	.2207	.1696	.2329
7. Social studies information	.2059	.2126	.1978	.2230
8. Social studies study skills	.2046	.2729	.1979	.3000
9. Science	.1679	.2238	.2548	.2498

[a] All partial correlations are significantly different from zero.

[b] The school year refers to the period between Ocotber 1971 and May 1972 for both cohorts; this was the fifth grade for the sixth grade cohort and the sixth grade for the seventh graders.

[c] The summer period refers to the period between May 1972 and October 1972 for the sixth grade cohort and the period between May 1971 and Ocotber 1971 for the seventh graders.

during the summer, while the effect of family income is smaller. The subtests are not independent of each other, in that all share a considerable amount of common variance; however, inferences regarding summer learning apply to each subtest. The actual amounts of gain differ, often inexplicably, as does the degree of discrepancy between the coefficients calculated for the school year and the summer by subtest. It would be a mistake, in my opinion, to interpret such differences as indicating relevant, substantively important distinctions between measured skills. Actual numeric values are frequently anomalous, and they are seldom consistent across test score metrics for the same subtest. The salient point for this analysis is the general consistency of results, irrespective of subtest. Although word knowledge yields the most reliable estimates of cognitive growth, the choice of this measure does not substantially affect the gross temporal patterns to be discussed.

CORRECTIONS FOR MEASUREMENT ERROR

Empirical work in sociology has devoted much attention to specifying causal models that include estimates of measurement error, in an effort to increase precision as well as to establish bounds for numerical interpretation (Bielby, Hauser, & Featherman, 1977a, b). Psychometricians have long been concerned with unreliability, and numerous techniques exist for generating estimates of the reliability of test scores (Stanley, 1971). Since longitudinal data with three or four tests taken by several thousand children are quite rare, this analysis initially aimed at assessing test score reliability in some detail. However, a number of difficulties emerged that cast doubt on the validity of the assumptions required for corrections for attenuation.

An independent estimate of test–retest reliability was not available for the Atlanta sample. Estimates of the internal consistency (KR-20) presented earlier were computed from the individual items, which were available only for the final testing period and thus could be computed only for a single form of the MAT. These results indicate that the Metropolitan Achievement Tests are as reliable for Atlanta as for the national norming sample and that the tests tend to be less reliable for black students than for whites. Reliability also differs for high- and low-scoring students and for students from relatively high-status backgrounds compared to disadvantaged students. Estimates of reliability are influenced by characteristics of the population; in the present case, the magnitude of the reliability coefficient is directly proportional to the variance of observed scores in the population studied. This is true whether one compares estimates of internal consistency or test–retest correlations calculated from the longitudinal data. More troubling, however, is the persistent tendency for test score reliabilities to depend on the point in time at which the tests were administered.

The definition of reliability found in classical test theory is the square of the correlation between the observed and the true scores (Lord & Novick, 1968). Coleman (1968b) proposed a method for separating the stability of test scores from the effects of measurement error using panel data, which Heise (1969a) explicated using standardized coefficients. Wiley and Wiley (1970) presented an alternative model, which does not require a constant reliability over time. If one is willing to assume either a constant ratio between error variance and observed variance or a constant error variance, it is possible to estimate the reliability and the temporal stability of coefficients from panel data containing three or more repeated measures. One must assume additionally that errors are uncorrelated with true scores and are serially uncorrelated, and that disturbance terms or random shocks are serially uncorrelated. Wiley and Wiley (1974) relax the assumptions of serially uncorrelated errors and present models for three waves of observations taken at fixed intervals.

The test score data from Atlanta were used to compare the models posited and to attempt to estimate the amount of measurement error present. The results do not justify accepting the assumptions required. First, there is substantial reason to believe that errors are correlated. Second, the longitudinal patterns suggest that the true score variance is not constant, but increases regularly over time. Third, the estimates of reliability and stability computed from these models yield unrealistic variance components. The computed value for the reliability is often as low as .75, while the estimated correlation between true scores often exceeds unity. Fourth, estimates of reliability differed markedly for subgroups; the coefficients seem more a function of the population studied than of the test instrument. Although the requisite data for assessing models with correlated error were not available, since the tests were given at unequal intervals, models incorporating correlated errors produced *negative* estimates for certain components of variance. Without a more pertinent theoretical basis for interpreting errors of measurement, corrections for attenuation do not appear to be appropriate.[5]

[5] One might argue that the construction of test scores does not permit the usual decomposition of measures into true score and error components that are necessarily uncorrelated. Imagine that the observed score for each individual consists of a number of correct responses which were known absolutely and a number of responses which were

As an illustration, the matrix of test score correlations calculated for the 739 seventh-grade students who took all four forms of the intermediate battery between the fall of 1970 and the spring of 1972 are presented in Appendix E, Table E.1, separately by metric. If one assumes that the test scores can be adequately described by a simple causal chain and that each successive test is uniquely determined by the prior test and by an error term, it is possible to estimate the correlations among errors implied. Given the assumptions of the model, the path coefficients are assumed to be exactly equal to the correlation between successive tests; the sum of the direct effect and the error term for each testing period is equal to unity. The correlations among residuals were calculated according to the assumptions of path analysis and are those that would be necessary to reproduce the zero-order relationships (Duncan, 1966, 1975). Figure 2.1 presents the estimates and the pattern of correlated errors that are a necessary consequence of accepting the stipulated causal chain.

The model is presented largely for heuristic purposes; it highlights the degree of autoregression in test scores and demonstrates the increasing magnitude of the direct effect of pretest on posttest observed at each subsequent date. The negatively correlated errors are substantial at adjacent time periods. The correlation among errors is at least partly the result of omitted causal influences. Socioeconomic status, for example, influences test scores at each date, independent of prior achievement. The pattern of correlated residuals and increasing explained variance persists, however, irrespective of what other variables are included.

As Wiley and Wiley (1970) point out, the assumption of a constant reliability presumes either a stable trait or a stable equilibrium between true score and error. As is evident in Appendix E, Table E.1, the

---

correctly guessed. The observed error variance would be determined to a large degree by the number of incorrect guesses. If one thought of an achievement test as being a sequence of n independent trials, corresponding to the n items included, and assumed that guessing was a stochastic process binomially distributed, and that every item was either known or not known, it could be assumed that all students would have the same probability of a random success, namely, $1/k$, where k is the number of possible responses. For the MAT vocabulary test, there are five possible answers for every item, and virtually no incomplete tests. If the errors for each specific test score follow a binomial stochastic process, the expected value for correct guesses would be $1/5(n-X)$, where X is the number of items known. Notice that the number of correct guesses would be inversely related to the student's knowledge; errors due to guessing would always be positive and negatively correlated to the number of items known. The variance of known items would tend to be greater than the variance of observed scores and would tend to increase over time if the mean observed score increased. Models incorporating a stochastic error term of the sort described have not to my knowledge been published, although the assumptions are at least as plausible as those of classical test theory.

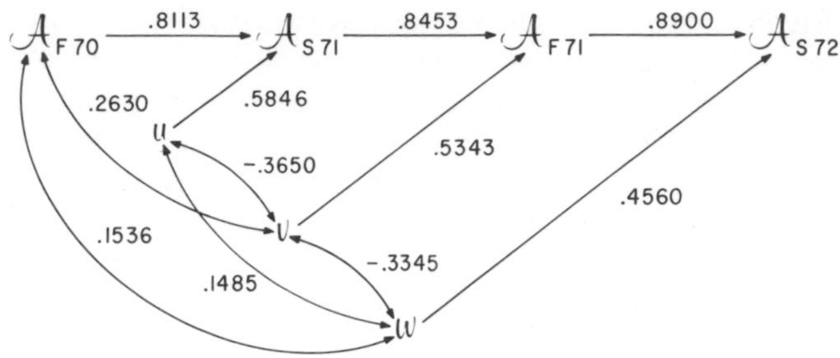

FIGURE 2.1. Achievement as a causal chain, for seventh-grade students, with test scores matched at all four points in time, and implied intercorrelations among errors.

variance of observed scores increases at each point in time, as does the correlation between pretest and posttest. To assume a stable error variance seems untenable, particularly since the increases noted do not seem to be a linear function of time or of time between tests. Assuming a constant rate of change would be equivalent to assuming that the rate of cognitive growth during the school year was equal to that of the summer. Reliability coefficients that differ markedly between subgroups and time periods are unwieldy to use or interpret. More complex models are possible, but those that depend on the restrictive assumptions of classical test theory do not seem plausible. Without additional *substantive* information, utilizing corrections for attenuation based on uncorrelated measurement errors and the structure of correlations observed does not seem likely to be fruitful.

The problem of estimating the reliability of test scores is confounded when metrics are compared. Although the correlations between raw scores and grade equivalents are quite high, as Appendix E, Table E.1, documents, reliability coefficients for grade equivalent scores tend to be lower and less stable over time. Classical test theory assumes homogeneity of error variance; but, unlike raw scores, grade equivalents have quite heteroskedastic disturbances.

If one assumes that learning is a linear function and can be described by the slope of the line relating pretest to posttest, an appropriate summary measure of the rate of change would be the unstandardized regression coefficient. Regression estimates differ among metrics, however, largely because of the tendency for raw score gains to decrease over time. Grade equivalents are scaled relative to time and therefore yield more similar learning curves during the equal time intervals. There is evidence, however, that regressions based on grade equivalent scores are affected by the degree of heteroskedasticity in scores. Although regression coefficients based on the assumption of homoskedasticity are unbiased and consistent estimates, they are not efficient, and the calculated standard errors of estimate and confidence intervals tend to be understated (Kmenta, 1971).

One tactic for dealing with heteroskedastic disturbances is the use of weighted least squares. Econometricians have used this technique to specify an earnings function, for example, when the disturbance terms tend to be positively related to income level. Since errors are systematically larger at higher average income levels, use of weighted least squares deflates the importance of these less precise observations by assuming that the variance of observations is a function of the independent variable.

A scatter plot of the joint distributions of pretest and posttest grade equivalent scores revealed a pattern of heteroskedasticity not unlike that found for income distributions. The variance of observations tends to be proportional to pretest scores, and it is reasonable to assume that

$$\sigma_i = k\,\chi_i^2$$

where k is a constant. Minimizing the function

$$\sum \frac{1}{k^2\,\chi_i^2}(Y_i - \hat{\alpha} - \hat{\beta}\,\chi_i)^2$$

yields the weighted least squares estimates. The technique and assumptions are fully discussed by Kmenta (1971, pp. 249–267), although the procedures used for estimating coefficients are those recommended by Wonnacott and Wonnacott (1970, pp. 132–135). Table 2.5 presents the series of equations describing the learning process over time for the Atlanta sample, based on ordinary least squares and weighted least squares estimation procedures for grade equivalent scores.

TABLE 2.5
Unstandardized Regression Coefficients Estimated by Ordinary Least Squares and Weighted Least Squares, Seventh Grade, Matched Sample

Dependent variable		Constant		Regression coefficient			R^2
				Weighted least squares solutions			
Spring 1972	=	.5359	+	1.0219(Fall 1971)	+	e_i	.7801
Fall 1971	=	.4324	+	.9154(Spring 1971)	+	e'_i	.6832
Spring 1971	=	.4761	+	1.0486(Fall 1970)	+	e''_i	.6458
				Ordinary least squares solutions			
Spring 1972	=	.7661	+	.9772(Fall 1971)	+	e_i	.7811
Fall 1971	=	.7027	+	.8540(Spring 1971)	+	e'_i	.6803
Spring 1971	=	.6636	+	.9872(Fall 1970)	+	e''_i	.6437

The differences between the sets of equations are suggestive. First, there are no substantial differences in terms of goodness-of-fit; the R^2 for the weighted least squares estimate is by definition less than that for the ordinary least squares; however, in this case the differences are never greater than .003. The R^2 varies between .643 and .781 for both sets and increases systematically over testing intervals for both models. Both sets of equations imply that the rate of learning, measured as the linear slope, is greater during the school year than during the summer, and both models suggest that learning during the sixth grade is somewhat slower than during the fifth grade and has a smaller constant increment. The heteroskedastic model, however, estimates a significantly higher rate of gain during each period than those obtained by the ordinary least squares solution. Accepting the conventional assumptions of homoskedasticity of error systematically underestimates the return to prior achievement level and overstates the constant gain. During the school year, the rate of learning estimated by weighted least squares exceeds unity; despite regression effects, grade equivalent scores yield estimates of learning that suggest a cumulative process is operating.

CONCLUSION

This chapter has dealt with preliminary matters, such as the sample and the dependent variables. The objective was to provide a brief overview of the study design and to justify the assumptions and analytic techniques to follow.

In sum, the data for this study consist of parental interviews and retrospective test scores for nearly 3000 sixth and seventh grade children enrolled in 1 of 42 elementary schools in Atlanta, Georgia. The measure of achievement which will be analyzed in depth is word knowledge, a very reliable test of vocabulary skills given with the Metropolitan Achievement Tests. The presentation of the results in subsequent chapters will take two forms: descriptive tabulations of gains by family income level for various categories of students using grade equivalent scores, and regression models based on the raw scores and presented in both standardized and unstandardized form. Whenever possible, analyses will be presented for both cohorts, separately by race. With these considerations in mind, let us turn to the substantive analysis and findings.

3
The Effects of Schooling

Does schooling have a demonstrable impact on students? Like the issue of learning, this question is deceptively straightforward. Although it has been debated, distorted, and subjected to heated controversy, it has yet to be posed in a manner that would permit a rigorous assessment. The purpose of this chapter is to review the discussion and the evidence on the subject and to elaborate the conceptual framework for an analysis of schooling. The initial sections will attempt to clarify the concepts prevalent in the literature and to provide an overview of the vicissitudes of research in this area. Then I will argue that the most appropriate method of specifying the effects of education is to compare learning rates during the school year with those observed in the absence of schooling. Finally, I will present the Atlanta results based on the conventional methods and ask to what degree equality of educational opportunity exists in Atlanta. This chapter is intended to be both a critique of the existing literature and a relatively nontechnical introduction to the general results.

Four sets of findings are customarily cited as evidence relevant to the issue of school effects. The first is that during the course of schooling, the achievement gaps between children from different backgrounds persist and may even increase. The second is that numerous short-term evaluation studies have shown children to have similar patterns of achievement irrespective of the characteristics of teachers or programs.

Although results differ somewhat, the most careful studies have rarely found that significant differences in learning could be unambiguously attributed to a specific program or curriculum. Third, when children who attend schools are compared to children who do not, as in studies of preschooling, achievement gains tend to be transitory; the cognitive advantage that results from attending a preschool program does not persist through elementary schooling. Finally, the differences in student achievement among schools are substantially less important than are the differences within schools. Which particular school a child attends is not consistently related to achievement once the socioeconomic status of parents is controlled.

Each of the four assertions is based on numerous studies of varying quality, and each invites several interpretations. Longitudinal data are conspicuously absent from the majority of studies, particularly those that involved comparisons among children at several grade levels or that attempted to assess learning over an extended period of time. The evaluations of preschooling programs are handicapped by the fact that test scores for young children are frequently unreliable. Most experimental studies have attempted only minimal modification of existing school programs, and the majority of interventions have been modest. Contrasting the effects of curricula designed to produce similar outcomes may not yield changes that can be measured by standardized tests, which tap general levels of skill. Hence, the fourth point mentioned above has become the lynchpin of the dispute. School effects are defined and operationalized as the differences between schools; the effect of education is taken to be the explanatory power of knowing which school a child attended.

The appropriate tactic for assessing educational effects is to compare the results of schooling with those that would obtain in the absence of schooling. Studies of differences among schools lose sight of the more general question of the impact of being in school at all. Operationalizing the effects of schooling when exposure is nearly universal is difficult; however, glossing the distinction between the effects of schooling as a whole and the differences among schools risks sophistry and conclusions that verge on the absurd.

Although the distinction between school effects and the effect of schooling is trivial semantically, it is crucial conceptually. By the effects of schooling, I mean the cumulative outcomes associated with an entire institutional complex and not the more narrowly defined issue of the patterning of outcomes among schools. If every school taught children to read, for example, but each did so in a relatively uniform manner, the differences among schools might be miniscule, but one could not argue that schooling had no impact on reading. It is a logical error to assume that negligible differences among schools imply that schooling has little effect, yet this is often the conclusion drawn.

By analogy, one might argue that legal institutions should be evaluated by comparing differences in the verdicts reached among judges or courthouses. If large disparities in the administration of a particular code of law by jurisdiction were discovered, one might conclude that justice was contingent on factors unrelated to the law. If, however, outcomes were found to be not predictably related to differences among courtrooms, one would clearly not infer that justice was independent of the courts, or that the law had little influence on outcomes. Inequalities in the distribution of justice would warrant scrutiny and investigation; similar outcomes would not. The research on schools and equality of educational opportunity embody this paradox. Assertions regarding the similar effects of schools slide easily into arguments about schooling and the impact of education generally.

Research on the differences among schools can be useful, although a major difficulty has been conceptualizing what should be studied. Sociological studies began by assuming that the social composition of schools had a direct bearing on achievement levels. The social context of education was thought to be identical to the school climate or ambience, but to be more generally an indicator of the total educational experience (Herriott & St. John, 1966; McDill, Meyers, & Rigsby, 1967; Rogoff, 1961; Sewell & Armer, 1966; Sexton, 1961; Wilson, 1959). Schools were chosen as the unit of analysis for pragmatic reasons; measures could easily be aggregated across students to yield an estimate of the socioeconomic context. Such measures were assumed to be proxies for a wide range of underlying factors, such as instructional materials, quality of teachers, motivation of peers, and the like. The causal mechanisms through which social context influenced outcomes were somewhat vague. At times, the authors inferred group processes or patterns of interpersonal contact and interaction; at times, the focus was more explicitly linked to school facilities, staff, or aspects of the physical plant.

Interpretations of the meaning and mechanisms were considerably more diverse than either the methods employed in constructing such variables or the predictive power of the variables once constructed. An underlying assumption common to all of the research was that there were good schools, with well-equipped classrooms and challenging teachers, which provided a superior educational environment; there were also inferior schools, which were overcrowded, underfinanced, and offered at best custodial services and inadequate attention. The quality of schooling was directly linked to the social class background of students. A cogent statement of such contrasts can be found in Conant's (1961) book *Slums and Suburbs.*

These initial studies confirmed, and indeed became, the conventional wisdom about the effects of schooling. Achievement levels, retention rates, and student aspirations tended to correspond to the impressions of most observers; there were substantial between-school differences that were directly related to the socioeconomic context of the school. Precisely how school differences caused differences in achievement was ambiguous, yet no one doubted that the inequalities among schools were a major source of unequal educational opportunity.

The Equality of Educational Opportunity Survey (Coleman *et al.*, 1966) provided the most massive documentation of the differences among schools yet to be compiled. Although greeted as "literally of revolutionary significance [Nichols, 1966, p. 1314]," the results confirmed rather than challenged much of the preceding research on schools. In terms of explaining individual variance, differences among schools contributed little to the prediction of individual achievement that was unrelated to family background. The major innovation of the Coleman report was to shift the burden of responsibility for unequal student outcomes to the schools and to link the notions of equality of opportunity to achievement outcomes in a compelling manner. As Coleman (1966) has written, "the principal focus of attention was not on what resources go into education, but on what product comes out [p. 71]." The thrust of the report was to clarify educational opportunity and to underscore the fact that the concept implied "*effective* equality of opportunity [Coleman, 1968a, p. 19]," not merely equal access to favorable educational environments.

Both the data and the methodological rationale employed have been widely criticized (Bowles & Levin, 1968a, b; Cain & Watts, 1970; Hanushek & Kain, 1972; Spady, 1976) and extensively reanalyzed (Heyns, 1971, 1974; Jencks *et al.*, 1972; Mosteller & Moynihan, 1972; Smith, 1972). Critics maintained that cross-sectional surveys, and particularly nonrandom samples, were inadequate for analyzing the effects of schools. Statistical models that controlled the effects of socioeconomic factors were argued to be inappropriate, since the differences in expenditures and quality among schools were confounded with individual differences in socioeconomic background. School resources were said to be poorly measured and their effects to be underestimated; either the critical factors were argued to be intangible and therefore not measurable or the effects of specific resources on aggregate outcomes were judged to be inadequate to specify how they were used and who benefited from their use within schools. Numerous complex nonadditive models of the effects of schools were suggested, and occasionally estimated, to account for the implausible results. The dominant reaction to the Equality of Educational Opportunity Survey was dismay and disbelief; the predominant criticism concerned issues of measurement and the appropriate specification of equations. The more fundamental question, of whether or not differences between schools could reasonably be assumed to measure the effects of education, was almost wholly neglected.

Neither school resources nor aggregate outcomes, even if perfectly measured, can be used to infer the effects of schooling. Without information on the learning process, one cannot conclude that schools are ineffective in redressing socioeconomic inequalities. Children are exposed to numerous educational influences unrelated to schooling that may substantially exacerbate cognitive inequality. The only method of assessing educational outcomes that can be unequivocally linked to schooling is to compare the patterns of cognitive growth in the absence of schooling. If all children learned the same amount whether or not they were enrolled, one could indeed conclude that education had little beneficial effect. This has yet to be shown. How might one explore the effects of education in this light? The next section attempts to provide an answer as well as the rationale for this study.

A CONCEPTUAL FRAMEWORK

The central premise of this study is that achievement is a continuous process, whereas schooling is intermittent. The effects of education are best judged by comparing the process and determinants of achievement during periods when schools are closed, such as the summer, to those processes at work during the school year. Summer vacation constitutes a time interval of sufficient duration to be studied as if it were nonschooling. As a quasi-experimental control for the effects of education, the summer months represent a plausible interval in which to contrast patterns of learning. When they are not exposed to schooling, children continue to be exposed to, and perhaps maximally influenced by, their families and peers. During the summer, it should be possible to disentangle the influences of schooling from those of social background and to attribute the appropriate importance to each. Since children are simultaneously exposed to both school and home environments for most of the time they receive education, the relative importance of the two environments can be contrasted only by holding constant the effects of one, while permitting the other to change. The two questions at the heart of the present analysis can be simply stated:

1. To what degree do the learning rates of children differ during the school year and the summer?
2. What differences exist among children from diverse backgrounds in the patterns of summer learning?

Summer is somewhat less than ideal as a temporal control. The time interval is short; therefore it may be difficult to infer whether change has occurred. Although most schools are closed, a number of children are involved in educational programs and activities similar to schooling that may influence achievement irrespective of family influences. Assuming a temporal control imposes bounds on the effect of education that may not be realistic; one might maintain that summer homework assignments or projects initiated during the school year had an impact even though schools were closed. Even granting that formal schooling is not a major influence on learning for most children during the summer, the nature of the schooling effect posited is somewhat abstract and not easily translated to policy. Describing the effects of schooling as a temporal interaction captures the gross impact of attending school but it leaves unanswered a number of relevant questions regarding how best to improve education during the year.

Although there are limitations to research on summer learning, the major argument in favor of such an approach is that there are few if any alternatives. An experimental study is impractical and certainly unethical. One risks confounding all seasonal variations in learning with the effects of schooling, but this is unavoidable. Once one has ascertained the relative influence of schooling as such, it may then be possible to specify the conditions and contexts that facilitate positive growth during the school year. Although imperfect, summer seems a reasonable facsimile of nonschooling and a plausible temporal control.

The criteria of learning chosen, standardized achievement tests, are also problematic, as discussed in Chapter 2. In addition, the dates of test administration do not correspond neatly to the summer–school year dichotomy. Fall tests are not given on the opening day of school nor are spring tests the last scheduled activity in June. The school year analyzed consists of the period between testing dates, from October to May, and not the complete period of instruction. Consequently, the summer is assumed to be 5 months long and to include 2 months in which children received at least some regular instruction.[1]

[1] Teachers and administrative personnel would argue that the results are more valid for this period, since children are less distracted by recollections or anticipation of summer vacation.

The influence of family and peers is assumed to be continuous and to operate throughout the year, whether or not schools are open. The aspect of parental influence that is considered to be central is the socioeconomic status of families. In this chapter, family income is the single measure considered, for purposes of simplicity; however, the models to be considered subsequently incorporate additional indicators of a child's background, such as parental education and household composition. The initial task is to disentangle the influence of schooling from that of parental status; in Part II, the focus is more specifically on the influence of families and the mechanisms through which socioeconomic status influences learning.

The analysis presented in this chapter is largely descriptive; a more rigorous presentation of the data and the quantitative models used is deferred to Chapter 4. The tabular results are based on grade equivalent scores; the more traditional raw score values will be used in the correlational analysis. In both cases, comparisons are based only on those students with test score data for at least three consecutive administrations of the intermediate battery and the requisite background information.

How does achievement vary during the school year and the summer? Table 3.1 presents the mean grade equivalents by race and family income level at each point in time and the observed achievement gains

TABLE 3.1
Mean Grade Equivalent Scores and Gains by Race and Family Income for Metropolitan Achievement Test, Word Knowledge, for Sixth-Grade Atlanta Students[a]

Race and income	Fall 1971	Spring 1972	Fall 1972	School gain	Summer gain
National average[b]	5.10	5.80	6.10	.70	.30
Total Atlanta sample	4.25	4.87	4.86	.62	−.01
White	*4.96*	*5.80*	*6.04*	*.84*	.24
Less than $9,000	4.21	4.86	4.93	.65	.07
$9,000–14,999	4.77	5.73	5.91	.96	.18
$15,000+	5.86	6.86	7.15	1.00	.29
Black	*3.93*	*4.44*	*4.32*	*.51*	*−.12*
Less than $4,000	3.62	4.04	3.76	.42	−.28
$4,000–8,999	3.84	4.35	4.23	.51	−.12
$9,000–14,999	4.08	4.67	4.55	.59	−.12
$15,000+	4.57	5.19	5.41	.62	.22

[a] The sample consists of all students with test scores available at all three points in time. Totals include those for whom family income was not available.

[b] These are the means predicted from the norming population for the particular test date.

TABLE 3.2
Mean Grade Equivalent Scores and Gains by Race and Family Income for Metropolitan Achievement Test, Word Knowledge, for Seventh-Grade Atlanta Students[a]

Race and income	Spring 1971	Fall 1971	Spring 1972	School gain	Summer gain
National average[b]	5.80	6.10	6.80	.70	.30
Total Atlanta sample	4.95	5.00	5.64	.64	.05
White	*6.11*	*6.28*	*6.98*	*.70*	*.17*
Less than $9,000	5.80	5.47	6.27	.80	−.33
$9,000–14,999	5.47	5.70	6.35	.65	.23
$15,000+	6.87	7.24	8.00	.76	.37
Black	*4.32*	*4.30*	*4.91*	*.61*	*−.02*
Less than $4,000	3.93	3.89	4.44	.55	−.04
$4,000–8,999	4.26	4.10	4.63	.53	−.16
$9,000–14,999	4.54	4.54	5.21	.67	0
$15,000+	5.20	5.57	6.45	.88	.37

[a] The sample consists of all students with test scores available at all three points in time. Totals include those for whom family income was not available.

[b] These are the means predicted from the norming population for the particular test date.

for the sixth-grade sample. Table 3.2 gives the parallel results for the seventh grade.[2] The raw scores, standard deviations, and sample sizes for these comparisons are found in Appendix F, with several other tables of less general interest. The national grade equivalent averages given in Tables 3.1 and 3.2 are those calculated by the test manufacturer for the periods in question (Durost *et al.*, 1962). It should be noted that the expected gain during a year is set exactly equal to 1.0 year of achievement; neither cohort achieved this value. In Atlanta, the greatest relative loss when compared to the nation occurred during the summer months. For the total sample of sixth-grade children, the annual gain between the fall of 1971 and 1972 was .61 years, rather than 1.0; hence, the achievement gap between sixth-grade students in Atlanta and in the nation as a whole increased throughout the year.

[2] It will be recalled that the grade designation of cohorts is that of the final testing period, during the fall of 1972. The intermediate battery is given only during the fifth and sixth grades. To avoid comparisons across batteries, which are based on nonparallel forms and different norming populations, only the fifth and sixth-grade test results are used. Throughout the analysis, the data for the sixth-grade cohort consist of the fifth-grade test scores and the fall of sixth grade while the seventh-grade cohort consists of students with complete test histories for the sixth grade and the last test of the fifth grade.

The patterning of gains and losses is more easily seen in graphic form. Figures 3.1 and 3.2 represent the mean observed scores plotted by months; the diagrams reflect the temporal shifts in the rate of cognitive learning by race and income level. Several observations are in order. First, no group maintained the rate of cognitive growth observed during the 7 months of the school term through the summer. Children of every income level, and within both racial groups, showed a slower rate of summer learning than they did when schools were open. Irrespective of socioeconomic background, schooling seems to boost learning. Second, socioeconomic differentials in learning were consistently exacerbated during the summer months. Summer losses were observed in both grades and racial groups for children from families with less than $9,000 income. In the middle-income levels, from $9,000–15,000, white children appeared to make modest gains, while black children did not seem to hold their own. Only high-income children, and high-income whites more than blacks, consistently improved their levels of cognitive achievement during the summer months.

The graphs offer dramatic support for the proposition that schooling increases the learning rates of all children and that the gains are far more equally distributed among children from divergent backgrounds

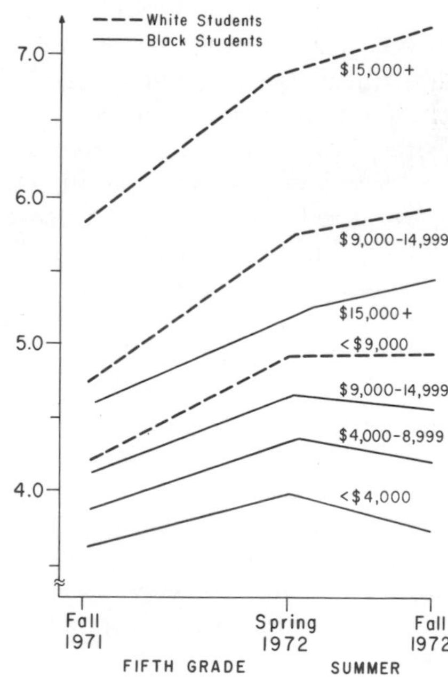

FIGURE 3.1. Rates of cognitive growth in word knowledge achievement, by race and family income, for sixth-grade students.

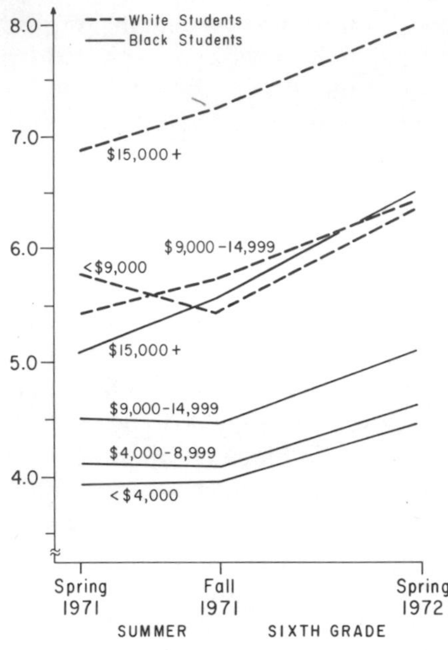

FIGURE 3.2. Rates of cognitive growth in word knowledge achievement, by race and family income, for seventh-grade students.

than is the case when schools are closed. Relatively advantaged children enjoy cognitive gains whether or not schools are open, presumably because their home environments foster intellectual achievement and growth independent of school influences. In stark contrast, poor children are the most dependent on schooling to increase achievement; without schooling, their rates of growth are slowed or reversed. Poor children profit less in absolute terms from schooling than do their more advantaged peers, and in no case are the rates of learning truly equal among children from varying backgrounds. Yet in relative terms, schooling must be seen as an equalizing force, mitigating but not overcoming the disadvantages imposed by economic inequality.

How much cognitive inequality should be attributed to the lack of schooling? The question does not admit an easy answer; as we shall see, there are several ways of quantifying the results. First, it is important to keep in mind the fact that the Atlanta sample viewed in its entirety is economically disadvantaged relative to the nation. Only children from the most affluent strata keep abreast of achievement levels observed nationwide. A comparison of the increasing gaps in cognitive achievement observed between sample children and the norming sample yields the conclusion that the summer differential is responsible for perhaps 80% of the gap. For sixth graders, the gap increased from .85

years to 1.24 years, as we have seen. This annual increase of .39 years between sixth graders in the nation and the sample can be separated into a school component of .08 and a summer portion equal to .31. Had Atlanta sixth graders accumulated achievement throughout the year at the rate observed during the school year, the discrepancy between their gains and those observed for the nation would have been reduced by four-fifths. The corresponding calculation for the seventh-grade cohort suggests an increase of .06 years in the achievement gap during the school months and .25 years during the summer, a figure quite close to that observed for the younger cohort. Apparently, the detrimental effects of economic disadvantage on learning afflict this sample relative to the nation in much the same way as that observed for children from varying backgrounds within the sample. Schooling in Atlanta cannot compensate for the disparity between these children and those of the nation as a whole; however, schooling does consistently reduce the relative differences when compared to those that prevail in the absence of schooling.

Among sample children, the impact of schooling influences relative gaps in a similar fashion. The most dramatic socioeconomic differential implies that between half and two-thirds of the annual learning gap among children accrues during the summer months. For the sixth grade, in the fall of 1971, black sample children from the lowest income level were 2.24 years behind white children from the highest income category; by the fall of 1972, this gap had increased to 3.39 years, and the summer months were primarily responsible. The discrepancy between seventh-grade children from the extremes of socioeconomic disadvantage increases from 2.24 to 2.82 years during the summer and rises to 3.39 years during the sixth grade.

The summer is not a very long time interval, nor is it devoid of educational experiences. As we have seen, learning during the school year, or rather the time interval between October and May, is substantially more rapid than during the summer. If a monthly rate of growth based on annual gains is computed and then compared with that observed during the school term, a summary impression is achieved of the order of magnitude of gains over specific time periods with the length of interval controlled. This comparison is presented in Table 3.3 for the race and income categories described above. If learning were a linear function of time, one would expect a ratio of unity between gains during the school year in months and annual monthly gains. Gains would accrue irrespective of whether schools were open, perhaps as a function of a child's age or mental development. Table 3.3 clearly implies that this pattern does not occur. In no case is learning during the

TABLE 3.3
Ratio of Monthly Gains during the School Year to Annual Monthly Gain, Grade Equivalent Scores, by Grade, Race, and Family Income Level

Race and income	Sixth grade	Seventh grade
White	*1.33*	*1.38*
Less than $9,000	1.55	2.92
$9,000–$14,999	1.44	1.27
$15,000+	1.33	1.15
Black	*2.24*	*1.77*
Less than $4,000	4.50	1.85
$4,000–$8,999	2.24	2.46
$9,000–$14,999	2.15	1.71
$15,000	1.25	1.21

summer as rapid as it is when schools are open. Monthly gains for the 7-month school year exceed monthly gains during the 5-month interval between May and October without exception, and typically by at least one-third.[3]

More important, Table 3.3 yields an explicit estimate of the relative importance of schooling for children from diverse backgrounds. Learning rates during the school year are invariably a larger portion of annual learning than would be expected if a linear function held. Equally, and perhaps even more striking, the relative importance of schooling is inversely related to a child's socioeconomic level. Without exception, children from more advantaged families learn at a more nearly linear rate with respect to time than do poor children. Schooling is critical for the achievement of children from poorer backgrounds, while schooling for the relatively advantaged appears to be supplemental. Well-to-do families are capable of augmenting achievement whether or not schools are open and at rates approximating those found in schools. Poorer families rely to a much greater extent on the schools and are seemingly unable to arrest declines in relative achievement when schools are closed. This pattern, I would argue, can be understood only by assuming that schools are an enormously important ingredient in the

[3] For example, white sample children in Atlanta in the seventh-grade cohort were estimated to be at the following grade levels in May 1971, October 1971, and May 1972: 6.11, 6.28, and 6.98. Thus, monthly gains during the summer were equal to (6.28 − 6.11)/5, while during the school year they were equal to (6.98 − 6.28)/7. School year gains were equal to .1 of a year per month, at parity with the nation, while summer learning accumulated at a rate of .034 years per month. Annual monthly gains for this group are equal to (6.98 – 6.11)/12, or .0725 years per month on average. The ratio of school to annual gains is thus equal to .1/.0725, or 1.38.

achievement process and an equalizing force in the dynamic interplay between family and school. The sources of cognitive inequality are to be found in the disparities among families; the opportunities offered by schooling systematically reduce this inequality and thus are a major factor in the opportunity structure for poor children. If opportunities for equal schooling did not exist, substantially greater inequality of outcomes associated to background would exist; the children most dramatically affected would be precisely those children with the fewest family resources to fall back upon. One might wish that schooling could equalize social disadvantage in absolute terms. Yet it is clear that for numbers of poor children, schooling is a critical means for obtaining educational levels comparable to those of their more advantaged peers.

The patterns of learning described are heavily dependent on the achievement metrics chosen; decomposing the annual gains for raw scores or standardized units would yield similar patterns but differing portions attributable to school and summer. Since the test scores are relative measures, the results cannot be interpreted as due specifically to either differential learning or retention.[4] Family income level is a relatively crude way to measure different home environments; without knowledge of the mechanisms that influence families, the patterns of learning are subject to numerous interpretations. Do families have a larger impact on summer learning than on achievement during the school year because children spend more time at home, or because the positive equalizing influence of education has been curtailed? Should the impact of schooling be construed as attenuating socioeconomic influences or as merely boosting the achievement levels of all children by an amount sufficient to produce greater equality of outcomes? These questions cannot be answered without strong assumptions regarding the constancy or variability of the measured effects of background over time; socioeconomic status represents a host of conceptually distinct but educationally relevant influences that cannot be empirically separated with much confidence.[5]

The configuration of test scores over time is, however, suggestive. At each date, the observed variance in achievement increases, which implies that the total amount of cognitive inequality rises whether or not schools are open. During the school year, however, the variability among the least advantaged pupils increases disproportionately; during the summer, the declines in the test scores occur in conjunction with a substantial contraction of the variability. It is as if certain poor children

[4] For a more complete discussion of metrics, see Chapter 2 and Appendix A.

[5] Mechanisms of parental influence will be dealt with at length in Part II.

are positively influenced by schooling a great deal, but that the gains do not persist when they are exposed to 3 months without schooling. The patterns of school learning are not in this sense incremental; for the relatively disadvantaged child, cognitive growth appears to operate in the fashion of an accordion. During the school year, a substantial number of lower-class children learn at rates equal to those of middle-class children; during the summer, when they are primarily influenced by family and friends, their achievement levels fall precipitously. Among middle-class children, the coefficient of variation, or the ratio of the standard deviation to the mean, is more nearly constant and does not fluctuate depending on whether or not schools are open. Both the achievement means and the standard deviations appear to increase in a more systematic manner through time. Such outcomes may reflect differential reliability, but the results are consistent with a theory that schooling both provides opportunities to children that would not otherwise exist and provides greater equality of outcomes than would exist if education were provided solely by families.[6]

DIFFERENCES BETWEEN SCHOOLS AND EQUALITY OF EDUCATIONAL OPPORTUNITY

For comparative purposes, it is useful to analyze the achievement differences between schools in Atlanta. Although this perspective adds little to our understanding of learning, since the results are similar to those that have been reported in several cross-sectional studies, such an analysis can shed light on the disparities and limitations of these data. If one asks to what degree achievement depends on which school a child attends, the answer is to be found in the conventional decomposition of variance within and between schools. Table 3.4 presents these figures for the 42 sample schools, separately by race, for the test dates.[7] For the total sample, the between-school variance is fairly stable during the school year and increases during the summer.[8] Paradoxically, the school effect, assessed as the between-school variance, increases in strength

[6] The standard deviations by race and income level are given in Appendix F, Tables F.3 and F.7.

[7] The proportion of variance among schools in the Atlanta sample is somewhat larger, particularly for white students, than is customarily found in the literature. This fact reflects the sample design, which tended to overrepresent extreme schools.

[8] The variance added by 41 dummy variables is less than 5.0% for either race when either socioeconomic status or prior achievement is controlled, for any single test. This value never attains significance for the school-year equation.

TABLE 3.4
Proportion of Variance in Achievement between Schools, by Grade, Race, and Test Date, Raw Scores for Matched Sample[a]

Grade and race	Spring 1971	Fall 1971	Spring 1972	Fall 1972
Sixth grade (N = 1499)				
White		.306	.286	.312
Black		.102	.143	.155
Total		.226	.225	.282
Seventh grade (N = 1460)				
White	.272	.321	.273	
Black	.164	.186	.194	
Total	.323	.329	.317	

[a] Uncorrected for degrees of freedom.

when schools are not open. Among white children, exposure to schooling actually diminishes the importance of which school is attended.

Residential location as reflected by where one attends school is a fairly sensitive indicator of a family's socioeconomic status. When schools are in session, family background or which school one attends becomes less important than the common experience of attending school; when schools are closed, the effect of school location serves as a proxy for socioeconomic differences; the increasing explanatory power of school location seems to be a function of socioeconomic differentials and not an effect of schools at all.

This conclusion is borne out by examining the impact of differences between schools once socioeconomic status is controlled. The results from the Atlanta study, like those of other studies of the differences between schools, suggest that once prior achievement and socioeconomic status are included in the prediction of achievement, the net effect of education is trivial. When the school effect is operationalized as the between-school variance, schools are shown to have little independent explanatory power.[9]

An extensive analysis of the differences between schools in Atlanta adds little to the discussion of school effects except to demonstrate that a significant effect of schooling is not incompatible with insignificant

[9] These data are for the total sample, separately by race. During this year, however, a number of black children had changed schools, many by integrating previously all-white schools. Black children were not, therefore, as segregated by socioeconomic status or achievement as were whites.

differences between schools. There are, in addition, numerous substantive reasons for expecting schools in Atlanta to be similar. Within a single district, expenditures and curriculum are relatively standardized. Policy decisions regarding resource allocation and the assignment of teachers are centralized; relatively few decisions of much consequence are made at the school level. These administrative arrangements produce a considerable degree of equity among schools; those disparities that persist are less a function of deliberate choices than of factors outside the control of the educators.

Atlanta schools differ in their facilities and the general quality of buildings and grounds; however, this is largely a function of the age of the buildings. Newer schools tend to be better equipped and to need less maintenance and renovation. Older schools tend to be located in either the very best neighborhoods or the very poorest, largely as a result of demographic changes. Central city schools tend to be all black, quite old, and deficient in key respects; schools in some of the more exclusive residential areas, however, are also aged and have similar deficiencies. Neither black nor white children nor children of particular income strata tend to be uniquely disadvantaged by such differences.

Educational expenditures are largely determined by staff salaries; in most systems, variations in the teaching staff constitute the major source of unequal resources. In Atlanta, teachers are randomly assigned to schools, except for concerted efforts to balance the staff in each school racially. Teachers' characteristics, therefore, tend to be similar in every school. Black schools are on average somewhat larger and are more likely to be overcrowded; but these schools are also more likely to sponsor costly programs such as breakfasts, supervised recreation after school hours, or extended day programs than are the schools in white neighborhoods. In general, budgetary allocations seem to favor the least advantaged children when there are differences, but such differences are minimal.

In sum, school resources are allocated remarkably equally throughout the district; differences among schools do not suggest that either racial or socioeconomic inequities are prevalent. Insofar as educational opportunity is measured by the degree of access to similar facilities, teachers, or other resources, Atlanta is quite egalitarian. The very equity of resources, however, implies that differences between schools will be negligible, and not necessarily related to achievement.

The most salient differences among Atlanta schools are not those of resources or facilities; rather, they are the socioeconomic composition and the correlated patterns of educational performance. These differences are pervasive, and they imply that children are exposed to classmates from backgrounds similar to their own. Although gains during the school year tend to be largely independent of which school is attended, the general pattern of outcomes supports one other conclusion. Table 3.5 presents the grade equivalent gains observed when comparing students enrolled in high- or low-status schools, determined by the proportion of students receiving a free lunch.[10] Excluding those students who changed schools during the year and those few students enrolled in a school in which most of their classmates were of a different racial background, one can compare the rates of learning by family income levels.[11]

The pattern of gains shown in Table 3.5 is intriguing. Although family income is associated with grade equivalent gains, the differences are significant only for white children in low-status schools. The differences between low- and high-status schools are statistically significant only for black children. For both races, however, the pattern of gains suggests considerably more equality of outcomes in the high-status schools. There appears to be an interaction between family income level and school status. Less advantaged children learn substantially more in schools in which the majority of their peers are from higher income families.

A common finding in a number of studies of school effects is that disadvantaged children do systematically better on achievement tests when they attend schools with middle-class peers. There are two interpretations of this result: first, that some aspect of this schooling experience contributes directly to their achievement; second, that the result is largely spurious and due to unmeasured individual attributes. Children from lower-status families living near middle-class schools are atypical; their families are perhaps not as disadvantaged as they seem. Such families may have chosen the school and neighborhood because of a special interest in their child's education and achievement.

Distinguishing between these two interpretations cannot be done unequivocally. Attributing causal importance to such contextual effects invariably risks confounding unmeasured background characteristics

[10] Atlanta schools were selected, it will be recalled, by dichotomizing the total sample by the proportion receiving a free lunch and cross-tabulating these schools by racial composition. (See Appendix B for details.) Table 3.5 replicates this division among schools.

[11] Although there would be some intrinsic interest in assessing the impact of minority status on achievement, or in comparing the gains in integrated schools, only 108 sample children were involved. This is partly the result of the sampling design, but also integration was a fairly recent phenomenon.

TABLE 3.5
Grade Equivalent Gains on Word Knowledge during the School Year by Family Income, Race, and School Socioeconomic Status, Sixth Grade[a]

	High-status schools		Low-status schools	
Race and income	Gain	*N*	Gain	*N*
White	*.91*	*329*	*.68*	*104*
Less than $4,000	.80	4	.49	20
$4,000–7,999	.78	40	.63	36
$8,000–14,999	.94	81	1.12	23
$15,000+	1.01	112	1.57	3
Coefficient of variation	1.147		1.389	
Black	*.65*	*410*	*.48*	*442*
Less than $4,000	.62	34	.43	108
$4,000–7,999	.61	116	.53	158
$8,000–14,999	.61	92	.53	56
$15,000+	.65	84	.62	12
Coefficient of variation	1.845		2.068	

[a] Totals exclude sample children who changed schools during the school year, children who were enrolled in schools in which they were the minority race, and children for whom income data were not available.

or individual attributes with the impact of a particular institution. The use of longitudinal data allows somewhat more certainty that the most important determinant of achievement has been controlled; however, conclusions about contextual effects in a nonexperimental study must remain tentative.

The Atlanta data lend support to the contention that the social composition of a school is modestly related to learning and that lower-status students benefit from attending class with more advantaged peers. One conventional interpretation would attribute this effect to the direct influence of interaction with more advantaged classmates; forming friendships with more academically oriented students is assumed to promote learning and cognitive development. However, these data also support a view of classroom organization that strikes me as more plausible. The most important difference between high-status and low-status schools is the number of children needing special attention from teachers in order to keep abreast of the class. If there are a few children falling behind, individual instruction is an effective teaching tactic; when a great many do not understand the lessons, such a remedy is impossible. The schools enrolling high-status students are distinguished by a relatively small number of children unable or unwilling to do the work; in less favorable circumstances, this number reaches a critical mass, and the instructor is relatively helpless to ensure that the material is learned by all. Learning rates are more equal in high-status schools for this reason, quite apart from how much one learns from peers. I suspect that the structural limitations and the organization of teaching have a great deal more to do with educational performance than the presence of middle-class peers, although neither explanation can be ruled out.

A limitation of studying contextual effects is the ease with which one can generate more explanations than can be tested. Social composition is an amorphous, perhaps even metaphysical, concept. Since we cannot specify the precise mechanisms through which children learn, our understanding of the social process is bound to be rudimentary. Although it is not possible to identify exactly how such influences operate, there appears to be an interaction between family income and the social composition of schools in Atlanta. The learning patterns of low-income children seem to be positively affected when they attend school with predominantly middle-class children, and this relationship is independent of prior achievement level.

The patterns of learning observed during the school year suggest an interpretation of school effects based on achievement outcomes that is considerably more favorable to schools than the current view. The most effective schools are also the educational contexts in which cognitive growth is most equal. The schools that foster the largest gains are also the schools that most effectively reduce the dependence of student achievement on parental status. To some extent, all schools attenuate the effects of background, when the comparisons are between schooling and no schooling. Yet during the school year, the best schools are also the most equal. The largest school effect, in terms of vocabulary gains, is found in conjunction with the greatest equality of outcomes. Although no school negates or reverses the relationship between background status and achievement, the best schools tend to equalize learning to the greatest extent.

In sum, this chapter has endeavored to describe the learning process and to reconceptualize the relationship between schooling and equal opportunity. The patterning of outcomes in one large urban school system suggests the complexity of the issues and offers an interpretation that is both more precise and a good deal more optimistic about the role of schools in furthering equality than are the conventional findings.

The process of schooling depicted strongly suggests that parental status, rather than schooling, operates to maintain and exacerbate inequality. Learning is substantially less influenced by family factors during the school year than it is when schools are closed. The argument is not that schools equalize in an absolute sense or that equality of opportunity has been realized; rather, the achievement gains suggest that the role of education is supplemental, contributing to create equality but not overcoming the impact of family background.

Although the Atlanta school system has achieved a remarkable parity of educational resources among schools, doubtless more could be done. The intent is not to offer a reprieve or an apologia for schools; rather, it is to stress that the effects of schooling do not operate in a vacuum. Children are exposed to numerous influences outside of schools that maintain or even increase unequal performance. A reasonable assessment of education cannot ignore the continuous and ubiquitous influence of families. Schooling, when viewed in contrast to nonschooling, seems to increase both the diversity of outcomes and the rate of cognitive growth. Equally important, superior schooling is associated with greater equality of outcomes, rather than with increased inequality among children from diverse backgrounds. Equality of educational opportunity need not mean leveling, as conservative analysts have been prone to imply. Although the Atlanta study offers few clues as to feasible policy alternatives, the data clearly suggest the importance of schooling for educational achievement.

Chapter 4 extends the analysis of the present chapter, with greater attention to the technical details of the analysis. The objective is to specify the achievement process more rigorously and to attempt to quantify the additive and interactive effects of schooling. The models to be used are drawn from the literature on status attainment, although many of the findings suggest revisions in the basic model. I hope to show that a substantial positive effect of exposure to schooling is compatible with other research in the area.

4

Socioeconomic Background and Schooling

In Chapter 3, I offered a critique of the research on school effects and a reinterpretation of the results. I argued that the effect of being in school was logically independent of the effect of attending a particular school or a particular sort of school. Second, I presented data that supported the contention that achievement varied as a function of whether or not schools were in session. In this model, schooling was argued to have both an additive and an interactive effect on achievement. Schooling both accelerated the rates of learning during the school year and mitigated the effects of family background on learning. Scholastic achievement was argued to result from the dynamic interplay of families and schools, the two institutions most directly concerned with socialization. The purpose of this chapter is to elaborate the achievement process in an explicit causal framework and to estimate the effects of schooling on the educational performance of sixth- and seventh-grade students over time.

The literature on status attainment has successfully dealt with education as a process. Schooling is conceptualized as a temporally ordered accomplishment, as part of the socioeconomic life cycle, which is marked by a sequence of transitions from an individual's origin in a family of a particular status to his establishment of independent adult standing. Education, measured as the years of schooling completed, transmits and mediates the impact of familial characteristics, while also providing a critical channel for upward mobility (Blau & Duncan, 1967;

Duncan, Featherman, & Duncan, 1972; Sewell & Hauser, 1975; Sewell, Hauser, & Featherman, 1976).

Conceptualizing stratification processes as a sequence of temporally ordered outcomes is a dramatic advance over alternative formulations; it has also led to some of the more insightful criticism of the literature on school effects. While carefully documenting the fact that differences between high schools explained at best a very small portion of the variance in achievement, course marks, and aspirations, Hauser (1971) also provided a cogent and compelling critique of studies that focused on school quality. Schooling, Hauser (1971) asserts, "is differentiated temporally, not territorially [p. 7]," and "being in school rather than out of school is far more important than the school one attends [Hauser, 1969, p. 590]." The dilemma for educational research, however, is to identify the processes through which schooling operates, since these do not seem to be variations in school quality, and to understand why schooling plays such an important role in adult attainment. This is aptly posed by Hauser (1969). "It is disconcerting that a definitive study of occupational stratification pictures education as loosening the ties between status origins and destinations, while recent school studies present the opposite interpretation [p. 587]."

The problem of determining how schooling operates has not been adequately addressed by models in the status attainment tradition. Although the models posit an explicit analytic separation of the effects of background and of education on later achievements, schooling is measured at completion. Scholastic achievement is taken to be a correlate of socioeconomic status, rather than a distinct process. The measured effects of schooling thus confound the importance of what is learned while staying in school with the importance of the credentials obtained while there.

In order to illuminate the causal nexus between family and schools in the achievement process, one must have an explicit substantive rationale for separating their respective influences. Viewing both parental status and years of schooling as causally antecedent to occupational achievements, status attainment models document profusely that the rewards of the stratification system are reaped largely as a consequence of years of education rather than as a consequence of paternal status positions. Nevertheless, this formulation leaves open the question of whether the institution modifies the attainment trajectory in any consistent way, or whether it serves only to sort and select candidates who are differentially endowed with talent. In every model of status attainment presented thus far, it is logically impossible to distinguish between an interpretation of schooling as imparting critical skills, knowledge, or opportunities from an interpretation of schooling as the passive agent of certification, screening individuals as they progress through the graded hierarchy. Although studies of the achievement process have proliferated, none have explicitly sought to estimate or test the effects of schooling on scholastic achievement, relative to the effects of families, in an appropriate manner.

Two logically distinct research traditions characterize the study of schooling in sociology. The two traditions are complementary in many respects and both have contributed enormously to our knowledge of educational processes. Nevertheless, the formulation of questions and therefore the pattern of findings are deficient in key respects; neither tradition has been able to address the institutional effects of education in a convincing manner. The first, which I have called school effects, assesses the differences between schools; levels of student achievement or other relevant outcomes are associated with characteristics of the school. The second, which is best exemplified by the status-attainment literature, asks to what extent do higher levels of schooling predict adult achievements of various sorts. Studying school effects leads one to pose the question of how differences in school quality are related to outcomes; however, it ignores the more dramatic impact of attending any school whatsoever. Asking to what degree educational attainment is relevant to the stratification system, as do models of status attainment, captures the importance of having been educated relative to the importance of having grown up in a certain family context; it does not, however, specify the social mechanisms or institutional context that shape later achievements. The quantity of schooling attained is clearly relevant to later achievements, but exactly how the cumulative exposure to schooling operates remains obscure. Interpretations regarding the mechanisms and processes vary; however, the models in and of themselves cannot answer the question of whether and to what extent the educational system either socializes students or simply allocates them to slots based on personal attributes (Kerckhoff, 1976).

The school effects literature has amply documented the relative stability of achievement differentials among children of different class and ethnic backgrounds and has shown that these gaps are largely independent of the particular school attended. The source of this stability, however, remains unexplored. Status-attainment models have conceived of education as a temporal process and as an influence rivaling that of socioeconomic background, but has not applied that insight to the study of educational performance through time.

The dual perspectives on schooling in the sociological literature are paralleled by research in economics. Two separate approaches to studying the economic effects of schooling have evolved, each with a distinctive operational criterion for measuring the effects of education and each with unique findings. In microeconomic models the assumption is that aggregate outcomes are the result of expenditures, resources, or other school characteristics. The production function for schooling is assumed to be the relationship between educational inputs and outputs, or between school characteristics and average achievement levels; the best studies control for the quality of the "raw material," or the characteristics children bring with them to school. This approach, which has been termed the factory model of schooling, is not dissimilar to that of the school effects literature in either the operationalization of concepts or the research results. Studying differences among schools, however they are measured, yields inconsistent and typically insignificant estimates for the effects of schooling (Averch *et al.*, 1975; Burkhead, Fox, & Holland, 1967; Cain & Watts, 1970; Hanushek, 1970; Murnane, 1974).

In sharp contrast, human capital theorists have taken the important question to be the monetary returns to investments in education (Becker, 1964; Hansen, 1970; Mincer, 1974; Weisbrod, 1962). This literature has documented the facts that years of schooling are related to levels of income and that there are substantial economic payoffs to remaining in school. Much like the sociological research on stratification, schooling when measured as credentials or the amount of time spent in school is shown to have a decisive impact on adult earnings and status. However, studies of human capital cannot prove that schooling augments individual capabilities, as opposed to merely screening and filtering students by ability.

Research on education tends to be divided both by method and by interpretation. Clarifying the terms of these debates clearly is desirable, but it does not lead directly to an appropriate technique for studying how, in what ways, or even whether schooling influences achievement. The problem lies both in specifying an appropriate model and in inferring the process when the determinants of achievement are inextricably confounded.

The strategy adopted here is to compare the learning rates of children in school and out of school; that is, to compare the determinants of achievement during the school year and during the summer. Cognitive growth, measured by vocabulary test scores on a single battery of the Metropolitan Achievement Tests, is the criterion for achievement. Families are assumed to influence growth year-round, while schooling is taken to have an intermittent effect, operating only while schools are actually in session. The critical dimension of family influence is assumed to be parental socioeconomic status, and this is taken to be a global indicator of the quality of a child's home environment. These measures are reviewed in the next section.

MEASURING THE EFFECTS OF SOCIOECONOMIC STATUS

The parental survey provided a wealth of information on the demographic compositions of households; regional origins, educational attainments, and occupational positions of both parents; and family income and its source. There were four criteria that guided the selection of variables: (*a*) theoretical relevance and comparability with other studies; (*b*) similarity of effects between the grade cohorts and racial groups studied; (*c*) independent predictive power; and (*d*) the response rates.

The coding of variables followed conventions established in the sociological literature. Educational attainments were scored as years of completed schooling; occupational positions were coded using the prestige scores established by Duncan (1961); family income, number of siblings, and household size were each coded in actual numeric values. The questions employed on the interview schedule were similar to those used by census surveys. This questionnaire is reproduced in Appendix C. The means, standard deviations, and correlation matrices used for the analysis are reported in Appendix E.

Initially, the three measures of socioeconomic status that were considered most relevant were paternal education and occupational attainment and the number of siblings, since these variables have figured strongly in most analyses of educational outcomes. However, the final measures chosen were family income, mean parental education, and household size. Family income proved to be the most sensitive measure of economic status, especially for black respondents. Mean parental education was more closely linked to achievement than was the value of either parent separately and had the additional advantage of providing a score for families with only a female head.[1] The number of siblings tended to be highly related to the household size, especially among white families; household size, however, captured to a greater extent the numbers of people who share fixed family resources, such as income and parent's time. Extended families and boarders are more common in the black community, and this variable is a more adequate description of the composition of the family unit than is the number of siblings.

These three variables taken together virtually exhaust the independent effects of family socioeconomic status on achievement, once prior achievement is controlled. Household size, although often insignifi-

[1] Among sixth-grade sample children in Atlanta, 85.7% of the whites lived with a male head of household and 60.8% of the black children.

cant, was retained in most of the equations to give comparability and to introduce some measure of household economies of scale. Variables such as the presence of a male head, the mother's employment status, and whether income was from earnings or transfer payments proved to have little additional impact on achievement once family income level, parental education, and household size were included.[2] Although there are differences between white and black families in the relative importance of particular variables, the final models suggest that these differences are slight.

The socioeconomic variables thus yield consistent estimates of the effects of parental status for each cohort and racial group at each point in time. Including all three variables, however, reduces the effects of each since they tend to be highly collinear. Since it was useful to have a composite measure of the effect of socioeconomic background for lucidity of exposition, a single index was created.[3] This composite permits summary statements regarding the strength of socioeconomic status in the scholastic achievement process, and a concise means of data reduction for graphic presentation.

THE BASIC MODEL

The basic model that will be elaborated in numerous respects can be briefly summarized. Two structural equations are taken to represent the patterns of learning over time. For the sixth grade they are

$$A_{F72} = \rho_{F \cdot S} A_{S72} + \rho_{F \cdot R} R + \rho_{F \cdot SES} SES + \rho_{SU} U \tag{1}$$

and

$$A_{S72} = \rho_{S \cdot F} A_{F71} + \rho_{S \cdot R} R + \rho_{S \cdot SES} SES + \rho_{SV} V \tag{2}$$

where A refers to achievement scores in raw form at a specific point in time, R is the race of the respondent, and SES, the child's socioeconomic status. The residual terms, U and V, are assumed to be serially uncorrelated and uncorrelated with the other independent variables included

[2] Regression equations including all the background variables are presented in Appendix F, Table F.9, p. 285.

[3] The SES index was constructed by weighting each of five standardized indicators by their factor loadings, and summing these values. The five indicators, in order of importance, were family income, father's education, mother's education, father's occupational prestige, and household size. Missing data on specific indicators were coded 0, the mean of each variable.

in the equation. Achievement is assumed initially to be completely determined by prior achievement level and background factors, although the model will be elaborated in an incremental fashion to include other intervening variables. The models will be estimated using multiple regression techniques and path analysis (Duncan, 1966, 1975; Heise, 1969; Land, 1969).

The initial question is whether the learning process specified to occur during the summer [Eq. (1)] differs in systematic ways from that posited for the school year [Eq. (2)]. Tables 4.1–4.3 present the results for each time interval for sixth-grade students separately by race. The unstandardized coefficients, b, their standard errors, σ, and the standardized coefficients, b^*, are presented for both the summer and school year.

Several observations are in order. The equations imply that fall achievement is more highly related to socioeconomic status than is spring achievement, whether or not prior achievement is controlled. During the school year, for blacks and for the total sample, only parental education is significantly related to test scores once prior achievement is controlled. Mean parental education has a consistently larger impact on school learning than on summer learning, but it is the only variable for which this is true. The racial background of students influences

TABLE 4.1
Partial Regression Coefficients of Posttest Achievement on Socioeconomic Status and Pretest, Sixth Grade, White Sample

Word knowledge	Family income	Parental education	Household size	Prior test	R^2
		*School Year (Fall 1971–*Spring 1972)			
b	.3664[a]	1.6506[a]	−.3491		
(σ)	(.1287)	(.2663)	(.3578)		
b^*	.1773	.3875	−.0451		.2805
b	.0511	.1408	−.2506	.9058[a]	
(σ)	(.0756)	(.1651)	(.2076)	(.0349)	
b^*	.0246	.0331	−.0324	.8382	.7600
		Summer (Spring 1972–Fall 1972)			
b	.4967[a]	1.4402[a]	−.5405		
(σ)	(.1316)	(.2726)	(.3663)		
b^*	.2380	.3347	−.0692		.2871
b	.1903[a]	.0605	−.2487	.8359[a]	
(σ)	(.0742)	(.1600)	(.2041)	(.0309)	
b^*	.0913	.0141	−.0318	.8276	.7799

[a] Coefficients at least twice as large as their standard error.

TABLE 4.2
Partial Regression Coefficients of Posttest Achievement on Socioeconomic Status and Pretest, Sixth Grade, Black Sample

Word knowledge	Family income	Parental education	Household size	Prior test	R^2
		School Year (Fall 1971–Spring 1972)			
b	.3390[a]	.7426[a]	−.3202		
(σ)	(.0803)	(.1806)	(.1844)		
b^*	.1735	.1753	−.0621		.1073
b	.0944	.3422[a]	−.0681	.8118[a]	
(σ)	(.0589)	(.1319)	(.1314)	(.0306)	
b^*	.0483	.0809	−.0132	.6882	.5368
		Summer (Spring 1972–Fall 1972)			
b	.4864[a]	.7992[a]	−.3554		
(σ)	(.0781)	(.1766)	(.1804)		
b^*	.2484	.1884	−.0687		.1652
b	.2432[a]	.2670[a]	−.1255	.7127[a]	
(σ)	(.0532)	(.1202)	(.1216)	(.0237)	
b^*	.1242	.0629	−.0243	.7157	.6224

[a] Coefficients at least twice as large as their standard error.

TABLE 4.3
Partial Regression Coefficients of Posttest Achievement on Socioeconomic Status, Race, and Pretest, Sixth Grade, Total Sample

Word knowledge	Family income	Parental education	Household size	Prior test	Race	R^2
		School Year (Fall 1971–Spring 1972)				
b	.3521[a]	1.1100[a]	−.2067		6.9276[a]	
(σ)	(.0714)	(.1535)	(.1970)		(.7453)	
b^*	.1742	.2464	−.0299		.2656	.2793
b	.0822	.2759[a]	−.2392	.8413[a]	1.8435[a]	
(σ)	(.0484)	(.1060)	(.1326)	(.0239)	(.5219)	
b^*	.0407	.0612	−.0345	.7373	.0707	.6741
		Summer (Spring 1972–Fall 1972)				
b	.4746[a]	1.0783[a]	−.2738		8.3051[a]	
(σ)	(.0799)	(.1506)	(.1932)		(.7310)	
b^*	.2268	.2314	−.0382		.3078	.3522
b	.2078[a]	.2381[a]	−.1174	.7570[a]	3.0610[a]	
(σ)	(.0451)	(.0982)	(.1230)	(.0195)	(.4843)	
b^*	.0993	.0511	−.0164	.7318	.1134	.7381

[a] Coefficients at least twice as large as their standard error.

both school and summer learning, but the effects are substantially larger during the summer, independent of prior achievement or socioeconomic status. The effects of prior achievement, by far the largest coefficient in each comparison, are without exception smaller during the summer months than during the school year. Despite the fact that the zero-order correlations between pretest and posttest are larger when based on the shorter time period of 5 summer months, the net effect of prior achievement is greater than the corresponding effect observed during the school year. The models yield, then, generally consistent support, for the interpretation that learning during the school year is based less on parental status and more on prior achievement than is the case during the summer; moreover, the impact of parental status is heightened during the summer, when schools are closed.

Diagrammatically, these relationships are summarized in Figure 4.1. The effect of socioeconomic status is based on the composite index described earlier. The relative importance of both race and socioeconomic status increases during the summer relative to the school year; achievement during the school year is determined by prior achievement to a greater degree than is achievement during the summer. As Figure 4.1 demonstrates, however, there are substantial correlations among the residuals that cannot be explained by the variables scrutinized.

The issue of autocorrelation raises the possibility that substantive errors of specification have biased the procedures. These are methodological issues of some import, which will concern us shortly. The model suggests that the combined influence of all independent variables increases between the spring and fall of 1972. Socioeconomic status is

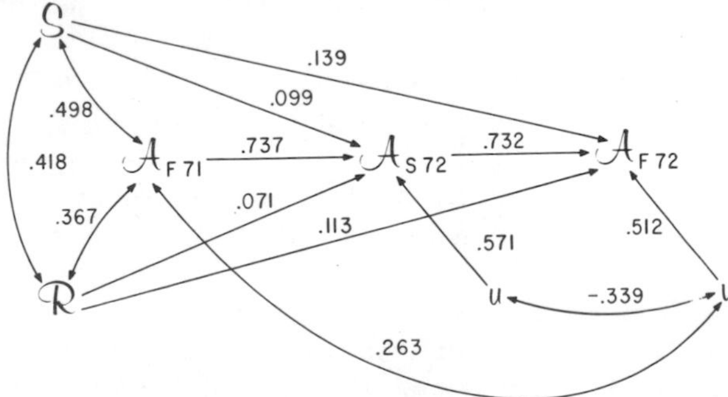

FIGURE 4.1 Model of the determination of achievement for sixth-grade students. A = Achievement; S = Socioeconomic status, R = Race.

not the singular variable to be magnified during the summer; rather, the summer effect is observed in conjunction with a more general increase in the variance explained at each date. This fact is even more troubling than the serial correlations posited among errors of measurement. Regression estimates in the presence of autocorrelation are unbiased and consistent; however, random errors of measurement depress the magnitude of the estimated effects and understate their relative importance. The increasing explanatory power of all variables suggests that test scores are more reliably measured over time. If test scores were measured more reliably in the fall of 1972 than in the preceding spring, perhaps the effect of social class during the school year is understated. Perhaps the true effect is relatively constant and does not interact with schooling in the manner hypothesized.

The reliability of test scores was discussed at some length in Chapter 2. I argued that corrections for attenuation should not be applied indiscriminately and that a close scrutiny of the longitudinal results suggested that the assumption of random, normally distributed errors was unlikely. Equally, test–retest models intended to separate the effects of stability and unreliability yielded unrealistic estimates, whether or not one assumed serially correlated errors.

The increase in the predictive power of the independent variables over time must be due to one of three causes, operating separately or in combination. First, an increase in the actual impact of background on achievement would suggest that parental status factors become more important over time. Second, a decrease in the reliability of socioeconomic status or race would produce a diminished effect on early test scores; one might argue that since the information on student background was collected during the fall of 1972, the relationship between this measure and earlier test results was attenuated. Finally, the reliability of test scores may have increased over time, due perhaps to student maturation, practice at taking tests, or other factors. This increased reliability could result from either an increase in the true score or a decrease in the error variance, relative to the total.

Each of these factors complicates the interpretation of schooling in different ways. The implications of an increasing true effect or of instability or unreliability in the measurement of socioeconomic status will be dealt with in the final section of this chapter. The immediate issue of concern is the implications for the model of schooling posited, if one assumes that the reliability of test scores is a function of the time period. The assumptions of either constant reliability or constant error variance do not fit the observed data very well. If the test scores are viewed as a sequence of repeated observations, every measure with any

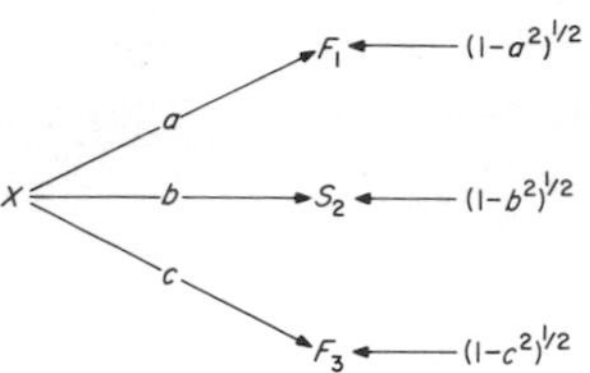

FIGURE 4.2. Model of the hypothetical variable *X* in the determination of achievement.

degree of association with test scores shows a similar pattern of increase. If either the reliability or error variance were constant, one would not expect such consistency.

The best estimate of the error variance, assuming that it is uncorrelated to the true score at a specific test date, is equal to $\sigma_A^2(1.00-R^2_{A \cdot 1 \cdots n})$, or the variance of observed scores times the proprotion of variance unexplained. Although it is true that the observed variances increase during the course of the fifth or sixth grade, this is not sufficient to account for the increase in explanatory power. The error variance appears to decline in absolute magnitude, as well as in proportion to the total variance to be explained, at each successive date.

One final exercise illustrates these patterns and provides a justification for the assumption that the true score increases over time. Let us imagine that a model such as that presented in Figure 4.2 describes the process. A single variable X is hypothesized to explain all of the variability in test scores at each point in time. The model assumes no causal order among test scores and no direct relationship except that between X and F_1, S_2, and F_3. Each test is completely determined by an effect parameter a, b, or c and an error term; errors are uncorrelated with each other and with X. Such a variable might be a composite of the effects of socioeconomic status, ability, and prior achievement. Using three-wave panel data, it is possible to estimate the magnitude of each coefficient, if the model were required to reproduce the observed correlations. The three parameters can be computed from the three structural equations implied by the diagram. For the sixth grade, these equations would be

$$r_{12} = ab = .81139,$$
$$r_{23} = bc = .84038,$$
$$r_{13} = ac = .83893.$$

The model is just identified, and the solutions are given by

$$a = (r_{12}r_{13}/r_{23})^{\frac{1}{2}} = .8999,$$
$$b = (r_{12}r_{23}/r_{13})^{\frac{1}{2}} = .9016,$$
$$c = (r_{13}r_{23}/r_{12})^{\frac{1}{2}} = .9322.$$

For heuristic purposes, the model casts light on the structure of correlations necessary to produce the stability of test scores over time. In order to replicate the matrix of observed scores, one would have to assume that any presumed cause of achievement increased, rather than decreased over time. The pattern of observed correlations, without the inclusion of any additional information, suggests that the true score variability of achievement is not stable. In the hypothetical model, c will always be greater than a if r_{23} is larger than r_{12}, and if the residuals are uncorrelated. One would therefore expect that any variable that covaried with the true score, or with increments in true score, would tend to increase over time. It seems likely that the true score increases and that it increases disproportionately to the observed variability at each successive test date.

The pattern of an increasing effect on achievement of particular variables and sets of variables is common to each subsample examined. Demonstrating that the true score is probably not stable, however, does not remove the difficult problem of the stability of posited effects. Since the true score increases, one would expect summer effects such as those hypothesized. The increasing relationship between achievement and socioeconomic status cannot, therefore, be taken as evidence that the influence of socioeconomic background is larger during the summer months than during the school year. If the analysis were based entirely on this cohort, such a pattern would clearly vitiate the major findings.

The seventh-grade cohort also took the fall achievement tests in 1972; these tests, however, were drawn from the advanced battery, rather than the intermediate form. These students took the three consecutive parallel forms at the end of the fifth grade and during the sixth grade; in the spring of 1971, the fall of 1971, and the spring of 1972, respectively. The summer occurs prior to the school year in time; an assessment of the achievement process that ends with the school term can thus be made. If the increase in the magnitude of socioeconomic status as a determinant of achievement is the result of the increasing reliability, one would not expect to find a decreasing effect of socioeconomic status for this cohort. Tables 4.4, 4.5, and 4.6 present these results. To an even greater extent than before, these data support the hypotheses. For both white and black students, all three measures of parental status are significant during the summer, while not one is significant during the school year. For both white and black students, the direct effect of prior achievement is consistently more highly related to spring scores than to fall scores, suggesting that the achievement process during the school year depends less on parental status and more on incremental learning. Although parental status and achievement are clearly correlated, their

TABLE 4.4
Partial Regression Coefficients of Posttest Achievement on Socioeconomic Status and Pretest, Seventh Grade, White Sample

Word knowledge	Family income	Parental education	Household size	Prior test	R^2
		Summer (Spring 1971–Fall 1971)			
b	.3209[a]	1.8145[a]	−1.1474[a]		
(σ)	(.1038)	(.2268)	(.3166)		
b^*	.1581	.4182	−.1536		.3285
b	.2518[a]	.4798[a]	−.5178[a]	.7132[a]	
(σ)	(.0678)	(.1586)	(.2081)	(.0307)	
b^*	.1240	.1106	−.0693	.7168	.7163
		School Year (Fall 1971–Spring 1972)			
b	.3114[a]	1.6882[a]	−.9234[a]		
(σ)	(.1003)	(.2191)	(.3058)		
b^*	.1607	.4075	−.1295		.3079
b	.0567	.2468	−.0120	.7944[a]	
(σ)	(.0584)	(.1360)	(.1791)	(.0279)	
b^*	.0292	.0596	−.0017	.8319	.7726

[a] Coefficients at least twice as large as their standard error.

TABLE 4.5
Partial Regression Coefficients of Posttest Achievement on Socioeconomic Status and Pretest, Seventh Grade, Black Sample

Word knowledge	Family income	Parental education	Household size	Prior test	R^2
		Summer (Spring 1971–Fall 1971)			
b	.5781[a]	.7430[a]	−.6623[a]		
(σ)	(.0756)	(.1700)	(.1713)		
b^*	.2937	.1729	−.1307		.2038
b	.2492[a]	.2512[a]	−.3228[a]	.7907[a]	
(σ)	(.0484)	(.1075)	(.1078)	(.0232)	
b^*	.1266	.0585	−.0637	.7458	.6889
		School Year (Fall 1971–Spring 1972)			
b	.6163[a]	.8039[a]	−.8007[a]		
(σ)	(.0848)	(.1907)	(.1922)		
b^*	.2815	.1683	−.1422		.1957
b	.0836	.1197	−.1908	.9209[a]	
(σ)	(.0499)	(.1095)	(.1100)	(.0023)	
b^*	.0383	.0251	−.0339	.8284	.7421

[a] Coefficients at least twice as large as their standard error.

TABLE 4.6
Partial Regression Coefficients of Posttest Achievement on Socioeconomic Status, Race, and Pretest, Seventh Grade, Total Sample

Word knowledge	Family income	Parental education	Household size	Prior test	Race	R^2
			Summer (Spring 1971–Fall 1971)			
b	.4401[a]	1.2301[a]	−.7451[a]		8.7620[a]	
(σ)	(.0643)	(.1414)	(.1886)		(7.0789)	
b^*	.2111	.2547	−.0994		.3223	.4236
b	.2354[a]	.3454[a]	−.3485[a]	.7626[a]	1.8963[a]	
(σ)	(.0409)	(.0919)	(.1194)	(.0191)	(.4781)	
b^*	.1129	.0715	−.0465	.7318	.0697	.7711
			School Year (Fall 1971–Spring 1972)			
b	.4572[a]	1.2106[a]	−.7925[a]		8.7644[a]	
(σ)	(.0681)	(.1498)	(.1998)		(.7496)	
b^*	.2112	.2414	−.1018		.3104	.4009
b	.0741	.1392[a]	−.1435	.8710[a]	1.1327[a]	
(σ)	(.0396)	(.0198)	(.1145)	(.0815)	(.4564)	
b^*	.0341	.0341	−.0184	.8386	.0401	.8062

[a] Coefficients at least twice as large as their standard error.

effects seem systematically patterned by whether or not schools are open.

The seventh-grade regressions are based on the correlations presented in Appendix E, Tables E.6, E.7, and E.8. A summary diagram is given in Figure 4.3, to which we now turn.

Both the sixth- and seventh-grade cohorts support the general conclusion that the learning process differs between the summer and the school year. Yet the regressions do not yield an answer to the question that is the central concern of this book. How important is schooling in the achievement process, and to what degree does exposure to education systematically alter outcomes by socioeconomic status? Schooling in each model is unobserved; education is the hypothetical construct accounting for the achievement processes depicted. Yet the goal is a precise quantitative estimate of the additive and interactive effects of schooling over time. The most reasonable model for estimating these effects will be deferred for the moment. Its value will perhaps be enhanced in contrast with the preliminary versions, which require a great deal more in the way of assumptions.

Figure 4.3 presents the seventh-grade model alluded to above, with the summary estimates for the effects of socioeconomic status, race, and prior achievement. The major distinction between this model and that of Figure 4.1 is the addition of a variable labeled "school." This variable

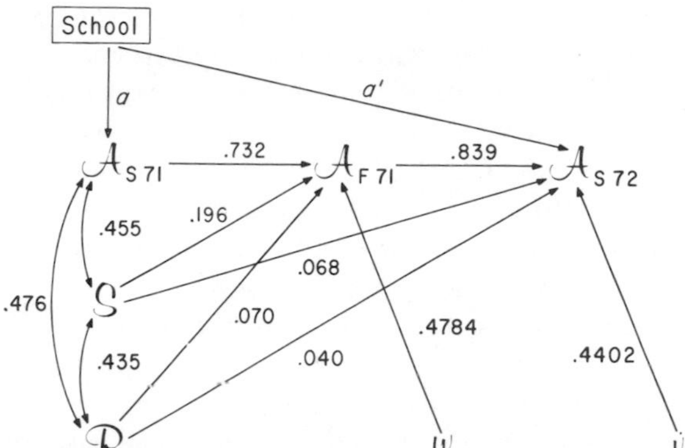

FIGURE 4.3. Model of the determination of achievement for seventh-grade students, with an additional hypothetical variable posited for schooling. A = Achievement; S = Socioeconomic status; R = Race.

is assumed to be uncorrelated with social class or race and to have a direct effect on achievement in the spring, and only an indirect influence on fall test scores. The two parameters, a and a', are assumed to be standardized coefficients and to influence achievement in the way described. The model makes the explicit claim that schooling has a direct additive effect on achievement only in the spring and that it does not operate during the summer, except through prior achievement levels. If one is willing to make certain assumptions about the achievement process, it is possible to estimate the magnitude of the paths a and a'.

If one were willing to assume that the true variability of test scores did not change through time and that the error variance was also constant, and hence equal in the fall and spring of 1972, one might infer that the absence of schooling accounted for the diminished variance explained in the fall of 1971. An estimate of a', the effect of schooling, would then be equal to the difference between the predictive power of the independent variables in the final testing period and that observed in the period preceding, since both equations contain similar variables. Given the observations on errors of measurement discussed above, however, these assumptions are quite unrealistic.

A second strategy involves assuming uncorrelated errors over time. The system of recursive equations for the learning process is overidentified; there is one additional correlation that was not used in the calculation of the paths. The observed correlation between the two spring scores, which is equal to .8497, should be equal to the value predicted by the sum of the direct and indirect effects. If one were to assume that the disturbance terms W and V were correctly specified as uncorrelated to A_{S71} and to each other, this correlation should be equal to .7669. One might then argue that the effects of schooling should be equal at both points in time, such that $a = a'$. An estimate of the effect of schooling would then be equal to the discrepancy between the observed correlation and the predicted value; a^2 would be equal to .0828, and the posited effect of schooling, a, would have the rather substantial effect estimated as equal to .2877.[4]

The deficiencies of both models are that they require rather strong assumptions about measurement error, which seem unrealistic in the context of empirical results. While it is possible to estimate the effects of schooling through other means, such as by constraining the parameters to be equal to fixed values or by introducing other measures of background and positing a model containing multiple indicators, such efforts have not proved particularly fruitful. The most plausible model, and one that permits an explicit test of the interactions posited, will be presented shortly. Before turning to an assessment of the effect of schooling, however, the next section will examine the achievement process when IQ is introduced as an antecedent factor.

THE EFFECTS OF IQ

The Atlanta school system routinely administers individual IQ tests to all pupils enrolled in the fourth grade; these records, augmented by the tests given to students who enter the system after this grade level, become part of the student's permanent file. When the test history files were assembled, IQ scores were retrieved for every sample child in the study.

Concepts of intelligence hold a sovereign position in most analyses of achievement or learning. Since any two sets of test scores tend to be highly correlated, analysts have generally accepted this as prima facie evidence that an individual attribute or capacity was causally related to educational performance. Measures of this attribute, whether defined as verbal skills, abstract reasoning, or a general learning potential, often eclipse the more modest association observed between parental status and achievement levels. This is commonly interpreted to mean that differences among families impart some advantage early in life, through

[4] In an earlier version of this monograph (Heyns, 1976b), I presented several alternative versions of this model based on the sixth-grade cohort. If one assumes that the effects of socioeconomic status and race are equal in the spring and fall, and that the observed diminished effect is entirely due to the temporal intervention of schooling, it is possible to estimate the direct effect of schooling (.39), and the indirect influence through prior achievement (+.14), socioeconomic status (−.33) and race (−.33).

heredity and/or environment, but that later academic achievements are the result of individual differences in intelligence.

The magnitude of the correlation between IQ and achievement test scores is not sufficient to establish its causal importance. The correlations are due at least in part to the common assumptions and similar techniques used in the construction of all tests of verbal ability. To argue that IQ is critical to the learning process, one must assume that it measures some aspect of verbal skills that is not more precisely captured by prior achievement levels. Although the individually administered IQ tests are probably more reliable, they lack the temporal specificity of the sequence of test scores. Consequently, the repeated measures of vocabulary skills based on parallel forms seem more useful for assessing the effects of schooling and the fluctuating patterns of growth over time.

In general, IQ behaves like a correlate of both achievement and socioeconomic status. When IQ is incorporated into models of the achievement process as a continuous influence, occurring prior to initial achievement, it tends to reduce the direct effects of both socioeconomic status and prior achievement level on all subsequent achievement. It does not, however, change the patterning of effects when achievement during the school year and the summer are compared. The discrepancy between the impact of family background on fall scores over that observed in the spring is not reduced. Although the zero-order correlations between IQ and achievement increase over time, much like the other variables studied, the direct effect decreases systematically.

These patterns are portrayed in the set of equations presented in Table 4.7, based on the total sample of seventh-grade students with test scores available at each of the four testing periods of the intermediate battery. The measures of socioeconomic status are family income and parental education, described earlier; both race and IQ are included in each equation. The relevant correlation matrix is reproduced in Appendix E, Table E.2, with the means and standard deviations of all variables. The coefficients in Table 4.7 are presented in both standardized (b^*) and unstandardized (b) form.

The effect of IQ is quite significant and of greater magnitude than the combined influence of the measures of socioeconomic status. The unique contribution of IQ declines over time, however, and the inclusion of this variable does not alter the fluctuation of effects observed over time. These patterns are consistent with at least two interpretations. First, one might argue that the effects of IQ on achievement are causal, in that the development of achievement is determined by some relatively stable attribute such as intelligence, as a consequence of

TABLE 4.7
Regression Coefficients of Posttest on Pretest Achievement, Family Income, Parental Education, Race, and IQ, Seventh Grade, Matched Sample

	Predetermined variables					
Word knowledge	Prior test	Family income (in thousands)	Parental education	Race	IQ	R^2
Spring 1972 (Sixth grade)						
b	.8581[a]	.1403[a]	.1349	1.6032[a]		
(σ)	(.0264)	(.0548)	(.1160)	(.6357)		
*b**	.8128	.0644	.0272	.0573		.8002
b	.6915[a]	.0862	.0659	1.3719[a]	.1782[a]	
(σ)	(.0333)	(.0527)	(.1109)	(.6064)	(.0234)	
*b**	.6550	.0396	.0133	.0491	.2298	.8189
Fall 1971 (Summer)						
b	.7227[a]	.2780[a]	.3670[a]	2.5394[a]		
(σ)	(.0265)	(.0563)	(.1207)	(.6622)		
*b**	.7049	.1349	.0781	.0959		.7548
b	.5433[a]	.1765[a]	.2619[a]	2.1714[a]	.2047[a]	
(σ)	(.0325)	(.0542)	(.1142)	(.6245)	(.0238)	
*b**	.5299	.0856	.0557	.0820	.2787	.7833
Spring 1971 (Fifth grade)						
b	.7872[a]	.1567[a]	.2944[a]	3.3818[a]		
(σ)	(.0338)	(.0652)	(.1394)	(.7529)		
*b**	.7096	.0482	.0642	.1309		.6891
b	.5648[a]	.0552	.1611	2.3411[a]	.2636[a]	
(σ)	(.0400)	(.0614)	(.1298)	(.7154)	(.0278)	
*b**	.5146	.0274	.0387	.0906	.3681	.7247

[a] Coefficients at least twice as large as their standard error.

biological maturation. Alternatively, one might argue that IQ has no independent effect on learning, but rather acts precisely like an early test score. Measured IQ is consistently related to achievement, largely through an association with prior achievement, and not because of a directly causal role.

In a highly collinear system, it is impossible to distinguish scientifically between these two interpretations simply by inspecting the equations. Since all test scores are highly correlated, they tend to absorb a disproportionate share of the joint variance, thus reducing the measured impact of other variables. It is clearly parsimonious in empirical work to omit variables that are redundant, but it is also possible that the most highly related variables are not the most important causes of an outcome of interest. The theoretical bases for distinguishing between achievement test scores and measures of ability are weak; the pattern of large observed correlations may be misleading with respect to causal importance. My argument for the importance of social class rests on the patterning of effects, rather than their magnitude. Although IQ does contribute unique variance, this is never great than 4%; socio-economic status operates temporally in the specified fashion, irrespective of IQ. These factors seem more relevant than the size of the coefficients in question.

ESTIMATING THE EFFECTS OF SCHOOLING

Each of the models examined supports the primary contention that the learning rates of children are contingent on socioeconomic status more directly during the summer than they are when schools are in session. Correspondingly, the determination of achievement during the school year seems more directly dependent on prior achievement level. The major determinant of these patterns has been argued to be schooling; attending school, I have argued, increases the achievement for all children, but also reduces the impact of parental status on outcomes to a significant degree. The present section extends the preceding analysis by attempting to quantify the effect of schooling in a temporal frame.

Substantively, the influence of schooling has been assumed to be a temporal interaction. One method of describing and estimating the effect of schooling would be to treat the set of repeated observations as if they were a time series. The relationship between posttest and pretest would be assumed to depend on socioeconomic status, race, prior achievement, and whether or not schools were in session. Schooling would then assume the status of a seasonal adjustment; it would be allowed to have both an additive and an interactive effect on achievement. In simplest form, the model would be described by

$$A_t = b_0 + b_1A_{t-1} + b_2Z + b_3ZA_{t-1} + e_i, \tag{3}$$

where A_t represents the posttest achievement score, A_{t-1} is the pretest, and Z is a binary variable introduced to capture the effects of schooling such that

$Z_t = 1$ if A_t is a spring test score, implying that schools were open during the interval and

$Z_t = 0$ otherwise.

The final parameter b_3 is an interaction term, or a slope dummy, that permits the relationship between posttest and pretest to depend on schooling. The model permits both the intercept and the slope of the achievement process to depend on schooling.[5]

The interpretation of the coefficients is straightforward. Observe that had separate least squares equations been estimated for the two time periods, summer and schooling, the models would yield parameters identical to those estimated from the single equation, provided there were no missing data. Thus, the two equations

$$A_{F72} = b_0 + b_1 A_{S72} + e_i$$
$$A_{S72} = (b_0 + b_2) + (b_1 + b_3)A_{F71} + e_i$$

yield identical parameters to those estimated by Eq. (3). The effect of schooling, b_2, is equivalent to the difference between the intercepts of the school and the summer equations; the interaction between schooling and prior achievement, b_3, is the difference between the two slopes. Extending the model to include other background variables that influence achievement and may interact with schooling is easily accomplished. This specification permits a parsimonious description of the effects of schooling and permits the strength of the relationships to be tested directly.

The models presented in Tables 4.8–4.10 were estimated in the fashion outlined. The posttest, which consists of the pooled test scores on the last two testing periods, was regressed on the pretest, which is set equal to the two initial observations, as well as the dummy adjustment for schooling, socioeconomic status, the schooling by achievement interaction term, and various combinations of background variables that interact with schooling. The three sets of equations reflect the outcomes for the total sample and separately by race. The sets of equations permit testing for the significance of the additive and interactive effects of schooling on achievement, calculated on the basis of annual increments in test score during the fifth grade and the subsequent summer. The coefficients are the unstandardized regression estimates based on those students with complete data for all the variables included; the input matrices used are included in Appendix E, Tables E.11–E.13, pp. 275–277.

Several observations are in order. First, for all three groups the main effects of prior achievement, socioeconomic background, IQ, and schooling are always positive. Family income has a statistically significant direct effect for all three subsamples irrespective of other variables included, with the exception of Model IV for white students. Parental

[5] Although such models are common in economics, they have not been widely used in sociology. Kmenta (1971, Chapter 11) provides examples of their use.

TABLE 4.8
Coefficients and Standard Errors for an Interactive Model of the Effects of Schooling and Background, Sixth-Grade White Students

		Predetermined variables									
							Interaction of schooling with				
	Constant	Prior achievement	School effect	Family income (in thousands)	Parental education	IQ	Ach.	Income	Education	IQ	R^2
Model I	3.811	.842	2.945	.211			.078	−.147			.7776
(σ)	(.92)	(.03)	(1.26)	(.06)			(.04)	(.08)			
Model II	−9.815	.635	4.228	.124		.197	.102	−.122		−.032	.8039
(σ)	(2.11)	(.04)	(3.05)	(.06)		(.03)	(.06)	(.08)		(.04)	
Model III	3.048	.836	2.928	.183	.108		.077	−.146			.7779
(σ)	(1.23)	(.03)	(1.26)	(.07)	(.11)		(.04)	(.08)			
Model IV	−10.059	.633	4.217	.114	.040	.196	.101	−.121	−.002	−.032	.8040
(σ)	(2.30)	(.04)	(3.35)	(.07)	(.15)	(.03)	(.06)	(.09)	(.22)	(.04)	

TABLE 4.9
Coefficients and Standard Errors for an Interactive Model of the Effects of Schooling and Background, Sixth-Grade Black Students

		Predetermined variables									
							Interaction of schooling with				
	Constant	Prior achievement	School effect	Family income (in thousands)	Parental education	IQ	Ach.	Income	Education	IQ	R^2
Model I	2.883	.735	2.622	.298			.084	−.133			.5798
(σ)	(.58)	(.02)	(.81)	(.05)			(.04)	(.07)			
Model II	−11.563	.577	6.078	.217		.195	.093	−.111		−.048	.6217
(σ)	(1.48)	(.03)	(2.18)	(.04)		(.02)	(.04)	(.07)		(.03)	
Model III	.037	.723	2.587	.216	.335		.083	−.133			.5842
(σ)	(.92)	(.02)	(.81)	(.05)	(.08)		(.04)	(.07)			
Model IV	−14.365	.567	7.010	.133	.348	.193	.097	−.084	−.113	−.047	.6252
(σ)	(1.74)	(.03)	(2.52)	(.03)	(.11)	(.02)	(.03)	(.07)	(.16)	(.03)	

TABLE 4.10

Coefficients and Standard Errors for an Interactive Model of the Effects of Schooling and Background, Sixth-Grade Total Sample

		Predetermined variables											
								Interaction of schooling with					
	Constant	Prior achievement	School effect	Family income (in thousands)	Parental education	Race	IQ	Ach.	Income	Educa-tion	Race	IQ	R^2
Model I	2.125	.800	2.941	.320				.080	−.146				.7011
(σ)	(.46)	(.02)	(.65)	(.04)				(.03)	(.05)				
Model II	.014	.761	2.822	.210	.283	2.524		.076	−.146				.7099
(σ)	(.73)	(.02)	(.69)	(.04)	(.07)	(.35)		(.03)	(.05)				
Model III	2.383	.771	2.806	.277		2.618		.084	−.136		−.532		.7076
(σ)	(.46)	(.02)	(.64)	(.04)		(.49)		(.03)	(.05)		(.69)		
Model IV	−11.861	.595	5.695	.190		2.299	.197	.100	−.112		−.512	−.044	.7387
(σ)	(1.19)	(.02)	(1.75)	(.04)		(.46)	(.02)	(.03)	(.05)		(.65)	(.02)	
Model V	−13.863	.585	6.237	.125	.264	2.464	.195	.102	−.093	−.074	−.558	−.043	.7402
(σ)	(1.38)	(.02)	(2.01)	(.04)	(.09)	(.46)	(.02)	(.04)	(.06)	(.13)	(.66)	(.02)	

education is not significant for white children, once prior achievement and family income are controlled, although it is for blacks. For black children, the effects of parental education are more nearly equal to those estimated for income.

The additive effect of schooling is consistently positive, for all three samples, augmenting the predicted achievement level by 3 to 7 points. The absolute magnitude of the achievement increment during the school year is larger for white children than for black children, except when IQ scores are entered, although the standardized gains yield the opposite interpretation. The magnitude of school learning, estimated as the mean increment in raw score points, is greater than that observed among black students; however, the increase measured in standardized units of black achievement suggests that school learning is relatively more important than summer gains, irrespective of other control variables. When IQ scores are entered, the estimated school effect increases markedly for all groups, as does the standard error. The models support the contention that schooling augments learning for both black and white children relative to what exists when schools are closed.

Schooling also interacts in the predicted manner with each of the other variables included. The returns to prior achievement levels are positive, suggesting that learning is cumulative and that the determinants of outcomes during the school year depend more on prior achievement than they do during the summer. The negative interactions between socioeconomic status and IQ imply that summer learning is considerably more influenced by the degree of relative affluence and the educational attainments of parents than is learning during the school year. The achievement by schooling interactions are of similar magnitude for both white and black students, although they do not attain significance among white students because of the small sample size. The same is true for the interactions between schooling and socioeconomic status. Although the interactions suggest that schooling consistently dampens the impact of parental status for both subgroups, the magnitude of this effect achieves significance only for the complete sample, when schooling is included.

Including measured IQ decreases the effects of each of the background factors, as one might expect given the strength of their covariation. The pattern of interactions suggests that IQ decreases the size of the interaction with socioeconomic background in absolute terms, but that the socioeconomic interaction is consistently more powerful. In no case is the magnitude of the IQ by schooling interaction even half as great as the income by schooling effect; although some portion of the summer advantage that accrues to more advantaged children is seemingly related to IQ, the major effect is clearly linked to differences in family income. The influence of family resources in the summer is clear in each equation; although both parental education and race yield negative interaction terms, neither are as large as their standard errors. The general conclusion that family influences are consistently more powerful when schools are closed is borne out in every case.

In sum, the models of schooling as a temporal interaction in the achievement process provide results consistent with those offered previously. Schooling is significantly related to achievement in each model and tends consistently to attenuate the effects of parental status on achievement. Although the equations provide little new substantive information, the effects confirm the prior observations about schooling and achievement. The models are a concise method for describing the process of schooling, and they provide a means for testing the significance of the results. For both black and white students, schooling seems to offer access to educational opportunities that increase achievement; the learning that results is substantially more equal than would prevail in the absence of schooling. Although the magnitude of the effects is not large, the patterns are consistent for both racial groups and for both cohorts. This suggests that such effects are real. Schooling must be compared to outcomes in the absence of schooling in order to infer the process at work. The Atlanta data suggest that schools are considerably more important in the achievement process than other analysts have shown. The next section pursues the implications of these results for sociological research on education and adult attainment.

IMPLICATIONS FOR MODELS OF STATUS ATTAINMENT

The argument of this chapter has been somewhat circuitous and necessarily technical. The conceptual framework that underlies the analysis is in the tradition of sociological research that has endeavored to sort out the processes of status attainment in American society. The focus, however, is not on adult attainment, about which much is known, but on socialization processes and achievement in the elementary grades. The central problem has been to elaborate and refine notions of the socioeconomic life cycle by examining the role of families in status transmission more completely than has been done previously and to estimate and interpret the role of schooling as a unique causal factor.

Although the strategies adopted are similar to those prevalent in the literature, the models differ in key respects from other work in this field. Educational performance is assumed to be determined by competing influences and is portrayed as the culmination of experiences and opportunities provided in and by families and schools. The majority of models have viewed achievement or ability as a correlate of background and as a relatively stable attribute. I have conceptualized socioeconomic status less as an ascribed attribute characterizing the starting point of one's career than as an indicator of familial influences operating continuously throughout schooling and perhaps well into the early career.

If the influence of socioeconomic status is continuous and approaches the magnitude estimated for the Atlanta sample, one must conclude that the effects have been seriously underestimated in the models prevalent in the literature. In particular, both the strength of the correlations between parental status and achievement and the persistence of the effect once prior achievement or intelligence is controlled suggest a substantially greater effect than most analysts have uncovered. The discrepancy between these results is due in part to sampling variability and the quality of data available; the Atlanta sample was based on parental rather than student responses, and considerable care was taken in the choice and measurement of background variables. Family income is not customarily available, nor do estimates of the educational level of both parents enter many models. Yet these factors are not sufficient to account for the differing results.

Models of the status-attainment process have relied on reports of parental status at a fixed point in time, typically after much schooling has been completed. Retrospective surveys, such as the Occupational Changes in a Generation (Blau & Duncan, 1967), inquire as to the father's occupation when the respondent was about age 16. The majority of studies based on students have relied on high school samples, rather than on studies of younger children. Since sociologists have been most concerned with stratification outcomes, and in particular with the transition between education and jobs, the relative inattention to the elementary grades is understandable.

High school students appear to give more reliable responses regarding parental status than do elementary students. The correlations between parental status and achievement are quite consistent for older cohorts, irrespective of the region or school system studied. However, sociologists have too readily inferred that the relationship between achievement and parental status is immutable through time and have accepted too quickly estimates of the stability of test scores over time derived from the psychological literature. Each of these points will be examined separately.

The critical links in the achievement process are those between socioeconomic status and achievement. Sociologists have used standardized tests of ability or achievement to estimate these relationships. In doing so, they have relied on measurement assumptions and estimates of reliability derived from classical test theory and have paid little attention to more complex models and scaling procedures found in the psychometric literature (Birnbaum, 1968; Lord, 1977; Lord & Novick, 1968; Rasch, 1960). In lieu of longitudinal studies of achievement and socioeconomic status, which do not exist, sociologists have borrowed estimates of this correlation and estimates of the stability of test scores based on small, relatively homogeneous samples. Psychometricians have observed that errors of measurement are neither normally distributed nor independent of true scores and that the error variance tends to decrease as one moves up the scale of observed scores (Lord, 1960). Similar patterns emerged in the Atlanta data, as discussed in Chapter 2 and Appendix A. The issue of metrics for the study of learning is most troubling for educational evaluation; however, there are clear implications for stratification research as well.

I have argued that by relaxing several assumptions of classical test theory, the available measures provide a more credible description of learning. If one assumes that the distribution of test scores is log normal, the grade equivalent metric yields superior estimates of learning patterns. Although the major findings of this study are sufficiently robust to persist irrespective of the metric chosen, it is worth underscoring the implications for educational research.

Numerous theoretical discussions of the impact of schooling posit interactions between a child's background or ability level and the process of schooling. The returns to education have been shown to depend on ability or achievement differences (Griffin, 1976) and to vary somewhat by socioeconomic background. The presence of theoretically significant nonadditive interactions has found modest empirical support in the literature (Taubman & Wales, 1973) but certainly none that would suggest they are critical aspects of the developmental process. This would, of course, not be the case if the achievement items were calibrated or scaled in a manner designed to yield a different distribution. The patterning of outcomes would be likely to reflect substantial interactions between socioeconomic background or ability and educational programs. The effects of educational institutions are interactive, as well as additive; schooling amplifies or depresses the influence of families and prior achievement. Such patterns can only be analyzed with longitudinal data and an adequate metric for assessing change.

Exploratory attempts to extrapolate status-attainment models encompassing the entire life cycle have appeared in the literature (Bowles & Nelson, 1974; Duncan, 1968a; Duncan, Featherman, & Duncan, 1972;

Jencks *et al.*, 1972). These models have typically estimated the test–retest reliability of early ability scores at .90, adopted from Bloom's (1964) seminal work on the stability of intelligence measures, and have estimated the correlations between socioeconomic status and IQ from the data available on high school students (Duncan, 1968a; Duncan *et al.*, 1972), from small studies such as the California Guidance Study (Bowles & Nelson, 1974), or from the data collected by the Equality of Educational Opportunity Survey (Jencks *et al.*, 1972). The models invariably estimate the correlations between paternal education and occupation and early IQ as being lower than the correlations between adult IQ, typically measured by the Armed Forces Qualification Test (AFQT) scores, and paternal status. Although Bloom (1964) and Neff (1938) cite studies that have found substantially higher correlations between childhood IQ and socioeconomic status, these studies have been ignored.

The central difficulties with such models are twofold: first, the dearth of longitudinal data on test scores; and, second, the implicit assumption that the observed stability over time results from an innate individual trait. The models do not allow education to play a major role in shaping achievement levels, nor do they permit parental influences to operate cumulatively. The Atlanta data provide evidence that both factors operate and that their effects are patterned in systematic ways, depending on whether or not schools are in session. The Atlanta data do not permit estimation of the cumulative impact of schooling on achievement, but they suggest that positing a considerable direct effect would not be unwarranted.

If schooling operates both to increase the level of achievement and to minimize the influence of parental status over time, one would expect to observe a decline in the degree to which achievement was dependent on parental status during the course of schooling. The paucity of longitudinal data during the course of schooling precludes a definitive statement. For high school students, the Project Talent data are still perhaps the best available on achievement patterns over time. Jencks and Brown (1975) report that socioeconomic status does not influence the test scores of twelfth graders, once ninth-grade scores are controlled, which suggests a diminishing effect. Inferences based on cross-sectional data involve comparisons among samples of diverse quality; since the most obvious explanation of differing correlations is that samples are heterogeneous, few analysts have systematically explored the possibility that schooling might actually reduce the dependence of achievement on social class background.

Cross-sectional comparisons of the effects of parental status over time are inherently problematic. Since the cohorts of students cannot be assumed to be strictly comparable and since the relationships between measured aspects of background and achievement are typically quite unstable when combined in a multiple regression, the tendency has been to attribute most of the observed fluctuations in effects to sampling variability or measurement error. Coleman *et al.* (1966) noted a slight tendency for family background to be more highly related to sixth-grade than to twelfth-grade achievement, particularly when using objective measures such as the type of reading material found in the home or the index of household possessions. The authors also commented that this relationship was probably understated, since the sixth-grade responses were less reliable. Hauser (1968) and Kerckhoff (1974) present results suggesting a decline in the effects across successive cohorts of students drawn from a specific bounded geographic unit, but do not infer any change (cf. Appendix D). Since it is well known that measures of socioeconomic status are highly collinear, and hence erratic indicators of the effects posited, analysts have tended to dismiss or ignore observed differences between cohorts that seemed inexplicable, if not random.

Through the 1960s, several studies accumulated cross-sectional results that utilized common variables and coding schemes. Given the importance of the question, it seems worthwhile to hazard an interpretation of the patterns. If schooling operates to increase systematically the variability in achievement that is unrelated to socioeconomic status, the strength of the relationship between parental status and achievement would be expected to decline during the course of schooling. The best evidence culled from numerous published studies suggests that precisely this pattern exists. The data from over 14 studies imply that the relationship between each measure of parental status is consistently larger for the younger cohorts of students than it is for those in the last years of high school.[6] Appendix D presents the detailed analysis of these results and provides a comparison with the correlations estimated from the Atlanta survey. For the studies that embodied common variables and coding techniques and were based on relatively large samples, the zero-order correlations between measures of achievement or ability and socioeconomic status are summarized by simple averages in Table 4.11. Among the approximately 30 correlations available for

[6] The 10 studies of high school cohorts included in Table 4.11 are Alexander and Eckland (1973), Griliches and Mason (1973), Hauser (1973), Jencks *et al.* (1972), Kerckhoff (1974), Kohen (1971), Morgan *et al.* (1974), Otto (1976), Thomas (1977), and Williams (1976a). The four sixth-grade samples include the Atlanta data, the Berkeley Growth Study (Honzik, 1957), Kerckhoff (1974), and Williams (1976b).

TABLE 4.11
Average of Published Correlations between Ability and Several Measures of Socioeconomic Status for Grade Cohorts[a]

Status variable	Sixth grade	High school seniors	
		Male	Female
Father's occupational prestige	.428 (5)	.248 (9)	.227 (3)
Mother's education	.341 (8)	.247 (7)	.249 (3)
Father's education	.371 (8)	.264 (9)	.255 (3)
Family income	.367 (4)	.207 (2)	—
Number of siblings	−.230 (5)	−.164 (3)	−.170 (1)

[a] Compiled from studies summarized in Appendix D, Tables D.1 and D.2. Number of studies or samples included are given in parentheses. The details of sample size, study date, and location as well as the coding of variables are given in Appendix D.

sixth-grade students, only 1 is smaller than the largest correlation reported for the corresponding variable calculated for the more mature students. Although the specific variables are not independent, since many were drawn from the same studies, the consistency of the results is noteworthy. The values are in all cases uncorrected for measurement error; if they were, the disparity would be likely to increase. Estimates of the reliability of student reports of parental status tend to increase with age, suggesting that high school students are, not surprisingly, more accurate informants than are younger students (Mason *et al.*, 1976). Corrections for attenuation would, therefore, increase the correlations for sixth graders disproportionately.

These correlations, taken alone, do not provide convincing evidence of the efficacy of education; this is perhaps the major reason why they have been overlooked. Nevertheless, the quantitative evidence clearly supports the contention that the relationship between parental status and achievement is attenuated during the course of schooling. Although one might argue that the cumulative impact of socioeconomic status is attenuated by extrafamilial influences or by maturation, the data on summer learning suggest that the role of schooling is instrumental. The importance of education in the socioeconomic life cycle, I would argue, is best depicted by the direct effects on learning during the school year and by the interactive influence of schooling with other measured attributes of students. While it is clear that the relative position of students in terms of achievement levels is not markedly altered over time, this stability must be understood as the result of the continuous influence of family background and the intermittent effects of schooling. A substantial correlation between pretests and posttests does not preclude either a considerable amount of learning or environmental influences of some magnitude. Schooling augments achievement in a relatively uniform manner, by exposing all children to a common academic environment, irrespective of differences in their backgrounds. Such an influence tends to encourage learning rates determined largely by prior achievement or ability and to reduce but not do away with socioeconomic differentials. Parental status reinforces socioeconomic inequality in achievement, and this effect is most clearly observed when schools are closed and family differences reassert an unmitigated vigor. Summer learning is substantially more contingent on the patterning of differences among families than is learning during the school year. Unless the fact that families exert a continual and decisive influence on achievement is acknowledged, the failure of schooling to equalize outcomes and the persistence of cognitive inequality cannot be understood. The importance of schooling in the generation of achievement and ultimate outcomes is underestimated unless we observe that education diminishes the effects of socioeconomic background and introduces variance to the prediction of achievement unrelated to parental status. Schooling in such a model is most important for children who have few alternative avenues available; although the effects of specific programs may appear transitory, I suspect that this is more compelling evidence of the strength of family influences than of the weakness of other influences. Although there is still much to be learned regarding the determinants of learning, and in particular how cumulative processes operate through time, the bulk of the evidence tends to support these conclusions rather than those common in the literature.

One final exercise is relevant both to the analysis presented thus far and to the more general issues raised by the status-attainment literature. Positing that the influence of parental status operates continuously poses certain dilemmas with respect to estimating the magnitude of the effects of background on ultimate outcomes. Although numerous studies have documented a considerable amount of fluidity in the stratification system, there has not been, to my knowledge, any discussion of the implications of this fact for assessing the impact of family background. One must logically assume that if the relative standing of parents is altered during the course of schooling, the relative impact of background cannot be assumed to be stable. During an individual's career, both occupation and income levels have been shown to change markedly, due to both intragenerational mobility and short-term fluctuations (Blau & Duncan, 1967; Duncan *et al.*, 1972; Sewell, Hauser, & Featherman, 1976). Data from the U.S. Department of Labor indicate that between 1965 and 1970, 34.6% of males between 30 and 50 years of age transferred to a different detailed occupational category (Sommers & Eck, 1977); income levels are likely to be even more unstable.

If parental status is assumed to operate continually, and if such relevant measures of adult status as occupation and income are unstable, the magnitude of the effect of background is likely to depend on the point in time at which it is measured. The sequence of transitions that mark the socioeconomic life cycle would be influenced by paternal status at the time a decision is made, rather than by status at an earlier stage of development. Entering college, for example, may well depend on family resources at matriculation, not at age 16. The probability of obtaining a job or promotion is likely to depend on paternal connections at the time of application. If, for example, one's father has become an alcoholic before one enters the job market, it is doubtful that his influence and support would be as helpful as it might have been in better years. Duncan *et al.* (1972) have argued that the effects of father's education and occupation are relatively stable and that the degree to which first job depends on origins is not appreciably different from the degree to which later career attainments depend on origins. Sewell and Hauser (1975) report that "intelligence becomes more important than socioeconomic status as progress is made through the educational system, but at no point does socioeconomic status cease to be an important determinant of who will attain the next step of the process [p. 9]." Both studies imply the continual importance of socioeconomic status; however, the relative magnitude of this effect may be underestimated.

Models of the attainment process reflect causality of a very abstract sort. The impact of numerous factors, operating at different points in time and through various mechanisms, are difficult to specify empirically. Inferences about the importance of such factors rest on the assumption that their strength is captured by the association between indicators at key junctures. If the causal influences are not stable, the amount of time elapsed between an event and its cause may attenuate the measured relationship. One is well advised to remember that the reality of the attainment process is a great deal more dynamic than our present analytic tools for portraying it. These observations are particularly pertinent to the Atlanta survey.

Throughout this study, family income has been used extensively as a measure of background status despite the fact that this variable embodies considerable measurement error. Unlike paternal occupations, which appear to be relatively stable over time, income tends to be subject to numerous short-term fluctuations. Since the data on achievement are retrospective and pertain to test scores taken prior to the measurement of family status, one might surmise that the magnitude of the estimated effect is attenuated during prior intervals. The observed correlations between each and every measure of status decrease progressively as one moves back in time; this pattern might result from retrospective data, with parental status measured concurrently with the final test. Perhaps the true effect of family income is attenuated due to the instability of measurement. Plausibly, consumption patterns and standards of living are influenced by the degree of stability of earnings as well as by the gross amount earned. If changes in family income produced changes in the allocation of time or resources to children, such fluctuations might influence achievement levels as well.

The Atlanta data are not sufficiently detailed to permit a longitudinal analysis of the effects of family income. However, if a number of simplifying assumptions are made, it is possible to estimate the likely effect random errors would have on the coefficients estimated at each point in time. Figure 4.4 presents the hypothesized model schematically. The seventh-grade cohort, which has the largest number of sequential tests available, has family income data based only on the fall of 1972, 5 months after the last test from the intermediate battery was administered. The correlations between test scores and income are assumed to be constant and to depend only on whether the relationship is observed in the fall (*a*) or spring (*b*). Income is assumed to be completely determined by prior income and an error term W_i. The expected correlation (q^t) between income at any two points in time is a

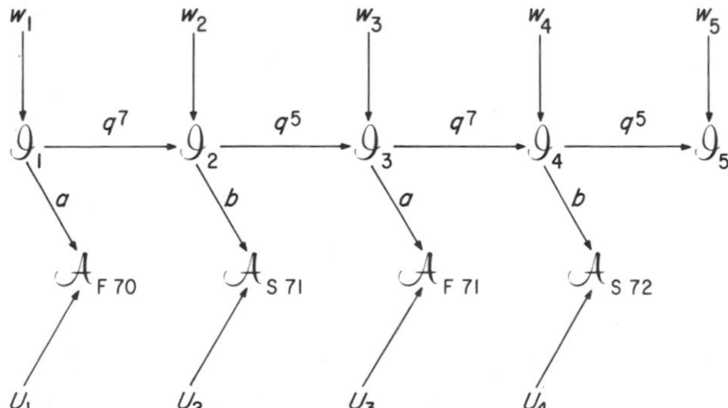

FIGURE 4.4. Hypothetical determination of the correlations between family income (*I*) and achievement (*A*) at each date of test administration.

function of t, the number of months that have passed between tests. The disturbances are assumed to be uncorrelated with test scores with income and with each other. Although the test scores are highly interrelated, the model is intended to reproduce only the gross correlations between income and achievement and to permit an examination of the resulting residuals. One question of interest is whether the increasing correlations between test scores over time could be attributed to unreliability of family incomes.

The four observed correlations between income (I_5) and achievement can be used to estimate q^t. The model specifies the following relationships:

$$r_{(I5)(A\cdot S72)} = bq^{5} = .54211$$
$$r_{(I5)(A\cdot F71)} = aq^{12} = .55189$$
$$r_{(I5)(A\cdot S71)} = bq^{17} = .45522$$
$$r_{(I5)(A\cdot F70)} = aq^{24} = .46955$$

The model has three unknown parameters, a, b, and q, and four observed correlations. Two separate estimates of q can be derived from the overidentified recursive system. Computing q from the two equations containing a yields an estimate of $q^{12} = .840$; from the two equations including b, the value of q^{12} would be equal to .851. The two values are quite similar and compare well with correlations reported in the literature. The estimates of q obtained seem plausible and suggest that income stability in the Atlanta sample over the course of 2 years is within the bounds of conventional estimates.

The values of a and b deduced from the model are quite consistent over time. Letting $q^{12} = .8455$, the geometric mean of the two estimates, one obtains a value of a equal to between .641 and .657; the values of b, the impact of income during the school year, varies between .577 and .581. The model implies that the expected correlations between income and achievement are constant except for seasonal variations. Unless one assumes quite implausible correlations among the residual determinants of income, it is not possible to replicate the observed correlations between income and achievement by assuming that the true effect is constant and of equal magnitude in the fall and spring. The general conclusion that family income is more highly related to fall achievement than to spring scores seems quite robust; this relationship is largely unaffected by the posited effects of instability in family resources. Whether one assumes that the increasing impact of parental status is due to instability in the measurement of income or to an increase in the reliability of test scores, the differential impact of income during the summer is supported. Assuming that the effects are attenuated by measurement error, the correlations suggest that the direct effect is larger in the fall than in the spring, and perhaps by an amount greater than that suggested by the original regression results.

CONCLUSIONS

This chapter has explored the effects of parental status on achievement in the context of an explicit interpretive framework. Each of the models supports the conclusion that socioeconomic status exerts an influence on achievement that is attenuated during the school year. The determinants of learning during the school year and the summer differ in both magnitude and relative importance. Summer learning is considerably more dependent on parental status than is learning during the school year. Spring achievement levels are contingent on prior achievement and at most a modest direct effect of family background; fall achievement reflects the impact of parental status to a much greater degree. The achievement process depicted is consistent with an interpretation of schooling as the major source of such differences. Education provides heightened opportunities for cognitive growth to all children, irrespective of parental background. This interpretation of schooling is both plausible and considerably closer to the liberal ideal than is the image of schooling found in either the popular or the academic literature.

The argument, to reiterate, is not that schools equalize achievement levels or that attending school will necessarily narrow the gaps between racial or socioeconomic groups. The patterns of learning do not suggest such outcomes. Schools do, however, provide a critical opportunity to learn skills and to augment cognitive achievement that is lacking at home. Schooling does, seemingly, reduce the dependence on background over the course of time in systematic ways.

Could schools be made more effective tools for promoting cognitive growth and socioeconomic equality? Such a question involves speculation, not evidence. Optimistically, the patterns of learning in the best Atlanta schools suggest that this would be possible. Yet even in these schools, the gains in cognitive achievement are equal, not equalizing. The impact of families on cognitive achievement seems ubiquitous; parental status is neutralized, rather than reinforced or reversed. Although the conclusions reached from studying summer learning suggest the importance of schooling in the achievement process, family factors appear to operate continuously, albeit with varying power, to produce unequal outcomes. Even if schooling were shown to influence learning quite generally in the manner described, this would not imply that complacency was in order.

Finally, it is not clear how the effectiveness of education might be increased; differences among schools in Atlanta shed little light on this question. Whether it is more important to increase the resources to education or to redistribute income among families seems a moot question; the impact of either would clearly depend on how they were spent. It would be reassuring to deduce a formula linking achievement to public expenditures or to the allocation of specific resources, but this is not feasible. Although schools matter, we need to know a great deal more both about what is taught and how before such questions can be discussed. It hardly needs to be added that we also need more precise measures of what is learned and what ought to be learned in schools.

The subsequent chapters are oriented to explicating the mechanisms of influence in several ways. Chapter 5 views exposure to schooling as one source of influence and reviews the evidence on attendance. In Part II, summer schools (Chapter 7) and related programs (Chapter 8) are assessed, as well as the patterning of individual activities, such as reading (Chapter 9), by social class and race. Although the relationships are complex, the data suggest several potentially fruitful ways of disaggregating the determinants of learning and academic achievement.

5
The Effects of Attendance

Exposure to schooling varies during the school year as well as seasonally. The amount of time children spend in school is structured by the length of the school day and the number of days in the session. Attendance rates are not constant but determine the amount of exposure a given child receives to the school curriculum. Several authors have suggested that the quantity of time is an important influence on school outcomes and that extending the school day or year could be a potent path for policy (Harnischfeger & Wiley, 1976; Wiley, 1976; Wiley & Harnischfeger, 1974).

Within a particular school district, the number of days in the school year and the length of the school day are legally mandated and the same for every school. The academic year in Atlanta consists of 180 days, with just over 6 hours per day of classroom instruction, which is quite close to national norms.[1] Several schools offer an extended day program, primarily for the benefit of working parents, and at least three elementary schools provide supervision and limited instruction year round. These programs are not compulsory, however, and the schools do not keep accurate attendance records for individual children. Reliable rec-

[1] Karweit (1976a) calculated a mean of 179.35 days per year and 5.96 hours per day based on the sixth grade in 2040 schools sampled in the Equality of Educational Opportunity Survey.

ords of absenteeism are available for the school year 1971–1972 and can be compared with achievement scores during the same period. Although the effects of lengthening the school day or year cannot be estimated from data for a single school district, the variability in absenteeism can perhaps shed some light on the effects of exposure to differing amounts of schooling. If the amount of time spent in school is a source of differential educational achievement, one would expect that students who were consistently absent would be further behind their classmates in achievement level. To the degree that exposure is related to the socioeconomic status of parents (Levanto, 1973), attendance may be one mechanism responsible for maintaining the learning gaps among children from different backgrounds. Examining the determinants of absenteeism in a single city for a given school year may provide some tentative evidence on the causes of differential truancy, as well as the consequences for achievement. Attendance, or rather nonattendance, has become a major problem in many large urban school systems since the early 1970s (Karweit, 1976a).

Several studies have been made of the effects of attendance on cognitive achievement, but these studies provide scant support for the proposition that missing school constitutes an important explanation for differential achievement. An early study in the New York City schools (Ziegler, 1928) found that differences in the average days absent throughout the elementary school career were not related to mental ability or educational development, although higher attendance did result in better grades in school. The study concluded that intelligence, measured by the Simon–Binet intelligence scale, was more predictive of school achievement than either attendance or age. Schultz (1958) found that high-achieving black pupils had slightly lower absentee rates than did low-achieving blacks. Neither study controlled the effects of socioeconomic status, however, nor attempted to explain differential attendance as a distinct phenomenon.

Several analysts have pointed out that it is difficult to separate the presumed causes of absenteeism from the consequences, or to infer that exposure to schooling is the principal factor mediating achievement. Poor attendance may reflect circumstances or attitudes that directly retard academic performance, irrespective of exposure. Achievement levels may be adversely affected by a chronic illness or a serious family crisis, whether or not such problems lead to missing school. Prolonged absence may disrupt a child's relationships with teacher and friends, as well as involving a setback in school work. Insofar as absence is a patterned response, children with lower rates of attendance may have greater distaste for school and less motivation to study even when physically present. Such factors cannot be disentangled unequivocally; insofar as the actual mechanisms linking achievement to schooling are confounded in complex ways, attempts to separate cause and effect are problematic.

Given such caveats, the data from the Atlanta study suggest a consistent but weak relationship between academic achievement and attendance levels. The relationships between achievement and attendance are presented in the next section. Subsequently, I will examine the determinants of differential school attendance. I will argue that the impact of social class, race, and such less tangible variables as family values and attitudes cannot be ruled out as the primary source of the hypothesized effect. Although attendance data are suggestive, the mechanisms of influence through which schooling operates must be presumed to be more complex than a linear function of time.

ABSENTEEISM AND ACHIEVEMENT

Attendance records in the Atlanta school system are based on 10 equal attendance periods, each roughly equivalent to a month of the school year. During 1971-1972, attendance levels in Atlanta were quite high, and truancy was not considered a serious problem by the administrative staff. The total days absent during the school year is the summed absences reported in each attendance period; the variable studied is the total annual days of schooling missed. In the Atlanta school system, the average child missed less than 1 day in each month. Not surprisingly, sample children were absent less often than the average pupil. Children absent from school on the days the standardized achievement tests were administered were excluded from the analysis due to missing data. Absenteeism also tends to be inversely related to socioeconomic status, and, relative to the average school in the district, sample schools were advantaged. Sampling and analytic strategies did, therefore, introduce a slight bias in favor of children who attended most regularly.

To assess the effects of absence on achievement, spring test scores were regressed on fall scores and on the total days absent during the year. Regressions were run separately by race and grade. The initial results are presented in Table 5.1. The unstandardized coefficients (*b*-weights) are presented, followed by the standard errors of estimation and the standardized parameters (b^*). The evidence indicates that the total days absent during the school year consistently depress spring achievement when prior achievement is controlled. For both grades,

TABLE 5.1
Regression Coefficients for Spring Achievement, 1972, Word Knowledge, on Fall Achievement, 1971, and Total Days Absent, by Grade in School and Race, Matched Sample

	Fall 1971 test score	Total days absent	R^2
Sixth grade, white students			
b	.9425[a]	−.0102	
(σ)	(.0256)	(.0258)	
b^*	.8722	−.0094	.7570
Sixth grade, black students			
b	.8412[a]	−.0885[a]	
(σ)	(.0260)	(.0251)	
b^*	.7131	−.0777	.5239
Seventh grade, white students			
b	.8289[a]	−.0470[a]	
(σ)	(.0207)	(.0213)	
b^*	.8679	−.0477	.7703
Seventh grade, black students			
b	.9432[a]	−.0660[a]	
(σ)	(.0190)	(.0204)	
b^*	.8484	−.0552	.7411

[a] Coefficients more than twice their standard errors.

and for either racial group, missing school tends to have an adverse effect on achievement, albeit not a large one. The influence is substantially more important for black children than for white children; among whites the relationship attains significance only for seventh graders.

Absenteeism is inversely related to socioeconomic status. The zero-order relationship between family income and absence is larger than the relationship between achievement and absenteeism. To test the relationship between attendance and achievement for children from roughly similar backgrounds, spring achievement scores were regressed on fall achievement, days absent, and the three measures of socioeconomic background: family income, household size, and mean parents' education. The coefficients for absenteeism are consistently lower when socioeconomic background factors are introduced, as Table 5.2 documents, although typically the effects are reduced by about .01 points of achievement. Absenteeism is still consistently negative, with the coefficients significantly different from zero only for black children. The equations tend to support the conclusion that attendance levels have a negligible influence on the achievement of white children once

TABLE 5.2
Regression Coefficients for Spring Achievement, Word Knowledge, on Fall Achievement, Days Absent, and Socioeconomic Status, by Grade and Race, Matched Samples

	Predetermined variables					
Grade and race	Fall 1971	Days absent	Mean parental education	Household size	Family income	R^2
Sixth grade, white students						
b	.9081[a]	−.0251	.1479	−.2491	.0564	
(σ)	(.0351)	(.0304)	(.1655)	(.2078)	(.0761)	
*b**	.8403	−.0182	.0347	−.0322	.0273	.7603
Sixth grade, black students						
b	.8048[a]	−.0722[a]	.3345[a]	−.1694	.0639	
(σ)	(.0315)	(.0299)	(.1346)	(.1572)	(.0612)	
*b**	.6823	−.0633	.0791	−.0293	.0326	.5415
Seventh grade, white students						
b	.7933[a]	−.0332	.2260	−.0186	.0454	
(σ)	(.0297)	(.0247)	(.1367)	(.1790)	(.0590)	
*b**	.8307	−.0337	.0546	−.0026	.0235	.7737
Seventh grade, black students						
b	.9138[a]	−.0591[a]	.1086	−.1984	.0693	
(σ)	(.0234)	(.0229)	(.1091)	(.1096)	(.0502)	
*b**	.8219	−.0494	.0227	−.0352	.0316	.7444

[a] Coefficients more than twice their standard errors.

socioeconomic status is controlled, while missing school tends to affect adversely the cognitive growth of black children. The data do not suggest, however, that the effect is sufficiently large to warrant dramatic policy recommendations. For black children, each additional full day of schooling would tend to increase achievement by less than .1 *SD*. Had the entire sample of sixth-grade black children had perfect attendance throughout the year, one would expect a gain of less than one vocabulary word per child.[2] Even for the group most directly influenced by attendance levels, sixth-grade black children, the number of days absent explains less than 8% of the residual variance left unexplained after initial achievement level is controlled. The original correlations between days absent and spring achievement vary between −.13 and

[2] Such calculations cannot, of course, be taken literally. An additional word has meaning only relative to a total set of items that might have been answered correctly; a given increment of score may reflect more learning than the number of vocabulary words indicate.

−.23, and most of this relationship is accounted for by prior achievement. Although one might argue that the cumulative effects of missing school would be substantially more important than the effects estimated for a single year, the evidence from Atlanta does not suggest that differential attendance could begin to account for the observed variance in achievement or the patterns of socioeconomic inequality.

The regression equations support the interpretation of a modest positive effect of school exposure on achievement, but these results are slightly misleading. The estimated parameters assume a linear relationship between days absent and achievement that does not exist. The independent variable of interest, absenteeism, is highly skewed; nearly half of the respondents missed 5 or fewer days of school during the entire year. The significant results depend almost entirely on a relatively small number of cases who missed more than 25 days of school, or better than 10% of the academic year. Comparing the achievement gains in terms of grade equivalent scores by level of attendance elucidates this fact.

Table 5.3 presents the mean gains in grade equivalent scores by race and grade for varying rates of attendance. The relationship is clearly

TABLE 5.3
Mean Grade Equivalent Gain, Word Knowledge, by Race and Days Absent during School Year 1971–1972[a]

Number of days absent, by race	Sixth grade		Seventh grade	
	$\bar{X}$	*N*	$\bar{X}$	*N*
White	*.84*	*470*	*.68*	*526*
0–2	.91	71	.74	71
3–5	.78	87	.78	86
6–10	.83	121	.60	159
11–25	.88	158	.73	167
26+	.59	33	.54	43
Black	*.53*	*1023*	*.61*	*959*
0–2	.56	294	.64	314
3–5	.54	225	.66	194
6–10	.62	223	.62	199
11–25	.41	237	.54	211
26+	.37	44	.29	41

[a] Within grade levels, a significant association between grade equivalent gains and attendance is not present for either race, when computed for five categories. Collapsing the attendance variable in order to compare children missing more than 10 days yields a significant relationship for sixth- ($F = 3.72$) and seventh- ($F = 2.91$) grade black children, although not for whites.

nonlinear; the only group for whom missing school is clearly detrimental to cognitive growth are those students who were absent a large number of days. Achievement levels for the white students who were absent less than 25 days are invariably within a tenth of a year of the total mean. A similar pattern holds for black students, although absenteeism begins to take a toll somewhat sooner; achievement gains among black children are decidedly lower if more than 10 days of school are missed.

If the grade equivalent gains are accepted as a reasonable measure of the expected increments in achievement, black children who missed more than 2 weeks of school lost more than 1 month of achievement in the course of the year. Children who were absent less frequently were largely unaffected. Attendance appears to operate as a threshold, rather than as a cumulative function of time. Within certain limits, missing school does not seem to be associated with a systematic loss of vocabulary skills; amassing a large number of absences, however, tends to dampen learning rates considerably. The patterns indicate that operationalizing exposure to school as a linear function of the amount of time may be inappropriate. Time in school is presumably a proxy for instruction; the relationship between learning and exposure may be more complex than is captured by a crude measure of elapsed time.

THE DETERMINANTS OF ABSENTEEISM

Students who miss large amounts of school are not, of course, just like students who attend more regularly. The most consistent predictors of the propensity to attend school were race and family income. Table 5.4 gives the average days absent by race and family income, separately by grade. It is noteworthy that the attendance levels of black students are consistently higher than those of white students at every income level. In Atlanta, black students averaged approximately 3 days more exposure to schooling than the white students in the sample during the year considered.

One apparent explanation for the racial differences in attendance is the political context. During the academic year, 1971–1972, the Atlanta school system was a tense and beleaguered district, attempting to satisfy the legal and moral imperatives of integration, while maintaining the support of white residents and taxpayers. The patterns of racial imbalance were being challenged by the black community in both the courts and the schools. To some degree, the attendance rates of white children may reflect their families' declining support for school policies and public education during this period.

TABLE 5.4
Mean Days Absent During the 1971–1972 School Year by Grade in School, Race, and Family Income Level[a]

Race and income level	Sixth grade[b]		Seventh grade[b]	
	$\bar{X}$	*N*	$\bar{X}$	*N*
White	*11.7*	*470*	*12.2*	*526*
Less than $4,000	16.8	26	18.6	29
$4,000–8,999	15.1	83	15.7	82
$9,000–14,999	10.8	115	12.1	118
$15,000+	8.7	124	9.3	180
No response	12.3	122	12.9	117
Black	*8.5*	*1023*	*8.4*	*959*
Less than $4,000	12.4	187	11.8	193
$4,000–8,999	8.1	325	8.3	312
$9,000–14,999	6.5	169	6.2	161
$15,000+	5.7	101	5.1	95
No response	8.7	241	8.8	198

[a] Variance in absenteeism explained by income (η^2):

Sixth grade:
White: .069, $F = 8.4$
Black: 0.62, $F = 17.8$

Seventh grade:
White: .070, $F = 10.2$
Black: .053, $F = 14.1$

[b] Grade level is that of the sample in the fall of 1972, not the attendance period 1971–1972.

The largest racial discrepancies in attendance were found in the schools most recently integrated; however, even in the relatively homogeneous all-white elementary schools, white attendance levels were lower than those for black sample children. The factors that produced lower rates of attendance among white children were not specific to any particular school, but tended to affect families throughout the district. Differences in attendance patterns among schools were generally quite small for both black and white children and depended primarily on the socioeconomic and racial composition of the schools rather than on circumstances peculiar to particular schools. Socioeconomic differentials in attendance are ubiquitous, however, and indicate consistent differences in exposure by socioeconomic background.

Family income explains between 5 and 8% of the variance in absenteeism within grades for either racial group. The relatively more advantaged a child was in terms of father's occupational status, parents' education, or family income, the less frequently did the child miss school. A significant negative relationship is present between each of these variables and attendance. Children with working mothers or from relatively small households were also more likely to attend school regularly, although these relationships were not significant.

A number of plausible explanations could be adduced to explain social class differences in rates of attendance. Unfortunately, the school records do not permit one to disentangle the reasons for missing school, short of the presumption that children claimed to be sick. It is not possible, for example, to distinguish legitimate absences from playing hooky; one cannot distinguish between absence on rainy days and Mondays (Karweit, 1973) and absence on days on which homework is due and tests are given. Low-achieving students tend to miss more school than do those with higher scores, irrespective of family status, but the effects are not large. Overt rebellion, in the form of truancy (Stinchcombe, 1965), might be a partial explanation of the patterns in missing school. Playing hooky could perhaps account for the fact that a disproportionate number of males missed more than 25 days. In Atlanta, girls' attendance rates are nearly equal to boys'; in contrast, other studies have found that girls, at least in high school, attend less regularly (Levanto, 1973). Students who are more than a year older than their classmates in the same grade tend to miss 1 full day more than the average student. These differences are not large enough to suggest that truancy is prevalent among elementary students in Atlanta. Neither the distance a child lives from school nor the customary mode of transportation are related to absenteeism in Atlanta.

Missing school because of illness might logically account for the socioeconomic differentials, since disadvantaged children might be presumed to have lower levels of health and nutrition. Serious illnesses have been reported to be two or more times as common among poor families as among the population as a whole (U.S. National Center for Health Statistics, 1964). These differences in health, assuming they applied to children as well as adults, would be sufficient to account for the observed attendance differences. Serious illness, however, cannot be assumed to be the major source of absence in this sample. Only four students missed more than 10 days in any single attendance period; the vast majority of days absent was not concentrated in a given time interval, but sprinkled throughout the year.

There are parallels between children's missing school and work stoppage among adults. Missing work is consistently related to both job status and income level, and apparently to a degree that cannot be explained by socioeconomic differences in health and morbidity. Kadushin (1964) argues that the positive relationship between health and socioeconomic level has declined for most of the twentieth century, largely because of rising standards of living and increased access to medical services. Among adults, work stoppage cannot be attributed to illness directly; rather, it is mediated by attitudes toward both work and health care. Lower-class adults tend to be more fatalistic regarding ill health, to utilize fewer medical services even when these are free, and to avoid and distrust the institutions and professionals providing health care. Instead of seeking a cure, less advantaged persons are likely to stay home until they feel better.

A similar argument could be made with respect to absences from school. Attending school, just like work, is a behavioral index of the commitment to an enterprise. Missing school indicates less interest. It is not necessary to argue that lower-class parents are in complicity with sick children who want to miss school; it is sufficient to assume that parents' attitudes toward school and sickness differ systematically by social class.

Missing school may also result from attitudes a child develops toward school, whether or not there is direct familial influence. There is circumstantial evidence that attendance reflects children's motivation and interest in school. Attendance levels are markedly better in free schools than in traditional ones; improved attendance has also been noted when an unstructured curriculum or innovative educational reform is introduced (Silberman, 1970). In Atlanta, children who chose to attend summer school in 1972 had missed significantly less school during the preceding year than those who did not attend (cf. Table 7.2, p. 129). Voluntary programs of all sorts tend to attract students who like school and who are interested in the subjects offered. I suspect that attendance during both the school year and the summer reflects positive attitudes toward school and learning by children.

In sum, there are numerous interpretations of differential attendance patterns. Although it seems useful to distinguish potential causal links, it is not possible to isolate the critical determinants. No direct measure of attitudes toward school was obtained from either the children or their parents, and inferring the importance of unmeasured processes is hazardous. More important, perhaps, the effects of differential attendance on school achievement are relatively small. Attendance rates seem to be neither a strong direct influence nor a powerful mechanism through which family characteristics might operate.

There is evidence that exposure to schooling is not equally valuable for all children, nor is absence equally detrimental. A final analysis was undertaken in an effort to specify more fully the relationship between missing school and achievement levels. Family income was collapsed into the four categories examined earlier, and spring achievement was regressed against fall achievement within income groups. These results

TABLE 5.5
Unstandardized Partial Regression Coefficient of Days Absent Predicting Spring Achievement 1972, Net of Fall Achievement within Income Groups, Separately by Race and Grade Level

Race and family income	Grade level	
	Sixth	Seventh
White	*−.010*	*−.047*[a]
Less than $9,000	−.041	−.083[a]
$9,000–14,999	−.008	−.031
$15,000+	.012	−.002
Black	*−.089*[a]	*−.066*[a]
Less than $9,000	−.126[a]	−.098[a]
$4,000–8,999	−.074[a]	−.052[a]
$9,000–14,999	−.069[a]	−.039[a]
$15,000+	−.023	−.007

[a] Coefficients more than twice their standard errors.

are presented in Table 5.5. The subsamples are not large, and most of the coefficients are not significant; however, the pattern of effects is instructive. The largest negative effects of missing school are invariably concentrated in the lowest income groups, while the unstandardized parameters tend to decrease in absolute value as family income increases. The data suggest that the costs of missing school are 4 to 10 times greater among families with fewer economic resources than they are among those more well off. Advantaged families seem to be able to offset achievement declines resulting from missing school more effectively than can families with less income. Perhaps high-income families ensure that children make up school work that is missed, or allow children to miss school only if they are not behind in school work. In any case, the relationship between high absence and low achievement is greater in low-income families, and absences are more frequent.[3]

CONCLUSION

This chapter has analyzed one aspect of school exposure, that measured by attendance patterns among sample children during the

[3] Since the relationships are small, an interactive model did not yield significant coefficients or explain much of the variance. Equally, the coefficients between adjoining classes are not significantly different from each other. The patterns support the general analytic framework, rather than a strictly statistical criterion for importance.

academic year, 1971–1972. The results are somewhat inconclusive. The available data do not support the contention that absence is strongly related to differential achievement, except possibly for children who are chronically absent. In part, this is because school attendance tended to be quite high and relatively uniform among sample children. The variability in exposure to schooling indicated by the data is not sufficiently large, nor is the number of children affected sufficiently great, to have a significant impact on levels of achievement. The average white child missed 1 day every 3 weeks, while the average black child missed less than 1 day a month during this school year. Less than 5% of the sample missed more than 1 month of school, and these absences were invariably scattered throughout the term. It could be argued that the limited variations in exposure introduced by absenteeism cannot be compared to missing several months of instruction during the summer months, in either intensity or duration. Perhaps these data are not a fair test of the proposition that greater exposure to schooling increases learning.

Attendance levels differ by social class and race. The data do not suggest, however, that differential absenteeism is an important mechanism for perpetuating socioeconomic differentials in achievement. The effects on learning tend to be interactive, rather than additive. The data suggest that missing a large number of days is most detrimental to those children who would benefit most from schooling. A relatively advantaged background may attenuate cognitive losses that accrue to less advantaged children when they miss school.

Separating the causes and consequences of school attendance is difficult, since numerous factors could potentially influence both missing school and learning rates. Attendance seems not to be related to sex or to characteristics of the school attended, at least in this sample. I have argued somewhat speculatively that attendance is in part a function of children's liking school and in part the result of class differences in values and attitudes. Disentangling the causal relations between such factors is difficult. Moreover, since the relationships are relatively weak, it does not seem likely that a remedy for absenteeism would influence learning appreciably. Exposure may be a potent path for policy, but altering the patterns of school attendance observed in Atlanta during a single year does not promise to influence achievement levels dramatically.

PART II
Socioeconomic Status and Achievement in the Absence of Schooling

6

Assessing Summer Activities: An Overview

Summer learning embodies a dual focus. Examining achievement gains in the context of a year's growth provides a basis for assessing schooling as contrasted to nonschooling; viewing the summer as a period in which family and friends are the dominant influences allows disentanglement of the sources of growth by holding institutional effects constant. The questions and the discussion in Part I were addressed to issues of school effects and equality of opportunity. Schooling was conceptualized as a process, rather than as a place, and observed as the distinctive pattern of outcomes relative to those prevailing in the absence of schooling. Socioeconomic status was presumed to influence children continuously, shaping educational outcomes whether or not children were attending school. Within such a framework, schools must be seen as a critical factor in cognitive growth, especially for disadvantaged children.

The complementary objectives to be addressed in Part II are to unravel the determinants of summer learning and to attempt to understand the causal links between family and achievement. Patterns of summer learning are viewed as the result of numerous discrete activities occurring in specific contexts. The central issues revolve around the distribution and the determinants of those summer experiences that are translated into educational gains. Schooling in the previous chapters was treated as an abstraction, with little specific content or substance; the activities to be examined in the following chapters are concrete.

Subsequent chapters are largely descriptive and exploratory. The results are suggestive but often inconclusive. This introduction is intended to give the reader an overview of the substantive conclusions and to serve as a theoretical and methodological road map. The chapters are organized around specific activities, but each seeks to answer or illuminate all of the following questions:

1. What activities and programs occupy children during the summer and why?
2. Which activities promote cognitive growth among participants and why?
3. How should one understand the workings of socioeconomic background in the process of achievement?

SUMMER ACTIVITIES: WHAT AND WHY?

Summertime offers children a respite from schooling as well as certain options for learning and play that are not available during the school year. The demands of extrafamilial institutions are minimized; summer programs and activities are all ostensibly voluntary. The ability to decide where and how children spend time distinguishes the summer from the regular school term in critical respects. Participation in activities is a choice made by children or their parents; the patterning of choices might be regarded as indicative of a world in which individual or family preferences dictated educational alternatives.

Conceptually, this view posits the summer as a free market for educational, recreational, or custodial services for children. Although public education is generally available, schools must compete with other institutions for the time and attention of children. Consumers are permitted to utilize public facilities and services at no cost, to purchase alternatives, or to provide for children's leisure at home. Aggregate rates of participation in such a model are a function of the preferences of families and the demand for particular services at a given cost. Parents and children are assumed to have sufficient information about alternatives to exercise choice and to be rational in their decisions; families are assumed to maximize utility through their choice of activities, subject to the constraints of cost and the availability of alternatives. The summer thus constitutes a natural experiment of sorts, permitting analysis of choices made in the absence of a compulsory institution with a monopoly on educational services. Although these economic assumptions are, in varying degrees, naive and indefensible, they do provide a useful framework for assessing behavior. The discrepancy between such a model and the actual choices made by families is as theoretically interesting as are the occasions in which the model fits the observations perfectly.

Summer activities are diverse, but, more important, particular activities are substitutable. The demand for programs involves choices among alternatives, or trade-offs, to preserve the economic metaphor. The appeal of a particular program or activity, measured by the enrollment, should reflect the demand for services. The curve would slope downward; the number of children participating in a given program would be a function of the relative costs and the preferences of families.

The costs of participating are in part monetary, such as camp fees or Little League outfits, and in part a function of the time, energy, and transportation expenses incurred by parents to get children involved and attending regularly. One would expect that family income and perhaps the number of children in the family to be accommodated would influence the demand for a given activity. Figure 6.1 posits a set of hypothetical demand functions for families of different economic levels that might obtain under the assumptions given. Activity costs, both monetary and nonmonetary, are assumed to be a more serious deterrent for low-income families, with a resulting inhibition on their rates of participation. The graph implies that the more expensive the program or activity, the fewer the number of children who would

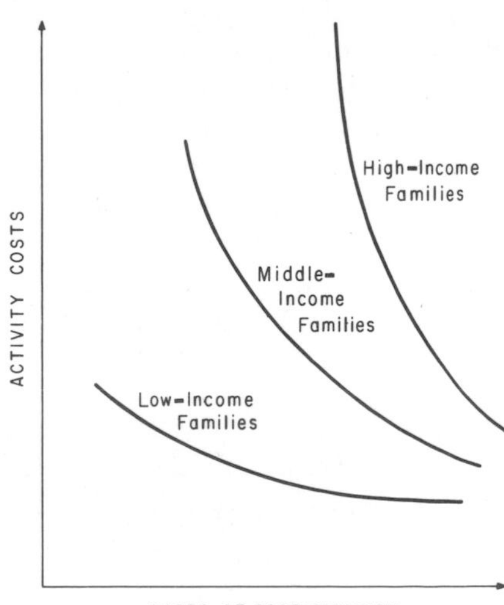

FIGURE 6.1. Hypothetical demand curves for summer acivities for families with differing resources.

attend. As a corollary, affluent families are predicted to consume more of a given activity, irrespective of costs, than poor families.

The usefulness of an explicit model, such as that presented, is largely heuristic. Figure 6.1 is a reasonably good representation of the pattern of participation in activities in Atlanta; yet the assumptions of the model are not directly testable. Little is known about the actual preferences of parents or about the specific outcomes or utility they might desire to maximize. Nonetheless, the model embodies a set of expectations and propositions; it is intended to sensitize the reader to relevant questions and to pose a basis for discussing the empirical observations of the summer activities of children.

What factors determine the choice of summer programs and activities? The first observation to be made is that the summer is not an appropriate time period in which to assess the demand for public education or for activities that directly promote achievement. The vast majority of activities neither claimed to be nor were particularly successful at enhancing intellectual growth to any significant degree. The summer is popularly regarded as vacation time and as a hiatus from school work; programs appear to attract participants quite apart from their academic utility. Summer schools, the largest single activity, were the only program that explicitly included educational goals, yet there is little evidence to suggest that either the schools or the students placed much emphasis on these objectives. Demand for summer schools as well as other structured programs seems to be a function of their relative convenience, rather than of their relative effectiveness in augmenting summer learning.

Figure 6.1 implies that the children from families with differing resources will participate at different rates and that the elasticity of demand is greatest for programs or activities that could be regarded as luxuries. Whereas both observations tend to be true among the summer programs examined, the patterning of activities is a good deal more complex. The model best describes the relationship between parental income and participation when comparing activities that involve a direct monetary cost, such as private camps or extended family vacations. Relatively advantaged children were not more likely to enroll in every program; rather, the total activity package consumed by families fits the hypothesized demand curves. Prosperous families provided their children with summer activities that are both more costly and more diverse in the aggregate. The scions of Atlanta were involved in both a greater number of activities and a higher proportion of expensive activities than their less privileged age mates, but numerous camps, clubs, and the like were oriented to the poor.

The major costs involved in participating in most summer activities were not fees or tuition, but parents' time; the majority of programs were free or involved only nominal expense. The utilization of public programs or facilities such as libraries, parks, or summer schools, tended to be a function of their relative proximity to a child's home. Children living near the library, particularly within walking distance, read more books than children living further away, irrespective of family income. Summer schools tended to be targeted to the poorest minority neighborhoods, and therefore to attract disproportionate numbers of children from less affluent families. Families with both parents employed full-time had a marked tendency to choose programs offering comprehensive, full-day care, rather than less extensive options. Each of these findings tends to support the basic notion that families choose activities on rational grounds subject to the limitations of time and resources, while at the same time suggesting that factors other than the immediate family resources are relevant.

SUMMER ACTIVITIES: WITH WHAT EFFECT?

The empirical analyses that constitute the major portion of this second half of the book are largely descriptive. The concepts and variables chosen, however, reflect an underlying presumption about why summer activities are important and how summer learning might be a major consequence of such experiences. The initial question is what effect, if any, does participation in particular activities have on learning? Socioeconomic background exerts a substantial influence on achievement during the summer, as we have seen. To what extent do summer programs mediate or amplify the influence of parental status on the achievement of children? Summer activities are considerably more diverse than those found in the typical elementary school classroom. Comparing the outcomes of children who were exposed to varying experiences may provide insight about sources of differential learning and suggest the contexts in which it occurs.

For example, one might hypothesize outcomes similar to those presented in Figure 6.2. A given program or activity could be described by its net effect on learning and by a pattern of outcomes specific to income strata. This relationship is assumed to be positive for all children. Activities have two measurable effects: the first, an increment in test scores relative to nonparticipants, and the second, an impact on the achievement process due to a change in the relationship between gains and income. Since access to programs is shaped by parental resources,

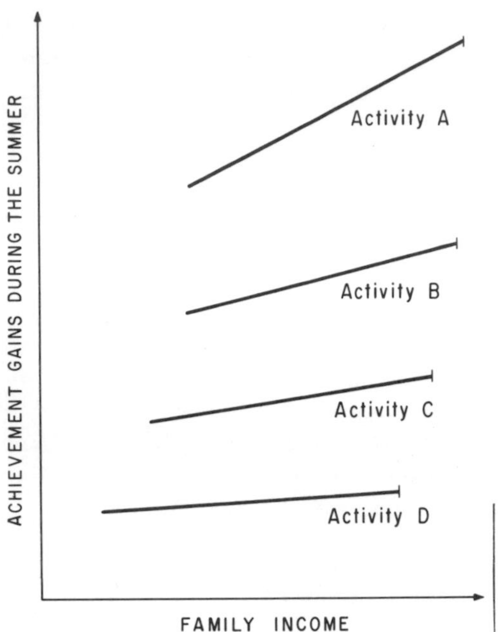

FIGURE 6.2. Posited relationship between achievement gains and family income for children participating in hypothetical summer activities, A, B, C, or D.

which have a major impact on summer learning, one might expect to isolate programs that were particularly instrumental in transmitting parental advantages. The schema posited in Figure 6.2 implies that the relationship between parental status and learning is positive, but that it varies across programs. The effects of programs are posited to be both additive and interactive.

The diagram does not exhaust the theoretical possibilities. One could imagine a summer program or activity that decreased learning or increased the verbal skills of poor children more dramatically than those of advantaged children. Neither pattern, however, is prevalent empirically. Figure 6.2 is a logical extrapolation of the effects one might find if schools or a surrogate for schooling were operating selectively and high-income children were the most likely to take advantage of them. The model suggests that one might construct a taxonomy of programs and activities, ordered by their relative effectiveness in increasing rates of learning for particular children.

With a number of rather substantial reservations, Figure 6.2 can be said to describe the patterns observed in Atlanta. First, and most important, the numbers of children involved in any particular activity are small and the magnitude of the effects quite modest. In only a handful of cases are the relationships sufficiently robust to produce significant summer gains once socioeconomic status is controlled. Second, Figure 6.2 is unrealistic for two reasons:

1. There is a considerable amount of segregation between racial and class groups during the summer, which truncates the relationship between income and achievement for any particular activity.
2. The activities are neither necessarily independent nor mutually exclusive.

Participation in one activity tends to be negatively related to participation in another, particularly among activities that consume a large amount of time. However, this relationship is relatively weak and varies by social class. Separating the effects of particular programs is thus quite problematic. Although the empirical effects do not contradict the graphic representation of Figure 6.2, neither do the outcomes offer a strong confirmation. While most activities benefited advantaged children more than poor children, only a small number of activities and no programs were significantly related to summer learning once socioeconomic background was controlled. Few activities constituted as prolonged an intervention as did exposure to schooling during the regular term. It is not possible to determine to what degree the interactions occurred because of the program or because of self-selection by children residing in families particularly concerned with their intellectual growth. Although cognitive gains appear to result from program participation, the role of particular activities is complex and cannot be unambiguously distinguished from the role of families. The next section summarizes the methodological issues posed by the patterns of summer learning.

INTERPRETATIONS AND NATURAL EXPERIMENTS

The dominant paradigm in educational research is the experimental method; although not always feasible, particularly for large-scale evaluations, experimental and quasi-experimental designs dominate the educational literature. The reasons are clear. Experimental methods provide an elegant solution to the ambiguities of causal influence. Isolating a single program or treatment that differentiates one set of students from another permits assessment of the unique effect of the treatment, ceteris paribus. The best method for ensuring that individual attributes do not confound the analysis is randomized assignment to treatment and control groups. The characteristics of the children are thereby held constant, while the program is varied. The difference between the two groups on some outcome measure is an unbiased estimate of the program effect.

Survey research does not approximate the degree of control possible in a carefully designed experiment. At best, one obtains numerous measures of individual differences, such as socioeconomic status or intelligence, that permit some degree of statistical control over the prediction of outcomes. There are, however, always unmeasured characteristics of children that may cause learning irrespective of environmental influence. The hypothesis that children exposed to one experience learned more because they were different in some way from children not so exposed is, in practice, virtually impossible to discount.

The survey of summer activities conducted in Atlanta is clearly not an experiment. Inferences about the magnitude or significance of program effects, or for that matter about noneffects, cannot be reliably assessed without a control group similar in every way but the treatment received by children actually enrolled in a program. Given the nature of the problem studied, controls for summer programs were impossible to institute.

Without control groups, what can be learned? By the canons of experimental design, little can be said with assurance about program effects. The initial research strategy was elaborated with such issues in mind, but with the expectation that if differences were significant, and the controls employed were sufficiently numerous, inferences were possible. One might be able to argue that summer programs were a viable policy tool and, most important, that they could arrest summer achievement declines among disadvantaged children.

The actual results are rather less promising, although perhaps not surprising. Although the achievement gains for black children attending a summer school averaged 1.5 months, which is the precise length of time of the program, these gains were barely significant. More important, they were not evenly distributed with respect to children's backgrounds. The largest gains were invariably concentrated in the highest income bracket. Once family income or parental educational levels were controlled, the net effect of program attendance was reduced to insignificance. The conclusion would seem to be that the program had at best a trivial positive influence on achievement once prior achievement and family background were controlled. A similar though less dramatic pattern existed for most structured programs. When the gains were significant, the program could not be interpreted as the unique cause, but at best as an interactive element. Although activities such as reading were consistently and significantly related to summer learning irrespective of controls, plausible reasons could be advanced for supposing that individual differences distinguishing children who read books were as important as reading per se.

Such results are not uncommon; however, they pose a dilemma for policy and analysis. If the central question is taken to be which programs most effectively raised summer achievement levels, the answer is those programs that enrolled the largest number of high-income children. If the question is which summer programs most reduced the gap between advantaged and disadvantaged children, the answer is that none did so very well. Summer programs do not explain learning, if by explain we mean make an independent contribution to variance, once socioeconomic status is controlled. The most persistent influence on learning was the child's family background, not the public or private programs attended.

There are numerous compelling reasons for supposing that the summer programs studied did not constitute serious educational interventions. By and large, the summer programs neither attempted nor expected to accomplish very much cognitive learning. Summer programs provided recreation and diversion, not academic instruction. Furthermore, summer is a very brief period, and most programs were in operation for less than half of that time. The data represent a cross section of programs available and were not collected so as to permit a careful evaluation of specific programs. With the exception of summer school, the programs were scattered and diverse in their scope, duration, and clientele. Seldom more than a handful of sample children were involved in the specific programs identified. In addition, the participation of children from varying family backgrounds was different in kind as well as amount. If the regular school session is taken as the norm, summer programs were quite homogeneous, tending to attract students similar to each other on every measured attribute; as a result, the average gains across both programs and summer schools were directly proportional to the socioeconomic composition. In sum, it could easily be argued that the poor showing of summer programs does not rule out their effectiveness as policy tools.

Such factors no doubt constitute a partial explanation of results. They do not, however, provide a satisfactory account of the prevalent patterns of learning. If programs did not augment achievement, yet learning occurred, it is incumbent to explain what influences were most important and through what mechanism they operated. Focusing on the narrow experimental question ignores the patterning of activities and of learning that occurred. The question that appears to be most fruitful is not which programs effectively promoted summer learning, but how are we to understand the persistent and pervasive effects of socioeconomic status on achievement? I would argue that socioeconomic status is not merely an individual attribute to be used as a control, but an active set of conditions that directly shape learning. Socioeconomic status is a convenient proxy for a host of differences between families, which, in the words of Davis and Havighurst (1946), "define and systematize different learning environments [p. 698]." The central cause of achievement is the continuous direct influence of families; the central dilemma for the analyst is to isolate those mechanisms through which socioeconomic status operates.

Parental status tends to be diffuse and poorly specified as a causal variable. Since measurement is imperfect, and since most indicators of background are highly interrelated, there has been a tendency to abandon efforts to identify the causal nexus. Analysts have often assumed that the quality of a home environment was indicative of social class operating as an attribute, rather than as an indicator of causal conditions and behavior critical for learning. Despite the fact that several of the indicators of adult status commonly used to measure background have been shown to vary considerably in the course of the life cycle, we assume that a child's status origins are fixed and immutable. Although many analysts have argued that environmental influences shape intellectual development, few have attempted to measure the impact of family circumstance as an ongoing process, or to relate such differences among families to learning.[1]

Efforts have been made to develop a theoretical framework for relating achievement to home life, although quantifying such relations has been somewhat problematic. Shulman (1970) argues that a unidimensional conception of environment along a single deprived–enriched continuum is inadequate; rather, that multidimensional measures are necessary. Bloom (1964) describes a study by Wolf, which found that such family process variables as parental aspirations, the emphasis on language and learning, and the intellectual climate of the home were more highly correlated to a child's IQ than were traditional measures of social status. Williams (1976b) argues that an assessment of family

[1] One reason for this deficiency is quite clearly the observed stability over time of measures of intelligence. Bloom (1964) argues that after Grades 5 or 6, the correlations are rarely less than .80 between test scores based on parallel testing procedures and repeated measurements. Although the strength of this relationship is enough to give pause to analysts familiar with quantitative models, it is not incompatible with substantial learning, nor with a substantial ongoing influence of background. For an elaboration of these arguments, see Appendix D.

environments should be based on social learning theory, rather than on notions of an environmental press, and should therefore be conceptualized as process variables, not attributes.

The strategy that underlies this analysis of summer learning is to document extensively those activities that distinguish students learning more from those learning less. Specific patterns emerge, and they constitute a plausible explanation of the role of family background on achievement; however, the nature of the inquiry is inherently speculative. The empirical results are in accord with our knowledge of social class differences in learning, which is reassuring; but they do not constitute proof of the propositions. What follows is a summary sketch of the significant results and an interpretation.

Children in Atlanta were involved in a large number of structured programs. The direct effects of these programs were generally negligible, but, in varying degrees, all structured programs interacted with family background. In addition, summer school programs were likely to be most successful in terms of cognitive growth for those children who attended summer school, despite the fact that their own school did not offer a program. Children who spent more time in school and who attended despite some inconvenience showed significant gains in learning irrespective of family background. It seems likely that either these children or their families were particularly motivated.

The number of books read during the summer is consistently related to achievement gains; the strength of this relationship often exceeds that of socioeconomic status when prior achievement is controlled. The use of a public library is, in fact, more predictive of vocabulary gains than attending summer school.

Taking a trip, and most especially a trip alone, is consistently indicative of gains in summer learning, irrespective of background. These gains tend not to be associated with characteristics of the trip, such as who was visited, for how long, or where they lived. Gains accrue to children who are permitted to travel alone, irrespective of the sort of vacation taken.

Between 70 and 85% of the children in the sample have a bicycle although, as one might expect, poor children are less likely to have one than more affluent children. The ownership of a bicycle is worth about 1 month of achievement for both males and females, even when parental income and other measures of status are controlled.

These effects are not large. The fact, however, that there are circumstances and activities that influence summer learning, quite apart from the effects of parental status, implies that cognitive growth can be systematically related to discrete events and activities. Even though 4 or

5 months is a very short time period, particular summer activities can be isolated that enhanced learning. Although the effects of socioeconomic status are ubiquitous, it seems possible to enumerate differences among families that are significantly related to achievement and are not inextricably confounded with socioeconomic background.[2]

Interpreting the substantive meaning and the importance of such findings is somewhat problematic. The effects are often as large as those attributed to socioeconomic status, yet they represent diverse experiences. It makes little sense to interpret such activities literally, because each seems only remotely relevant to school performance. Although it might be possible to construct an index of effective experiences, it seems far more useful to deduce how such individual activities might serve as mechanisms of family influence, in addition to the more easily measured social class differences.

One tactic would be to view the activities as indicative of interfamily differences reflecting parental attitudes and behavior conducive to learning. Each of the activities could be argued to be representative of either of two underlying dimensions of childrearing, dimensions one might call "directed resources" and "independence training," respectively.

The single variable that has proved to be the most strongly associated with summer learning is family income. The amount of income earned is probably a reasonably good indicator of family life styles, consumption patterns, and cultural or social opportunities. Family income would be expected to promote cognitive growth insofar as it enables families to provide an enriched home environment and educational experiences for their children. Each of the summer activities described requires that a portion of family resources or time be specifically targeted to the sixth-grade child. Families of varying degrees of affluence differ in the degree to which they are able to spend money on children, although this relation is far from perfect. Family income enables parents to invest in their progeny, but parents who do so despite low income, and perhaps at some sacrifice, are more likely to be interested in and supportive of their children's intellectual and emotional well-being. Buying a bicycle, providing transportation to an out-of-the-way summer program, or subsidizing a trip to visit relatives, even if the family cannot join, are behavioral indicators of this commitment. The mechanism influencing summer learning is the ability and the willingness to

[2] The criteria imposed were relatively strict and purely statistical; these activities had a unique influence on the determination of fall achievement after spring achievement and parental status were included, were significantly different from zero, and were consistent for both white and black sixth-grade children.

commit resources directly to children; family income reflects the ability to do so; participation in activities independent of family income is assumed to tap the variation among families in devoting resources to children not captured by status alone.[3]

A second dimension measured by individual activities is the degree of independence permitted or expected of the child. Each of the variables examined might reflect the parents' stress on independent initiative. Taking a trip alone requires not only directed resources, but a measure of confidence in the child's ability and competence. Attending a summer program in a strange and distant neighborhood requires greater autonomy and self-confidence than drifting into the local program with one's friends. Having access to a bicycle facilitates independent mobility and initiative. Sontag, Baker, and Nelson (1958) found that children's IQ gains were associated with emotional independence. Kohn (1963) has argued quite eloquently that the middle-class values toward child-rearing emphasize independence, rather than obedience or conformity, and that this fosters achievement. The patterning of summer activities suggests that such values, translated into behavioral differences in the degree of independence allotted to children, may play a role in achievement differences. Although such behavior is generally assumed to be part of middle-class socialization, perhaps lower-status families who encourage independent activities also further the achievement of their children.

In sum, the data on summer activities present more puzzles than solutions. Disentangling the mechanisms through which a family influences a child's performance in school is a complex task. The patterns are suggestive, although there is no altogether satisfactory method of ascribing unique effects to the web of causal relations present. The analysis underscores the general observation regarding the pivotal importance of family circumstances and provides two theoretical dimensions likely to be implicated in socialization and social class transmission. Specific activities will be examined in greater detail in subsequent chapters with more attention to empirical reality and less to theoretical conjecture. Chapter 7 explores the impact of summer school programs. Chapter 8 describes other structured activities, the use of time, and vacation trips. Chapter 9 presents the data on reading and library use during the summer.

[3] It could also be argued that the patterns of expenditure are more stable than those of income; perhaps families who direct larger portions of their income to their children are actually better off than those who do not, but have suffered a temporary financial setback. Such an argument implicitly assumes that directed resources are errors of measurement in the specification of family income variable, rather than independent effects.

7
The Effects of Summer School

Summer school provides an opportunity to study learning in another context. The virtual absence of mandatory summer schooling in this country offers a tailor-made contrast between voluntary programs and compulsory schooling and between school and nonschool environments. The ability of summer programs to attract students and to increase cognitive achievement can perhaps furnish additional evidence on the effectiveness of formal schooling. Summer school is also a unique setting for innovation and experimentation.

Traditionally, summer vacation offered a break from the classroom regimen and an opportunity to synthesize and integrate materials. Increasingly, however, summer vacation has been viewed as an anachronism dating from an agrarian cultural context and as a period of time that might be better spent educationally. The demand for summer schooling increased dramatically throughout the 1970s, although few districts have yet instituted a set curriculum. Summer school tends to be administratively decentralized and relatively loosely organized. These factors are unique assets in that small experimental programs could be initiated with little difficulty. Since it is often possible to hire noncredentialed aides, summer school might be a means for building direct links with the community by using parents or other interested adults, or for bringing imaginative new talent to the classroom.

The initial section of this chapter provides an overview of the summer programs in Atlanta, drawing heavily from the field work, anecdotal sources, and a series of reports produced by the Atlanta public schools. I then review the evidence on the effectiveness of summer programs for sixth-grade students in Atlanta, based on cognitive achievement scores. Finally, I compare differential summer gains by family income. The general results suggest that summer school is only marginally effective in raising test scores or in promoting more equal outcomes. Despite their popularity, Atlanta's programs do not seem to make a dent in educational inequality.

ATLANTA SUMMER SCHOOLS

Summer school in Atlanta is neither an extension of formal education nor a systematic attempt to introduce alternatives. The school district sponsors one of the largest ongoing summer school programs in the nation. Since 1969, Atlanta has offered a wide range of summer classes on diverse topics. The programs attract fully one-fourth of the elementary students and an even larger proportion of students in secondary schools for a fourth quarter (Anderson, 1972; Rice, 1970).[1] Of the 42 sample schools, 23 offered a summer program in Atlanta during the summer of 1972, enrolling one-third of the sixth-grade sample. The typical program lasted 6 weeks, ending in mid-July, and was limited to 3 or 4 hours of instruction in the morning. Several community schools, however, stay open year-round and supervise summer activities throughout the day. At least 2 sample schools began with a free breakfast program in the morning and ran extended day programs until 6:00 p.m. One-fifth of the students attending summer school were involved in programs longer than 6 weeks, and about one-tenth participated for more than 5 hours per day.

The curricula varied considerably across schools, although all programs included some reading and math instruction, often remedial in nature. The emphasis in every school studied, however, was not on academic subjects but on recreation and enrichment. Summer programs included arts and crafts, music, drama, and team sports. In addition, some classes not generally available to sixth-grade students were added to the summer program, such as typing and home economics. Particular

[1] The size and quality of Atlanta's summer school programs was one of the principal reasons for choosing this city as the research site. The decision of the school board and key administrative personnel to cooperate was based on a desire to accumulate evidence on the effectiveness of the summer programs, perhaps to facilitate legislation and funding in the future.

schools built an integrated program around a theme, such as developing library skills or future careers. Students in one school organized a theater group, which put on elaborate puppet shows, while another published a school newspaper filled with children's stories, poems, and artwork. Field trips were common and were frequently mentioned as a memorable part of the summer experience.

A fairly extensive internal evaluation of the programs in 11 of the sample schools was initiated by the central administration during the last week of the summer session. These schools enrolled over half of the sample children attending summer school. Questionnaires regarding the summer school experience were distributed to principals, teachers, and a number of students and parents. Although the results do not represent a random sample of the summer school programs or participants, the responses are instructive. They indicate that students, parents, and staff felt that the program was a great success. Principals reported that nearly one-third of the summer staff in the 11 schools were not regular employees, but special teachers, community aides, or volunteers. Although not routinely taken, attendance varied considerably across schools, with estimates ranging from 55 to 89% of enrollment. Although attendance was often cited as a problem, the teachers felt the students had learned a great deal and assessed the program favorably.[2]

The reasons given for the success of the summer programs were far more consistent across different schools than were the criticisms. Without exception, teachers mentioned the smaller class size and the informal and relaxed atmosphere, which allowed more individual attention. Classes tended to be ungraded and less structured than during the school year, and teachers believed that students were more interested and involved in school. Teachers had far more autonomy in structuring classroom activities and organizing a curriculum, and this apparently contributed to their positive assessments.

The responses of selected students in the 11 schools were also unambiguously favorable. Most children (94%) went to summer school "because it was fun." A few mentioned making up work or skipping a grade; the vast majority, however, attended for pure enjoyment and stated that they preferred summer school to regular sessions. The reasons given were seldom academic. "You don't have to stay as long," "Teachers are nicer," or "Because it's easier" were common refrains. When asked what would have improved the summer program, they

[2] The two most frequent suggestions were to expand services by hiring additional staff and to install air-conditioning units in particularly uncomfortable classrooms. Attendance was third on the list.

typically wanted more of the same activities offered, such as field trips, or the addition of swimming to the curricula.

Parents also overwhelmingly endorsed the summer school programs. Several working mothers commented that the extended day program was entertaining and "kept the children off the streets." The children of working mothers were disproportionately likely to attend summer school, although they were no more likely to attend full-day or throughout the summer. Parents whose children attended a free, full-day, year-round program frequently mentioned the benefits for parents as well as children. Unlike those of the students, the parents' responses tended to stress the educational component of the summer experience, rather than the fun, as foremost. Summer school was viewed as a means of helping children read better, or of receiving individual attention often lacking during the regular academic year. A common theme, well expressed by one parent, was that summer school helped children "to advance themselves more and more in education."

The general enthusiasm among the participants no doubt partly reflects the interviewing process. Respondents were selected during the last week of summer school, and no effort was made to find malcontents. The results suggest, however, that the programs' successes were based on both student interest and parental aspirations. The near-unanimous acclaim seems to be because motivated children were attracted, who probably liked school better than the average child, and whose parents were interested and supportive of educational goals. Such factors are clearly relevant to an assessment of the effects of summer schooling and difficult to control adequately in a nonexperimental study. The next section examines who went to summer school, summarizing the determinants of program attendance in Atlanta and providing a rationale for the various controls introduced in evaluating program effects.

THE DETERMINANTS OF SUMMER SCHOOL ATTENDANCE

Demographically, children attending summer school were more likely to be black, to have a working mother, to be from lower-income families, and to live near a school that sponsored a program. Black children were more than twice as likely to enroll in a summer program as were white students, irrespective of program location, employment status of mother, or family income level. Of those students regularly enrolled in one of the 23 sample schools that offered a summer program in 1972, 48% of the black students and 18% of the white students attended. Among those students whose own school did not have a program, 28% of the black students and 12% of the white students attended. Table 7.1 summarizes these relationships by employment status of mothers.

Attendance at summer programs is wholly voluntary, and the choice of school or program is less restricted than during the school year. Summer schools in Atlanta are substantially less integrated than are schools during the year. Over half of the white sample, irrespective of the racial composition of the neighborhood school, was concentrated in three predominantly white schools in the Northeast section of the city. Whites were nearly twice as likely to attend a summer program in a

TABLE 7.1
Proportion of Students Attending Summer School by Race, Employment Status of Mother, and Whether Child's School Offered a Program, 1972, Sixth Grade[a]

Race and school program	Employment status of mother: Employed full-time		Employment status of mother: Not employed or part-time		Total	
	Percentage	*N*	Percentage	*N*	Percentage	*N*
White	*19*	*139*	*13*	*331*	*15*	*470*
Regular school offered program	26	62	15	181	18	243
Regular school did not	14	77	11	150	12	227
Black	*44*	*514*	*41*	*509*	*42*	*1023*
Regular school offered program	50	359	45	358	48	717
Regular school did not	30	155	27	151	28	316

[a] Variance explained (η^2) in attendance, main effects.

White: Employment status: .081, $F = 5.75$
School location: .92, $F = 6.13$

Black: Employment status: .017, $F = 7.38$
School location: .093, $F = 12.83$

school other than their own, but did not choose to attend majority black programs. Discretionary attendance does not seem to encourage racial integration.

The ecology of summer school programs in Atlanta tends to confound the relationship between attendance and family socioeconomic status. Predominantly black schools and schools in low-income neighborhoods were more likely to be chosen as program sites than were schools in the more affluent neighborhoods. Consequently, economically disadvantaged children were more likely to attend. Comparing only children regularly enrolled in the schools that offered summer programs, however, the relationship between family income and attendance is slightly, although not significantly, positive for both black and white students. When the employment status of mothers is controlled, this relationship disappears altogether. Although the summer school population tends to be from lower-status families, this is almost entirely due to the distribution of schools rather than to the influence of family factors.

Among black children, the relationship between attendance and family income is not linear. For example, a small number of families in the highest income bracket tends to follow patterns characteristic of upper-middle-class white families: employed male heads earning over $15,000 annually, mothers not employed, and only 15% of the children attending summer school. For neither white nor black children does family income or parents' education explain more than 1% of the variance in summer school attendance when program location and mother's employment status are controlled. In general, it seems as if the socioeconomic status of families is neither strongly nor consistently related to the propensity to attend summer school when such characteristics as program accessibility or family needs for child care are controlled.

One might assume at the outset that children attending summer school were likely to be those who had fallen behind during the school year and had to complete additional work before promotion. This does not seem to be the case in Atlanta. Both black and white summer school students had slightly higher school year achievement levels when socioeconomic status was controlled. In fact, school year gains tended to be positively related to the decision to attend summer school for children enrolled in an elementary school that offered the program. The relationships were barely significant, but persisted when family background was controlled. If summer programs were intended as a means for achieving academic parity or making up school work, they do not attract the lowest-achieving students. Parents do not perceive summer school as a place to make up work; only 21 parents, or less than 4%, reported that their child's teacher had recommended the summer program. Nor do those children who missed a great deal of school during the year enroll in large numbers. Children attending summer school tended to have had the best attendance records during the preceding year, as Table 7.2 documents. It would seem that at most a very small fraction of children were enrolled in summer school in order to make up academic work. Moreover, very few students were accelerated a grade through attending summer school during 1972.

For the slight majority of the children attending summer school (51%), the parents reported it had been the child's idea; for the remainder, respondents indicated it had been the parents' idea. This factor was seemingly unrelated to either the causes or consequences of attending. There was a slight tendency for higher-status parents to report that summer school had been the child's idea rather than their own; this may, however, reflect more about class values toward childrearing than about the actual responsibility for such decisions. In virtually no case, whether the child attended a school nearby or farther away, did the imputed source of influence on the decision affect outcomes.

In sum, summer school programs in Atlanta recruit students disproportionately from certain neighborhoods and from families with particular needs. The location of the program explains the socioeconomic composition, although not the racial makeup, of the summer school student body. Irrespective of other family characteristics, black children were more likely to attend summer school, to attend

TABLE 7.2
Proportion of Students Attending Summer School in 1972 by School Attendance, 1971–1972, by Race, Sixth Grade[a]

Days absent during 1971–1972	White		Black		Total	
	Percentage	*N*	Percentage	*N*	Percentage	*N*
Less than 2	19.7	71	54.4	294	47.7	365
2–5	20.7	87	38.7	225	33.7	312
6–10	16.5	121	39.0	223	31.1	344
11–20	10.8	158	36.3	237	26.1	395
21–30	8.0	25	31.7	41	22.7	66
31+	0	8	0	3	0	11
Total	*15.1*	*470*	*42.3*	*1023*	*33.8*	*1493*

[a] Variance explained (η^2).
Total: .035, $F = 5.6$
White: .017, $F = 1.7$
Black: .027, $F = 10.8$

full-day programs, and to be enrolled for a larger part of the summer. In Atlanta, black children appear to get more exposure to schooling in the summer as well as during the school year.

The location of summer programs has a dramatic impact on the likelihood a child will attend. Decisions as to which schools would offer a summer program are made centrally; in part, they probably reflect the demand for programs as well as bureaucratic exigencies. Summer school is currently provided at no cost to parents, although in the past tuition fees were levied. Although these educational expenses are not as great as those budgeted during the school year, it is clear that the distribution of subsidies is remarkably progressive. The allocation of funds for summer school programs tends to be inversely related to family income levels in the district. For whatever reasons, the school system allocates disproportionate funds to those schools serving relatively underprivileged children.

The major factors examined thus far do not begin to account for the variance in attendance. School location, family income, and employment status of mothers explain less than 10% of the variance for either racial group. Since programs are voluntary, it seems quite probable that students who like school best decide to attend. Although there is no direct evidence that motivation or interest were critical factors, the attendance data presented earlier are suggestive. The reports of teachers regarding student interest and enthusiasm during the summer indicate considerable self-selection. Although it is not clear that the summer students were eager for an academic curriculum, they seemed at least willing to hazard a little school work in order to participate or perhaps to be with their friends. Factors such as self-selection are crucial in assessing the effects of summer school, to which I now turn.

ACHIEVEMENT IN SUMMER SCHOOL

Summer school programs in Atlanta were not designed primarily to raise test scores; it seems somewhat gratuitous to observe that they did not do so with overwhelming success. The objectives and curricula were diverse; the staff and students enthusiastic; the time available short. Perhaps it is to be expected that few gains could be attributed unequivocally to summer school.

Looking first at the general pattern of gains by race and school location, Table 7.3 presents the grade-equivalent gains for the entire sample. White students tend to gain nearly 2.5 months during the summer, whether or not they attend summer school; black children lose

TABLE 7.3
Mean Grade Equivalent Summer Gains, Word Knowledge, by Race, School Location, and Whether Child Attended Summer School, Sixth Grade[a]

Race and school attendance	Location of summer program: Own school		Location of summer program: Other school		Total	
	Gain	*N*	Gain	*N*	Gain	*N*
White	*.14*	*231*	*.34*	*218*	*.24*	*449*
Attended summer school	.11	43	.40	26	.23	69
No summer school	.16	188	.33	192	.24	380
Black	*−.19*	*692*	*.06*	*294*	*−.12*	*986*
Attended summer school	−.09	327	.17	87	−.03	414
No summer school	−.28	365	.02	207	−.18	572

[a] Within locations, attendance is not significantly related to summer gains.

a little over 1 month, while summer school appears to offset the decline, albeit not by a large amount.[3] For the total sample of blacks, the achievement difference between those attending summer school and those who do not is barely significant ($F = 4.7$); within the school location variable, the number of cases is less, and the differences for neither group attain significance. The achievement gains suggest that attending summer school is worth perhaps 1.5 months of achievement relative to not attending, which is, coincidentally, the exact amount of time the programs were in operation. This pattern is consistent for each of the nine subject area tests in addition to word knowledge; however, the differences are not large in any area.[4]

The differences in gains experienced by students attending a summer program in their own school and those attending a different school are

[3] It is important to remember that the grade equivalent scores are scaled relative to national norms; an absolute gain in learning is not incompatible with a loss in relative position, as measured by grade equivalents.

[4] The parental survey asked which subjects children had studied during the summer as well as what sorts of programs had been attended. An effort was made to match the subject tests to the subjects studied during summer school. Students who studied those particular subjects did not have larger gains on specific subtests than did students who just attended. The achievement gains tend to generalize across subjects, but to be unassociated with particular courses.

curious. Since summer school programs were located in relatively disadvantaged neighborhoods, the gains might be expected to reflect higher socioeconomic status. However, the students going away to a summer school were quite like those who attended in their own neighborhoods. The socioeconomic status of black summer school enrollees was similar regardless of their origin school. The summer school programs tended to attract the least advantaged children within the more affluent schools, not the most well-to-do. Irrespective of family income, as Table 7.4 documents, children from other schools gained the most from summer school.

One might assume that students attending a summer program farther from home may have chosen the better programs and hence improved their achievement as a result of a superior educational setting. Program effects are intrinsically interesting from a policy perspective, in that

TABLE 7.4
Mean Grade Equivalent Summer Gains, Word Knowledge, by Race, School Location, and Family Income, Sixth Grade

	Attended summer school				
	Location				
Race and family income	Own school	Other school	Total	Did not attend	Total
White[a]	*.11*	*.40*	*.23*	*.24*	*.34*
N	*43*	*26*	*69*	*380*	*449*
Less than $9,000	−.23	.40	−.14	.09	.06
N	12	2	14	87	101
$9,000–14,999	.24	.26	.25	.19	.20
N	11	10	21	88	109
$15,000+	.26	.50	.39	.32	.33
N	11	9	20	99	119
Black[a]	*−.09*	*.17*	*−.04*	*−.18*	*−.12*
N	*327*	*87*	*414*	*572*	*986*
Less than $4,000	−.38	.15	−.22	−.28	−.26
N	51	21	72	104	176
$4,000–8,999	−.09	.07	−.06	−.17	−.12
N	116	25	141	173	314
$9,000–14,999	−.23	.04	−.19	−.06	−.11
N	57	10	67	100	167
$15,000+	.33	.90	.46	.17	.23
N	36	11	47	52	99

[a] Totals include 120 whites and 230 blacks for whom income data were missing.

identifying particularly successful schools can provide insight on how best to structure programs. However, differences among the summer programs in Atlanta do not account for achievement differences among summer school students. The composition of summer schools was more homogeneous than that of the schools during the regular school year and there was greater between-school variance; however, gains tended to be directly proportional to those expected on the basis of the school composition.[5] Few programs produced either dramatic success or dismal failure with respect to summer achievement gains. Children who attended summer school in spite of the fact that their own school did not offer a program tended to choose the school closest to their own home, irrespective of the quality of program. White children clustered in certain schools much more often than black children, but with little effect on their scores. The other schools chosen were roughly those that might be expected from the housing patterns. Few children traveled very far to attend summer school, nor does the evidence suggest that gains were due to particularly effective programs.

Although the observed differences between schools do not suggest that programs were differentially valuable, one aspect of the summer school experience deserves attention. The duration of programs varied considerably across schools. Certain schools provided a full day of supervised activity rather than a half-day; a few schools remained in session for the entire summer, rather than just 6 weeks. Such differences are clearly relevant to a discussion of the effects of exposure to schooling. If academic exposure during the summer were an important factor in achievement, the effectiveness of schooling should be proportional to the duration. Although relatively few children were involved in full-summer or full-day programs, Table 7.5 suggests that program duration did have a modest impact on children's achievement patterns. Children enrolled for more than 6 weeks consistently gained more than those enrolled for only half the summer. The gains suggest that a full-summer program is worth an additional month of achievement; this difference persists irrespective of student socioeconomic status or school location. The data for full-day programs are rather less encouraging; children who stayed at school for more than 4 hours per

[5] The proportion of variance in fall achievement between the 23 schools offering summer programs was 27.3% for those students attending summer school. For all students enrolled in one of these schools during the fall, the between-school variance was 22.4%. There were 13 schools with more than 10 black children enrolled for summer school; in 11 of these schools, gains for summer school students were larger than those for their peers who did not attend. In every school, children enrolled in another school during the regular session gained the most.

TABLE 7.5
Mean Summer Grade Equivalent Gain, Word Knowledge, by Program Duration and Location of Summer School, Sixth-Grade Black Children[a]

	Location of summer program					
	Own school		Other school		Total	
Attendance	Gain	*N*	Gain	*N*	Gain	*N*
Attended summer school	*−.09*	*327*	*.17*	*87*	*−.03*	*414*
6 weeks or less	−.12	270	.17	75	−.06	345
More than 6 weeks	.06	57	.19	12	.08	69
4 hours or less per day	−.06	268	.20	70	−.01	338
More than 4 hours per day	−.28	50	−.19	11	−.26	61
Did not attend summer school	*−.28*	*365*	*.02*	*207*	*−.18*	*572*
Total	*−.19*	*692*	*.06*	*294*	*−.12*	*986*

[a] Within school location, differences in duration are not significant.

day tended to gain less than children attending fewer hours.[6] The patterns are similar for white students, although there are too few cases to be meaningful.

The gains by program duration should be interpreted cautiously since so few children are involved. One plausible explanation consistent with the evidence would be that children who received greater exposure to instruction, not just schooling, gained the most from summer school. Extended day programs were largely custodial during the afternoons; academic materials were seldom if ever presented. Since children enrolled for a full day were given little additional instruction, the hours per day attended would not be expected to enhance achievement systematically. Children attending for more than 6 weeks, how-

[6] The comparisons of programs of differing duration are not significant if only students attending summer school are compared; however, the achievement levels among children attending longer were invariably higher, irrespective of other controls. It could be questioned whether the specific information on programs supplied by parents was very accurate. A fair number of children were reported to be in full-day programs but were enrolled in a school that did not offer an extended day. I suspect the parents may have been either confused or misled on the subject. Roughly one-fifth of the parents also reported that their children did not study academic subjects during the summer, despite the fact that all schools had minimal instruction. It seems likely that such responses were indicative of a degree of disinterest, by either the parent or the child, in the academic instruction.

TABLE 7.6
Mean Grade Equivalent Summer Gains, Word Knowledge, by Race, School Location, and Family Income, Sixth Grade

	Attended summer school				
Race and family income	Own school	Other school	Total	Did not attend	Total
White	*.10*	*.40*	*.22*	*.24*	*.24*
N	43	26	69	380	449
Less than $9,000	−.23	.40	−.14	.09	.06
N	12	2	14	87	101
$9,000–14,999	.24	.26	.25	.19	.20
N	11	10	21	88	109
$15,000+	.26	.50	.39	.32	.33
N	11	9	20	99	119
No response	9	5	14	106	120
Black	*−.09*	*.17*	*−.04*	*−.18*	*−.12*
N	327	87	414	572	986
Less than $4,000	−.38	.15	−.22	−.28	−.26
N	51	21	72	104	176
$4,000–8,999	−.09	.07	−.06	−.17	−.12
N	116	25	141	173	314
$9,000–14,999	−.23	.04	−.19	−.06	−.11
N	57	10	67	100	167
$15,000+	.33	.90	.46	.17	.23
N	36	11	47	52	99
No response	67	20	87	143	230

ever, were exposed to instruction all summer. Their gains, it could be argued, reflect this fact.[7]

Summer achievement gains, as I have shown, are consistently related to the socioeconomic status of a child's family. Since the summer school programs tended to attract relatively disadvantaged children, the gains due to such schooling might be expected to equalize cognitive achievement among children from different socioeconomic strata. This does not seem to be the case. Table 7.6 presents the grade equivalent gains by race, family income level, and school location for the Atlanta sample children. A substantial interaction is consistently present between fam-

[7] The gains for children attending exactly 6 weeks were slightly larger than those for children attending less time, although not by much. The children attending less than 6 weeks presumably dropped out of summer school without completing the program.

ily income and summer school gains, with students from the most advantaged families benefiting disproportionately. Although black children at every income level achieved more than expected through summer school participation, the higher the family income bracket, the larger the relative gap between those who attended and those who did not. For black children from families earning less than $4000 annually, attending summer school was worth approximately 2 weeks of achievement; for black children from families earning over $15,000, the gains attributable to summer school averaged nearly 4 months. The relationships are similar for white children. The influence of family background on achievement is mitigated during the summer among children of either race who did not attend summer school rather than among those attending. Such patterns imply that summer schools, unlike educational programs offered during the regular term, tend to amplify rather than to diminish cognitive inequality. This is an important issue for educational policy, and one to which we will shortly return.

The links between summer learning and summer school presented thus far detail the major relationships uncovered in the course of the analysis. The gross differences are not large and in most cases do not attain significance except for black children. Grade equivalent gains have been used to describe learning patterns in terms that could be readily translated into meaningful units. It seems reasonable to compare briefly the grade equivalent results with estimates obtained from a regression model, based on raw scores. Table 7.7 presents these data for the sample of black children.[8] The regression results summarize the patterns observed for several alternative models of the achievement process during the summer and the role of summer schooling.

Several observations are in order. First, the single largest effect is between prior achievement levels and fall scores, as expected. Second, attending a summer program is positively related to achievement, although the effect is not large; attendance never explains as much as 5% of the variance in achievement. This relationship is not significant when either family income or mother's employment status is controlled. Including family income reduces the explanatory power of summer school by half. Most of the income effect, however, is interactive. Family income has a much more decided impact on the achievement of students attending summer school than on students who do not choose to attend. During the summer, the effects of family background tend to

[8] The coding of variables is identical to that used in Chapter 4; school location is a dichotomy, with children attending a summer school at their own elementary school receiving a code of 1.0. The employment status of mothers was scored as a dummy variable, with full-time employment coded 1.0.

TABLE 7.7
Regression of Fall Achievement Test on Spring Score, Summer School, and Family Income, Black Sixth-Grade Children

	Predetermined variables						
Regressions	Spring score	Attend summer school	School location	Mother works	Family income (in thousands)	Income × attendance	R^2
b	.779[a]	.705[a]	−1.36[a]				
(σ)	(.02)	(.36)	(.48)				
b^*	.777	.041	−.058				.5991
b	.723[a]	.481	−1.62[a]		.378[a]		
(σ)	(.02)	(.41)	(.05)		(.05)		
b^*	.721	.022	−.069		.193		.6271
b	.775[a]	.594	−1.31[a]	1.38[a]			
(σ)	(.02)	(.42)	(.48)	(.45)			
b^*	.773	.025	−.056	.063			.6029
b	.721[a]	.371	−1.79[a]	.32	.041	.286[a]	
(σ)	(.02)	(.49)	(.06)	(.48)	(.04)	(.04)	
b^*	.718	.018	−.073	.00	.006	.127	.6304

[a] Coefficients at least twice as large as their standard errors.

increase cognitive inequality primarily among the children attending summer school, not among those who do not. This interaction is not a product of the grade equivalent metrics or other nonlinear relationships; the interaction persists across metrics and irrespective of other controls.

The interaction of family background and attendance is pervasive. Within categories of summer school programs, the association between parental income and achievement gains is largest for the most successful programs. Every distinct program or social category that could be judged marginally effective in raising summer scores is most effective for the relatively advantaged child. Table 7.8 presents the relationship between income and gains within the set of summer programs and variables examined. For every program type, the largest gains were invariably realized by children from the most affluent families.

The income-by-attendance interaction is of substantive importance because of its policy implications for voluntary summer school programs. It implies that the implementation and targeting of successful summer programs where disadvantaged children would be the major clientele would not necessarily ensure greater equality of outcomes. The Atlanta programs present both a puzzle and a dilemma in this regard.

TABLE 7.8
Total Association between Mean Grade Equivalent Summer Gain and Family Income by Summer School Attendance Variables, Black, Sixth Grade

Summer school attendance variables	Did not attend summer school		Attended summer school, 1972	
	η	N	η	N
Total sample	*.092*	*429*	.227[a]	*327*
School location				
Own	.123	280	.216[a]	260
Other	.098	149	.333	67
Mother works full-time	.088	223	.268[a]	178
Mother does not work	.061	206	.166	149
Students attending summer school				
Academic subjects studied			.243[a]	154
Other subjects studied			.186	73
Program under 5 hours per day			.247[a]	282
Program 5 or more hours			.119	45
Attended 6 weeks or less			.223[a]	272
Attended more than 6 weeks			.281	55

[a] Significantly different from .0.

Although schooling has been shown to equalize outcomes during the school year, the patterns during the summer do not support the assumption that all educational programs will have this effect.

As we have seen, summer school programs in Atlanta were somewhat successful in terms of achievement gains. The gains do not, however, prove that the programs were the critical factor. Since there is good evidence to presume that the children attending were a select group, it is not possible to discount the possibility that summer school contributed little to the educational progress of children that might not have occurred in the absence of programs. The hypothesis that self-selection was a critical component in achievement gains is relevant when comparing differences by school location. As we have seen, attending a school other than the one in which the child is regularly enrolled influences achievement positively, irrespective of socioeconomic status, race, or other measured characteristics. Programs enrolled students disproportionately from nearby neighborhoods, presumably because they were easily accessible. Children who attended despite the greater inconvenience or distance may have been more highly motivated, more interested in school, and more likely to receive greater parental encouragement for studying. Children attending their own school may have drifted into the program because they knew the teacher or had friends attending. The pattern of gains by income suggests that family factors were the most important component of achievement gains among children attending, even though few advantaged children were enrolled.

Summer schools in Atlanta are targeted to relatively poor neighborhoods; as such, they constitute an educational subsidy to the neediest families. Cognitive outcomes suggest, however, that summer schooling may exacerbate socioeconomic inequality. Despite the fact that the provision of programs is equitable, even redistributional, the benefits are not. As we shall see in Chapter 9, when examining libraries and summer reading, this somewhat paradoxical pattern characterizes other public sector educational institutions. They are undeniably mechanisms for transmitting parental status during the summer, especially for black families. However, this is not because they cater to elites or overtly discriminate against the poor. If such services did *not* exist a great many poor families would have even fewer opportunities than currently exist. I suspect these findings are central to an understanding of both equality of opportunity and equality of outcomes. Summer learning is more unequal than school learning because the programs are less structured and depend on the motivation and interest of children to a greater extent. When open classrooms are compared to more traditional approaches, the average amount of reading accomplished is similar, but socioeconomic inequality is greater (Bane, 1972). The provision of educational resources is not sufficient to guarantee equal use or equal benefits. Demonstrating that outcomes are not equal is, however, not evidence that schools have failed or that programs are ineffective and should be curtailed. These points are elementary, yet they are frequently misunderstood and misconstrued.

In sum, the pattern of gains suggests that summer programs of the sort described may have limited effects on cognitive achievement. The programs were of limited duration, and the majority of children did not enroll for academic reasons. The programs were popular but did not have a significant influence on achievement levels independent of family background. Given the diversity of program objectives, it could be argued that summer schools do not constitute an educational intervention. The more critical question, however, which cannot be answered at present, is whether a more demanding program oriented toward formal instruction would increase summer achievement, particularly among poor children. As a corollary, one might wonder whether an interest in school and a high level of attendance could be maintained if the programs were like formal schooling, but not compulsory.

8

Socioeconomic Background and Summer Activities

Summertime is commonly thought to be that part of the year in which children are quite free, unencumbered by the demands of formal schooling, rigid schedules, or other obligations. Judging from the experience of Atlanta children, such notions are naive and fanciful. As the last chapter indicated, the schools in Atlanta do not necessarily close in June; children preferring nonacademic settings can find a plethora of organized activities. Although summer activities are clearly voluntary, the evidence suggests that discretion is not given free rein.

This chapter explores the distribution and patterning of summer activities. The results are largely descriptive and exploratory, adding depth to the images of summer, although digressing somewhat from the major themes. The chapter is divided into four sections, devoted to structured activities other than summer school, sex differences, the use of discretionary time, and vacation trips. The educational effects of these activities are modest. As discussed before, the effects of activities are not independent of differences among families; it is therefore difficult to prove that particular experiences were uniquely valuable.

STRUCTURED SUMMER ACTIVITIES

Sixth-grade children in Atlanta spend quite a lot of time in group activities. Nearly three-fourths of the black children and just under two-thirds of the white children were involved in organized group activities for at least part of the summer. In terms of structure, periods of nonschooling seem to differ from those of schooling only by degree. A sizable amount of a child's waking hours is free time during the school year; during the summer, the majority of children are engaged in some structured activity, often for 6 or more weeks, even though schools are closed. Although it is convenient to contrast the time periods and the types of activities pursued, for most children a sharp dichotomy is not very realistic.

Structured activities tend to attract children from all backgrounds. Table 8.1 presents the distribution of a number of summer activities by the race and income level of families. For black children, summer school programs were far and away the most popular vacation time activity; no single structured activity attracted as large a proportion of white children. In general, the types of summer programs and their sponsorship distinguish activities of black and white children more than do the patterns of interest or attendance. Black children are about as likely as white children to study music or dance; they do so, however, by joining the school band or signing up for a dance class at the community center. White children are three times as likely to take tennis or swimming lessons, although participation in organized sports, such as Little League, is roughly the same. Black children attend day camps and summer school; white children are nearly twice as likely to go to a residential camp. Black children use the public services almost exclusively—schools, parks, community centers—or attend subsidized camps. White families patronize private facilities and are much more likely to pay for services.

Like summer school, structured programs tend to be racially segregated, although apparently not by design. The prevalent imbalance could be due to residential housing patterns, cultural differences, relative access to or cost of available programs, children's preferences, or overt discrimination. Although the opportunities for participating do not seem enormously disparate, it is clear that the public schools are more integrated than are most other activities. Since summer programs tend to be relatively more homogeneous, in terms of both class and race, peer contacts during the summer are likely to be restricted to children from similar backgrounds. Although evidence is limited, this could be one explanation for the persistent differentials in summer learning.

The rationale for considering structured group activities as a class of phenomena is theoretical. The notion of structure pertains to the organizational framework of activities, rather than to the content. If by *structure* one means a routinized curriculum with clearly defined objectives and an educational mission, every one of the programs was un-

TABLE 8.1
Proportion Participating in Structured Summer Programs by Race and Family Income, Sixth Grade

Race and family income	Any structured activity	Overnight camp	Day camp	Summer school	Music or dance lessons	Organized sports: All lessons	Organized sports: Little League	(*N*)
White[a]	*61.5*	*20.3*	*13.2*	*15.2*	*7.2*	*8.1*	*15.5*	(*470*)
Less than $4,000	57.7	19.2	11.5	12.0	3.8	7.7	3.8	(26)
$4,000–8,999	50.6	14.5	14.5	14.5	3.6	2.4	13.3	(83)
$9,000–14,999	55.7	20.0	12.2	18.3	6.1	3.5	12.2	(115)
$15,000+	77.4	28.2	14.5	16.9	7.3	17.7	22.6	(124)
η	.2356**	.1311*	.0012	.0508	.0638	.2459**	.1583*	
Black[a]	*71.3*	*10.1*	*21.6*	*42.6*	*7.4*	*2.6*	*13.7*	(*1023*)
Less than $4,000	68.4	7.5	21.0	41.4	3.2	2.1	10.7	(187)
$4,000–8,999	72.6	10.5	24.0	45.8	6.2	3.1	9.8	(325)
$9,000–14,999	74.0	8.3	19.6	40.5	14.2	4.1	20.7	(169)
$15,000+	80.2	13.9	21.8	48.0	17.8	3.0	13.9	(101)
η	.0776*	.0682	.0043	.0560	.1851**	.0392	.1276*	

[a] Includes 122 white and 241 black nonresponses on income.
* $p < .05$.
** $p < .01$.

structured. In this context, structured programs include all organized group activities under the supervision of one or more adults who are typically not members of the child's family.

Structured programs are similar to schooling in that they require and perhaps teach many of the same social skills. Participants are expected to attend regularly and to arrive promptly at specified times and places. Children must learn to work in a group cooperatively, sharing the time and attention of the adult. The activities are to a large extent planned, directed, and supervised by adults rather than by the participants. The groups tend to be composed of children of roughly similar ages, backgrounds, and levels of skill; such groups are typically several times larger than the average family. The size and composition of the group and the role of an unfamiliar and perhaps judgmental adult combine to create a social situation more typical of a classroom than of a family or a set of friends.[1] These characteristics dictate to a large degree the patterns of authority and social control and the strategies for manipulation available to both adults and children.

Structured programs replicate, in varying degrees, the social relations of schooling. A number of theorists have argued that the function of schooling is to inculcate social norms and patterned behavior, as well as to transmit cognitive skills. The structure of schooling enables children to learn norms and expectations that cannot be imparted by the family. The relationship between the structure of schooling and student outcomes has been variously described. Dreeben (1968) has argued that the critical function of schooling is to teach such norms as universalism; achievement and peer competition; independence; and affectively neutral, role-specific relations to authority. Bowles and Gintis (1976) have argued that school structures correspond to the authority relations of the workplace and that these social relations reinforce and reward such personality traits as docility, passivity, and obedience. Schools, in

[1] Structured activities demand unique skills from the adult organizer as well as from the children; such skills are not dissimilar to those possessed by a competent teacher. The adult must communicate the objectives, demonstrate how to realize them, and involve children in the learning and doing of an activity. Since the adult is typically more proficient than the children, he or she is often in the position of evaluating how much and how well the children have learned a skill. It is frequently impossible in such situations to provide very much individual attention; it is often difficult merely to keep the group interested in the activity. The resulting social context is not unlike that found in classrooms. The tactics for gaining and keeping a group's attention are much the same. A coach or camp counselor must assert authority and manipulate rewards and sanctions as skillfully as any teacher. Overt punitive actions tend to be ineffective if not specifically disallowed. To maintain an orientation toward the collective task, the adult leader must retain some sense of being in charge as well as an atmosphere of goodwill.

such a model, transmit socioeconomic status not by teaching skills, but by inculcating appropriate noncognitive traits and behavior. The notion implicit in linking school structures to outcomes is that the hidden curriculum of the school determines educational success. Placing children in age-graded, relatively large and homogeneous classrooms, under the supervision of an adult who has specific tasks and authority, ensures the learning of essential norms and behavior. The structure of programs is not coincidental, but contrasts with family life in critical ways. Family relationships are necessarily open-ended, particularistic, diffuse, and affectively charged; the contrasting structure of schools in terms of duration, composition, and the patterning of authority provides a complementary form of socialization.

The common social structure of group activities might, therefore, foster similar patterns of learning. Perhaps the exposure to programs during the summer reinforces the learning of norms or noncognitive traits that generalize to school performance. Perhaps such social skills enhance verbal skills or achievement, even if the stated objectives are making potholders or perfecting a backstroke.

The Atlanta data suggest that the skills learned in structured summer programs are not readily cashed in for cognitive achievement. Grade equivalent gains for participants by race and family income level are presented in Table 8.2. The general pattern is not unlike that observed

TABLE 8.2
Mean Grade Equivalent Summer Gain, Word Knowledge, by Race and Family Income Level for Participants in Selected Structured Summer Activities, Sixth Grade

Race and family income	Any structured activity	Music or dance lessons	Organized sports: Lessons	Organized sports: Little League	Total gain	*N*
White	*.26*	*.27*	*.21*	*.28*	*.24*	*470*
Less than $9,000	.04	.02	−.08	.09	.07	109
$9,000–14,999	.33	.42	.18	.24	.07	115
$15,000+	.47	.71	.32	.36	.29	124
N	288	33	38	73		
Black	*−.10*	*−.04*	*−.06*	*−.11*	*−.12*	*1023*
Less than $4,000	−.22	−.21	.27	−.20	−.26	187
$4,000–8,999	−.13	−.09	.16	−.15	−.12	325
$9,000–14,999	.02	−.06	.02	.01	−.12	169
$15,000+	.28	.34	.59	.07	.23	101
N	729	76	27	140		

for summer school programs in Chapter 7, in that the largest gains accrue to the most advantaged children. Yet the gains are invariably quite small. Although attending a program may benefit relatively advantaged children, the net effect is trivial. Programs that are structured like school but do not include academic instruction seem to foster little cognitive growth.

SEX DIFFERENCES IN SUMMER ACTIVITIES

Pronounced sex differences exist in the patterning of summer activities, particularly for the less structured uses of leisure time. Although there are more sex-segregated group activities in the summer, the opportunities to participate in a structured program seem to be roughly equivalent for boys and girls. Girls tend to take more music lessons, enroll in more dance classes, and play fewer organized sports. Boys are less likely to attend church-sponsored activities, but more likely to be in Scouts. The organizations that sponsor sex-segregated activities, such as the Girls' Club and the YMCA, are more active during the summer; yet, in terms of sheer numbers, the coeducational programs such as summer school attract the most children. Girls attend a larger number of supervised activities but tend to spend proportionately less time at any single activity. Team sports and Little League acquire overwhelming importance during the summer for many boys, displacing other pursuits and more sexually mixed activities. Disregarding athletics, the sex composition of most structured programs, and the amounts of time spent, suggest that boys and girls invest similar amounts of summer leisure time in group activities.

Among the more active and gregarious unstructured activities, however, boys clearly dominate the field. Parents reported that their sons spent more hours on a typical summer day playing with friends, doing chores, pursuing hobbies, and playing outside. The two activities in which girls averaged more time than boys were reading and watching television, both fairly sedentary domestic activities. Both boys and girls were reported to spend nearly 6 hours a day playing; boys, however, spent almost all of this time outside and away from home. Girls read nearly an hour more than boys each day and watched 30 minutes more television. The impression gained from numerous sources was that girls spent a larger amount of their free time in relatively solitary activity.[2]

[2] These sex differences in leisure activities apparently persist well into adolescence. As Coleman (1961) has shown, leisure pursuits among high school boys include active

When families included more than one child, girls reportedly spent more time playing with their younger brothers and sisters than did sixth-grade boys. Some portion of this time was probably child care, although parents did not apparently perceive this as a household chore. Twice as many parents volunteered that their sons were responsible for household chores as mentioned the same about their daughters.[3] I suspect that it was taken for granted that girls would help around the house whereas for sons it generated family controversy. Perhaps boys complained more bitterly or demanded monetary rewards more frequently than did girls. Given the larger proportion of time spent at home, it seems doubtful that girls actually helped with household chores less often than boys.

Boys are seemingly permitted, or perhaps not restrained from enjoying, a broader range of independent activities than are girls. Boys take more trips alone, attend camps more often and typically for longer time periods, and tend to be subject to adult supervision more sporadically. Boys are more likely to have bicycles, and the differential widens as the socioeconomic level declines.[4] Parents credit their sons with both more activities and more time spent at each particular activity. Unless we believe that sixth-grade males sleep less than their female counterparts, the observed patterns must in part be due to parental misreporting. While I suspect that the reports of behavior may be of questionable

---

outdoor activities far more often than is the case among girls. He notes, "whether it is athletics, or cars, or hunting or model-building, our society seems to provide a much fuller set of activities to engage the interests of boys. Thus, when girls are together, they are more often just 'with the group' than are boys [p. 13]."

[3] The information collected on household chores was not precoded nor routinely asked of all parents; therefore sex differences in the actual amounts of time spent doing chores cannot be compared. The kinds and types of chores reported were tabulated only in cases where parents volunteered the information.

[4] The patterning of unstructured activities suggests that boys and girls are treated more similarly and behave more alike in relatively affluent families. Reading books or taking a trip, for example, is reportedly equal for sons and daughters. In contrast, the structured activities such as camp, music or dance lessons, or clubs, which are most popular among the middle class, are typically sex segregated. Conversely, lower-income children spend considerably more time in coeducational structured programs, but tend to live in families in which rather large sex differences in play activity are the rule. One reason seems to be sponsorship. The organized activities for lower-income children tend to be publicly supported, by schools or the recreation department, and are typically designed to include both boys and girls. Children's programs chosen by high-income parents are smaller, more exclusive, and conform to more traditional forms of social organization, thereby retaining a somewhat archaic division by sex. The patterns suggest a curious reversal in sex-specific socialization: private, family-centered activities are more equal among the relatively well-to-do, but public life is segregated sexually; lower-income families tend to treat boys and girls separately and differently, but the public sphere does not.

validity, the data suggest that boys' activities are more salient to their parents.

The differences in activities are consonant with a large number of studies of sex differences in childrearing. Boys are subject to more intensive socialization (Maccoby & Jacklin, 1974). Boys tend to receive more resources, attention, and time from parents (Hill & Stafford, 1974). Parents are less likely to value independent initiative from their daughters, and these differences tend to increase in working-class families (Kohn, 1963).

Whatever their role in socialization, sex differences in activity patterns do not seem to be related to summer learning. Although boys tend to learn at a slightly faster rate during the summer and girls tend to excel during the school year, sex differences in achievement are small and not statistically significant. Moreover, when a particular activity is associated with gains, it tends to be equally effective for both males and females. Reading, for example, is positively related to summer learning, but watching television is not. Yet both males and females are positively benefited by reading books, and both tend to be negatively influenced by large amounts of television viewing.

THE ALLOCATION OF DISCRETIONARY TIME

The use of discretionary time has become a topic of increasing interest to social scientists and policymakers alike. The field has even adopted a separate disciplinary label, *chronosophy,* to identify a unique perspective on research about work and leisure. The Atlanta survey included a series of questions on how much time children spent engaged in particular activities on a typical summer day. Although neither the questionnaire objectives nor the format allowed treatment of the data as a comprehensive time budget, the results allow comparison of gross patterns of time allocation and establishment of a descriptive basis for further research. This section will focus on socioeconomic and racial differences in use of time among sixth-grade children.

Studies of the use of time have without exception focused on adults. The units of analysis have been individuals, or occasionally households; if children's activities are mentioned at all, it is in the context of family activities. This seems largely to be the result of the pragmatic and applied concerns of the field, which tend not to see children as a special group. The dominant theoretical perspective generally has been that of economics, in which time is treated as a commodity to be effectively utilized or invested. Becker (1965) argued that time and money are interchangeable resources and attempted to analyze household decisions as examples of utility-maximizing behavior. Urban planners have applied, or proposed applying, time budgets to evaluate communication and transportation systems, recreational facilities, and other social services (Brail, 1969; Gutenschwager, 1973; Meier, 1959). Sociologists have maintained a more pristine interest in the field. Studies have explored socioeconomic and racial differences in the use of leisure (Chapin, 1974; Ferge, 1972; Lundburg, Komarovsky, & McInerny, 1934) and cross-cultural differences in the use of time (Szalai, 1973). Occasionally, sociologists have disputed the notion that man is rational in the allocation of time, or questioned the degree to which time is a comparable concept across different social groups (Henry, 1965; Horton, 1967).

A comprehensive review of this literature clearly exceeds the purposes of this study (see Converse, 1968; Rubin, 1974). My objective is rather to draw attention to how little is known about children's use of discretionary time and to suggest some implications of children's activities for educational policy.[5] The analysis will be restricted to those leisure time pursuits for which parents provided estimates of time in hours spent, including hobbies; watching television; and playing at home, alone, or with friends. Reading will be discussed later. Although it is possible to establish only rather gross patterns, the data suggest that time allocation does not vary markedly between socioeconomic strata or racial groups. Sex differences are larger and more prevalent than status ones.

Conceptually, time is a zero-sum commodity. Yet for a number of reasons, parents' estimates of the total time their children spent on activities during a typical summer day varied enormously. Children were reported to have been playing, reading, watching television, or pursuing hobbies for between 5 and 14 hours, a considerable range. One might expect, for example, that children attending summer school or a day camp for most of the summer would have less time to play with their friends or to watch television; this seems not to be the case. Among the specific categories mentioned, the expected inverse relationship holds, suggesting that trade-offs between activities exist. However, time allocation is not related to the propensity to participate in other activities. Most parents apparently did not consider a day they were on vacation or the child was at camp to be typical. Since the question did not specify a given day and parents were not asked to detail an hourly schedule, it seems most reasonable to conceive of the

[5] The data gathered cannot adequately deal with children's preferences, since parents supplied the information.

responses as subjective impressions of the relative importance of particular activities during a day when children were at home.

The actual number of hours spent on every activity tends to be directly related to the socioeconomic background of families. Either relatively advantaged children spend more time on every activity, or higher-status parents systematically exaggerate the time spent. If the proportion of time spent on each activity is compared, however, the effects of family background tend to disappear. Although the associations between background and time allocation are not large, as presented in Table 8.3, the observed differentials are largely accounted for by patterns of parental reporting. Children of all backgrounds apparently spent remarkably similar proportions of time doing each of the leisure activities studied, provided the children were involved at all. Socioeconomic and racial differences are more predictive of whether or not a child was involved in the activity than of the amount of time spent.

Playing occupies the largest block of time spent by sixth-grade children, and in terms of the proportion of the total day it is the single most important summer activity. Nearly 6 hours a day are devoted to playing, and roughly 80% of this time is spent with friends. Neither race nor family socioeconomic level is related to any appreciable degree to the total time spent playing, as documented by Table 8.3. The ratio of time spent playing at home to total time spent playing is more strongly related to family income and race. Low-income children, boys, and those from larger families are consistently more likely to play away from home. It would seem that higher-status families tend to be more protective of their children or tend to prefer them to play at home. Alternatively, one might infer that children are more likely to play at the homes of friends who have more toys or more space.

Playing alone tends to be a much less time-consuming activity. For both blacks and whites, and for families at any income level, playing alone rarely occupies more than an hour of the typical summer day. Playing alone tends to be a function of family size, but not much else. Fully one-fourth of the sample of only children spent more than 2 hours per day playing alone; fewer than 8% of children with siblings did so. Playing alone tends to have a curvilinear relationship to both achievement levels and social status, albeit not a large one. Children who spend no time alone during the day tend to be relatively disadvantaged in terms of both background and school achievement. I suspect that economic disadvantage would account for both, since it is not difficult to imagine that an overcrowded environment provides little privacy or seclusion, whether for playing or studying.

TABLE 8.3
Distribution of Selected Summer Activities by Family Income and Race, Sixth Grade

	Mean hours spent		Hobbies		Television	
	Playing alone	Playing with friends	Percentage with hobby	Mean hours spent/day	Mean hours spent watching TV/day	N
White	*.91*	*5.2*	*62*	*.85*	*2.63*	*470*
Less than $4,000	.77	5.1	46	.50	3.06	26
$4,000–8,999	.90	5.1	50	.88	3.08	83
$9,000–14,999	1.03	5.4	70	.93	2.89	115
$15,000+	.84	5.3	67	.89	2.23	124
η	.071	.014	.187[a]	.096	.217[a]	
Black	*.81*	*5.3*	*65*	*.98*	*3.07*	*1023*
Less than $4,000	.81	4.9	67	.92	2.94	187
$4,000–8,999	.74	5.1	59	.95	2.98	325
$9,000–14,999	.80	5.6	70	1.01	3.39	169
$15,000+	.96	5.8	77	1.05	3.05	101
η	.053	.091	.137[a]	.041	.091	

[a] Significantly different from zero.

The negative impact on school achievement experienced by the relatively few children who spent more than 6 hours per day playing alone is more difficult to explain. Such children were not particularly disadvantaged in terms of home background, nor were they especially likely to be only children. Perhaps a large degree of social isolation is symptomatic of psychological distress, or perhaps children preferring to play alone constantly are less likely to enjoy or to adjust well to school. Except for the very small number of children who seem to be socially isolated, the relationship between playing and measures of school performance is quite trivial. Playing clearly occupies a central role in the lives of children, but does not relate to socioeconomic status or achievement in obvious ways.

Hobbies are also unrelated to other social characteristics of the Atlanta sample. Having a hobby is more indicative of higher status than is the number of hours one spends on it. Atlanta children devote less than an hour a day to their hobbies, although over half of the sixth-grade children reportedly have them. Neither having a hobby nor investing a large amount of time in it is significantly related to achievement gains.

Television occupies a large block of time during a typical summer day, second only to playing with friends. More than 3 hours per day were devoted to television by 30% of the white children and 40% of the black children. Among white children, a significant inverse relationship exists between watching television and socioeconomic status of families, whereas black children tend to spend equivalent amounts of time watching television irrespective of family income. While 2 or 3 hours per day may seem excessive, Atlanta children do not seem atypical by national standards.[6] Commentators have argued that television rots the mind, inculcates violence, and destroys family life; in Atlanta, it does not significantly affect achievement. Large amounts of television, much like excessive quantities of other activities, tend to be associated with lower achievement. The pattern is consistent, but few children are implicated, and the differences are not statistically significant. The most that can be said is that television has a consistently detrimental but rather trivial impact on learning.

Perhaps the most striking finding regarding children's use of leisure is the similarity between socioeconomic strata and racial groups. For

[6] The earliest data collected on children's television habits (Maccoby, 1951) found that a sample of children in Cambridge, Massachusetts, watched an average of 2.4 hours during the weekday and 3.5 hours during weekends. Adults in America also spend a large amount of time watching television. Chapin (1974, pp. 128–129) found that adults in Washington, D.C., watched between 1.0 and 2.8 hours during the average weekday; race and socioeconomic differences were consistent with those found in Atlanta.

each of the activities, sex and family composition are substantially more important than social class. The number of hours spent on any single activity or on a combination of activities is only marginally related to background; only reading is related to achievement. If one aspires to understand the effects of background on learning, patterns of time allocation do not seem a particularly fruitful place to begin.

THE EFFECTS OF SUMMER VACATIONS AND TRIPS

For a great many Americans, summer is synonymous with vacations. A casual perusal of the statistics reveals the large and growing importance of trips as a leisure time activity. This section is devoted to the extent and the distribution of vacations taken during the summer of 1972 and their effects on the academic achievement of the sixth-grade children involved.[7]

In Atlanta whether a family takes a vacation is highly related to the socioeconomic status of the family. Just as most studies of leisure have demonstrated, the propensity to take a vacation, the average distance traveled, and the number of family members participating are all related to family income level. The distribution of trips and vacations for the Atlanta sample are presented in Table 8.4. A comparison of the proportion taking family vacations with the proportion taking a trip to visit friends or relatives outside of Atlanta reveals several interesting patterns. The difference between the two distributions is the proportion of families taking at least one vacation that was not combined with a visit to friends or relatives.[8]

[7] The parental survey conducted in Atlanta asked two sorts of questions regarding family vacations: one on whether the sample child stayed overnight with friends or relatives during the summer, and one on whether the family took a vacation together during the same period. The questions were formulated so as to ensure that the information would be collected on the summer trips of the sample child, rather than the family. If the child spent at least 1 night with friends or relatives away from home, parents were asked who was visited and his relationship to the child, the duration of the visit, where the person visited lived, and whether other family members accompanied the child. The only information solicited about vacations was the length of time involved. This created some difficulty, since the majority of visits outside of Atlanta involved the entire family. For the purposes of analysis, vacations were defined as either a trip or a visit that took the family outside of Atlanta for more than 2 nights. The tables present separate tabulations on visits and vacations, although it should be remembered that they are not strictly independent categories.

[8] These trips might be considered vacations proper; although more costly in terms of family expenditures, they are also likely to involve greater choice of location and fewer social obligations.

TABLE 8.4
Distribution of Vacations and Trips by Family Income and Race, Sixth Grade

	Family vacations		Trips to visit friends and relatives (in percentages)			
Race and family income	Took vacation (in percentages)	Mean days	Outside Atlanta	Alone	Alone outside Atlanta	*N*
White[a]	*62.5*	*2.8*	*23.9*	*19.1*	*8.6*	*470*
Under $4,000	23.1	4.5	7.8	11.5	0.0	26
$4,000–8,999	44.6	1.6	22.9	13.3	8.4	83
$9,000–14,999	66.1	2.7	29.6	20.0	11.3	115
$15,000+	73.4	3.1	30.6	19.4	8.1	124
η	.313**	.219**	.141	.084	.101	
Black[a]	27.6	4.4	15.8	14.3	4.5	1023
Under $4,000	13.5	5.0	11.8	10.7	3.7	187
$4,000–8,999	23.2	4.2	12.9	14.8	3.7	325
$9,000–14,999	37.3	3.1	20.1	18.3	7.7	169
$15,000+	51.5	3.6	23.8	15.8	5.9	101
η	.273**	.130*	.122*	.074	.077	

[a] Total includes 122 white nonrespondents on family income and 241 black nonrespondents.
* $p < .05$.
** $p < .01$.

The data suggest a hierarchy of summer vacationing, primarily determined by family income. The most expensive vacations are the most unequally distributed in the population. The trips most characteristic of low-income families involved visiting friends and relatives, typically near Atlanta. The majority of low-income and black families devoted their vacations to trips that might be characterized as instrumental rather than purely recreational. Presumably, such trips allowed families to spend less for food and lodging than they otherwise would.

The data on length of vacations are less clear; less advantaged families spend more time on each single trip, but rarely enjoyed multiple vacations. Upper-income families tend to take shorter trips, but to take them more frequently. A weekend trip or a prolonged vacation is still largely the prerogative of middle- and upper-middle-class white families.

Class differentials in the propensity to take vacations have frequently been noted in the literature on leisure (Allen, 1964; Perlman, 1973; Wilensky, 1961). Irrespective of family income levels, there are substantial differences between blacks and whites. In Atlanta, black families are consistently less likely to take a vacation of any sort than are whites.

The distribution of vacations by income for white families mirrors national averages to a remarkable degree.[9] Within every income class, black families are less likely to vacation and more likely to combine a vacation with a visit to friends or relatives than are white families of similar economic status. This could be because black families tend to be larger and are more likely to be native southerners; perhaps there are more relatives to be visited. Among the sample families, this is not the case. Blacks do not visit relatives as often as do white families, nor do they visit a more diverse set of relatives. Although cultural and economic factors may account for the differences, I suspect that aspects of family life are more salient. Substantially larger proportions of black families have two or more breadwinners; presumably arranging a family vacation is especially difficult when several different schedules must be accommodated. Equally, black workers are more likely to be employed in peripheral, nonunionized industries; they often lack the contractual guarantees for annual paid vacations enjoyed by white workers (Allen, 1964; U.S. Committee on Education and Labor, 1967). Since black respondents also report using the parks and picnic grounds in Atlanta more than do whites, it seems likely that family recreation typically involves local facilities and outings of no more than 1 day.

Visiting friends and relatives is not primarily a family activity. The sheer number of times children spent the night with a friend or relative is considerably larger than the distribution of family vacations would suggest. More than half of the sixth-grade children spent at least 1 night away from home during the summer. Such visits were typically for less than 2 nights, and almost without exception they did not involve leaving Atlanta. The relative most frequently visited, by a wide margin, was the grandmother. Fully one-third of the black children and just over 40% of the white children stayed with grandparents at least 1 night during the summer. There were a handful of visits to other relatives. Girls spent more nights away from home with friends and slightly less time with relatives. White children were substantially more likely to spend a night with friends than were black children; approximately 38% of the white sample and just over 12% of the black sample spent a night with friends during the summer. Slumber parties or staying over do not seem particularly popular in the black community.

Vacations might be expected to increase the intellectual growth of

[9] For example, Morgan (1966) reports that "the proportion who took a vacation in 1964 varies from 27% for those with incomes under $1000, to 72% for those with incomes of $15,000 or more [p. 291]." Eight years later, almost exactly the same differences were reported for white families in Atlanta.

children in a variety of ways. Exposure to diverse places and people may expand horizons and stimulate interest in the world outside of one's family or neighborhood. The data on summer achievement suggest some support for such a proposition, although the effects are small and in most cases are not independent of family background and prior achievement.

To test the effects of summer trips on children's learning, fall achievement scores were regressed on spring achievement, socioeconomic status, and several variables measuring different aspects of visits and vacationing. These equations are presented in Tables 8.5–8.7, separately by race. Family vacations are more strongly related to income level and general social status than are solitary trips; however, the latter have a more direct impact on school achievement. The influential trips are those on which a sample child was trusted to travel alone. For black children, visiting alone was significant independent of socioeconomic background only when the trip involved leaving Atlanta. For white children, the solitary trip significantly increased summer learning whether or not the child left the city. The regression coefficients are not large, barely twice their standard errors in both cases, but the results tend to be consistent.

Interpreting such differences is a speculative enterprise. The individual trips do not seem to be different in any way from the family trips. A few children visited a parent, presumably because the parents were separated or divorced, but visiting particular relatives in particular places for a given length of time does not distinguish the trips children take from those their family takes. Comparisons among trips reveal inconsistent relationships. For black children, trips alone to visit relatives in rural areas were substantially less favorable to achievement gains than visits alone to urban relatives. For white children, the reverse was true; visits to rural places were associated with higher gains. Family visits to either place, however, followed the identical pattern for both white and black children. A plausible explanation would be not that the visits were responsible, but that rural origins were associated with lower socioeconomic status for black children, while the opposite held for southern whites. Although factors that distinguish family trips cannot be isolated from those that distinguish trips alone, it seems logical to presume that solitary trips are different primarily because the children went alone. I suspect that those families that allowed children to visit relatives on their own are different from families that did not; the achievement gains are a reflection of parental trust and willingness to devote resources to children, rather than to the vacation per se.

TABLE 8.5
Regression of Fall 1972 Achievement on Selected Summer Activities, Spring 1972 Achievement and Socioeconomic Status, for White Sixth-Grade Students

	Predetermined variables					
Activity	Spring test	Family income	Parental education	Household size	Activity	R^2
Bike ownership						
b	.8749[a]				2.0275[a]	
(σ)	(.0232)				(.7801)	
*b**	.8661				.0597	.7741
b	.8350[a]	.0878[a]	.0453	−.2004	1.1001	
(σ)	(.0309)	(.0376)	(.1605)	(.2083)	(.9452)	
*b**	.8267	.0842	.0105	−.0256	.0324	.7808
Took a trip alone						
b	.8839[a]				1.7026[a]	
(σ)	(.0227)				(.6238)	
*b**	.8751				.0614	.7745
b	.8387[a]	.0906[a]	.0376	−.2281	1.3171[a]	
(σ)	(.0308)	(.0370)	(.1599)	(.2037)	(.6282)	
*b**	.8303	.0868	.0088	−.0292	.0479	.7821
Took a trip outside Atlanta						
b	.8866[a]				.9421[a]	
(σ)	(.0228)				(.4465)	
*b**	.8777				.0383	.7719
b	.8376[a]	.0928[a]	.0542	−.2467	.5660	
(σ)	(.0310)	(.0372)	(.1604)	(.2043)	(.6138)	
*b**	.8292	.0890	.0126	−.0316	.0241	.7803
Took a trip outside Atlanta alone						
b	.8870[a]				1.3999	
(σ)	(.0228)				(.7245)	
*b**	.8781				.0424	.7726
b	.8383[a]	.0914[a]	.0562	−.2426	1.0291	
(σ)	(.0309)	(.0372)	(.1600)	(.2041)	(.6619)	
*b**	.8299	.0876	.0130	−.0311	.0391	.7808

[a] Coefficients at least twice as large as their standard error.

TABLE 8.6
Regression of Fall 1972 Achievement on Selected Summer Activities, Spring 1972 Achievement and Socioeconomic Status, for Black Sixth-Grade Students

	Predetermined variables					
Activity	Spring test	Family income	Parental education	Household size	Activity	R^2
Bike ownership						
b	.7658[a]				2.0305[a]	
(σ)	(.0202)				(.4718)	
b^*	.7636				.0869	.6028
b	.7178[a]	.1129[a]	.2538[a]	−.0870	1.0721[a]	
(σ)	(.0237)	(.0270)	(.1201)	(.1230)	(.5030)	
b^*	.7158	.1153	.0598	−.0168	.0478	.6243
Trip alone						
b	.7731[a]				1.1157[a]	
(σ)	(.0203)				(.5532)	
b^*	.7708				.0395	.5969
b	.7183[a]	.1214[a]	.2564[a]	−.1207	.4412	
(σ)	(.0237)	(.0267)	(.1212)	(.6434)	(.5546)	
b^*	.7163	.1240	.0604	−.0233	.0156	.6226
Trip outside Atlanta						
b	.7728[a]				1.0171	
(σ)	(.0203)				(.6009)	
b^*	.7706				.0342	.5965
b	.7179[a]	.1203[a]	.2653[a]	−.1219	.3871	
(σ)	(.0237)	(.0268)	(.1203)	(.1218)	(.6691)	
b^*	.7159	.1228	.0625	−.0236	.0103	.6226
Trip alone outside Atlanta						
b	.7712[a]				2.5944[a]	
(σ)	(.0203)				(.8874)	
b^*	.7690				.0591	.5989
b	.7176[a]	.1190[a]	.2600[a]	−.1059	1.8002[a]	
(σ)	(.0237)	(.0266)	(.1201)	(.1219)	(.9014)	
b^*	.7155	.1216	.0612	−.0205	.0410	.6241

[a] Coefficients at least twice as large as their standard errors.

TABLE 8.7
Regression of Fall 1972 Achievement on Selected Summer Activities, Spring 1972 Achievement and Socioeconomic Status, for the Total Sample of Sixth-Grade Students

	Predetermined variables					
Activity	Spring test	Family income	Parental education	Household size	Activity	R^2
Bike ownership						
b	.8553[a]				2.3472[a]	
(σ)	(.0149)				(.4125)	
*b**	.8268				.0817	.7127
b	.7897[a]	.1336[a]	.1262	−.1867	1.1762[a]	
(σ)	(.0185)	(.0218)	(.0968)	(.1061)	(.4842)	
*b**	.7634	.1277	.0271	−.0293	.0410	.7297
Trip alone						
b	.8651[a]				1.6649[a]	
(σ)	(.0148)				.4411	
*b**	.8363				.0539	.7091
b	.7907[a]	.1409[a]	.1212	−.2181[a]	.9570	
(σ)	(.0185)	.0215	(.0972)	(.1048)	(.4971)	
*b**	.7644	.1347	.0260	−.0343	.0310	.7292
Trip outside Atlanta						
b	.8665[a]				1.3351[a]	
(σ)	(.0148)				(.4602)	
*b**	.8376				.0415	.7080
b	.7904[a]	.1403[a]	.1377	−.2262[a]	.6079	
(σ)	(.0185)	(.0216)	(.0968)	(.1048)	(.5152)	
*b**	.7641	.1341	.0295	−.0355	.0189	.7286
Trip alone outside Atlanta						
b	.8639[a]				2.5907[a]	
(σ)	(.0148)				(.6009)	
*b**	.8351				.0616	.7100
b	.7896[a]	.1378[a]	.1373	−.2104[a]	1.7338[a]	
(σ)	(.0185)	(.0215)	(.0966)	(.1047)	(.6730)	
*b**	.7633	.1317	.0295	−.0330	.0412	.7299

[a] Coefficients at least twice as large as their standard errors.

In sum, the mosaic of summer activities does not shed much light on the implementation of effective programs. The influence of social class on learning persists or is amplified in each setting described. Insofar as activities contributed to summer learning, their direct causal importance is ambiguous. The patterning of outcomes is quite consistent with an interpretation stressing differences among families as the critical factors in achievement. Parents willing or able to encourage participation also foster cognitive growth, irrespective of the activity pursued. Allocating family resources, such as time and money, to children's activities, and encouraging children to exercise initiative and independence are plausible strategies for augmenting summer learning; however, it is difficult to conceive of voluntary structured programs that could compensate for such pervasive differences among families. The programs in Atlanta tended to be effective in capitalizing on such differences, rather than overcoming them. In the next chapter, the discussion will be more optimistic. Reading and the use of public libraries are highly related to summer gains irrespective of parental status. The results also suggest that such behavior should be taken into account in formulating policy.

9

Reading, Libraries, and Summer Achievement

The single summer activity that is most strongly and consistently related to summer learning is reading. Whether measured by the number of books read, by the time spent reading, or by the regularity of library usage, reading during the summer systematically increases the vocabulary test scores of children. Although related to differences in parental status, summer reading has a substantial effect on achievement that is largely independent of family background. Although unstructured activities such as reading do not ordinarily lend themselves to policy intervention, I will argue that at least one institution, the public library, directly influences children's reading. Educational policies that increase access to books, perhaps through increased library services, stand to have an important impact on achievement, particularly for less advantaged children.

The subsequent section provides a brief review of the literature and a rationale for inferences based on nonexperimental research. I will then document in some detail the effects of reading on achievement. The concluding section will be devoted to disentangling the determinants of reading and assessing the extent to which reading might be responsive to the levers of public policy.

RESEARCH PERSPECTIVES ON THE "FIRST R"

Despite the very general assumption that reading is one of the most important skills children learn in school, little empirical research exists on the amount read outside of school, the literary preferences of children, or the relationship between reading and academic performance.[1] Research on reading tends to be narrowly focused. A highly technical literature in both education and linguistics deals with learning to read. The research questions most frequently broached regarding older children, however, have concerned the effects of reading programs and school libraries or the quantity and quality of reading materials available in the home.

Studies that sought to assess the effectiveness of school reading programs have been largely inconclusive. Silberman (1970) reports anecdotally that reading programs are essential to the curriculum of successful ghetto schools, using as an example the John H. Finley School in Harlem. In contrast, analyses of the Equality of Educational Opportunity Survey (Coleman *et al.*, 1966) suggest that neither the provision of school libraries nor the number of volumes available is strongly related to the average level of student achievement in a school, once socioeconomic background is controlled. Gaver (1963) found that the type of library program was unrelated to either the quantity of books students read or their expressed interest in reading. Austin and Morrison (1963) argue persuasively that reading instruction should be coordinated with library programs and that existing school facilities provide only fragmentary services; their central contention, however, that "a successful library program will substantially improve the total reading program [p. 18]" remains unproved.

Although analysts have found the presence of reading materials in the home to be consistently related to school achievement (Jencks *et al.*, 1972), this has been interpreted as resulting from general features of

[1] Estimates of adult reading patterns are available, but the data on which they are based are suspect; published government statistics appear to understate seriously the degree of functional illiteracy in the United States (Harman, 1970). Several despairing essays lament in a more or less apocalyptic fashion the demise of the printed word and the general impoverishment of the intellectual life of Americans (Bagdikian, 1971; Disch, 1973; Steiner, 1972). Although it is sometimes implied that the blame for this abysmal state of affairs lies with the public schools, little substantiating evidence exists. The explicit assumption that the quality or quantity of written material consumed by Americans has seriously declined is rarely supported in a rigorous manner. Data presented by Hyman *et al.* (1975) suggest that at least since World War II, Americans have read increasing amounts of material of all sorts.

family background and cultural environments. Books and magazines have been assumed to be indicative of status differences rather than to be an independent causal influence on cognitive skills. This is, perhaps, a logical inference, since the requisite empirical linkages between the availability of materials and the behavior of children have not been available. The data on summer learning among children in Atlanta suggest, however, that reading should be viewed as a decisive factor in learning that operates irrespective of parental status.

The literature evaluating school programs designed to increase reading is problematic on several grounds. Since both the survey results and the experimental evaluations concur in finding few relationships between reading and libraries, and since the results I will be presenting differ substantially on both counts, it seems worthwhile to examine one experimental study in some detail. Cleary *et al.* (1968) conducted a very carefully designed study of the effects of library exposure experienced by fifth graders in a school in the rural South. The authors sought to compare the reading activities, attitudes, and skills of children under varying degrees of exposure to library materials. Three groups were randomly chosen and assigned to separate experimental treatments; the treatments were designed to represent a continuum of program intensity, from no library exposure to a carefully structured, intensive introduction to the school facilities. The group slated for the intensive treatment was regularly exposed to the library and the school librarians; films, discussion, and guidance in library use were freely provided. The intermediate group received the normal program, which was described as typical of elementary schools in the nation. One library hour per week was scheduled, but without special preparation or instruction. Children were permitted to browse, use reference materials, ask questions, and check out books at will. The third group, intended as the control, received neither treatment. These children were assigned to an alternative project, unrelated to reading or library use. These students met weekly for outdoor activities, arts and crafts, or science films on nature, astronomy, and marine life.

To the chagrin of the research team, the most effective treatment was that enjoyed by the control group. Both the first and third groups improved somewhat in their reading attitudes and behavior, whereas the traditional program apparently changed participants slightly if at all. The most enthusiasm for their particular program was clearly shown by those children who were provided the least access to libraries, the group offered outdoor activities and science films. This group was not less likely to read books or to use the library than the group most actively encouraged to read. For all three groups, reading achievement, as measured by the Iowa Test of Basic Skills, was largely unaffected by the particular treatment. Although the data were not analyzed in a manner that would permit this conclusion to be drawn, the tabulations suggest that within each group higher reading achievement scores were associated with a larger amount of actual reading. The differences were not sufficiently strong among groups, however, to yield a significant positive effect for the programs that encouraged more access to books. The authors conclude, characteristically, that more research is needed.

This study typifies the limits of educational experimentation. The focus is on structured programs and group differences, not on the learning process. The presumption, which is rarely tested, is that reading influences achievement. The objective, therefore, is to establish and evaluate a program designed to promote reading, yet without asking how much was read or for what purposes. A control group is exposed to a nontreatment, which it is assumed will not encourage reading. It is rarely deemed useful to inquire what or why children read. It is assumed that the control groups are given an actual placebo, rather than an alternative program that might have educational benefits quite independent of the study design.[2] The causal influence is assumed to flow directly from the program, and nonadditive interactions are seldom analyzed. Since the experiment is designed to measure program effects, researchers systematically ignore the more important question of why certain children read or learned more. The experiment is generally of limited duration and bounded in terms of potential influence. Customarily no attention is paid to the role of parents or peers in reinforcing or subverting the goals and processes studied. The most thoughtful studies mention the possibility of confounding variables, such as social class or social contacts outside the program, but such variables are frequently too complex to study. Experimental biases, such as a Hawthorne effect, are mentioned in passing, but their impact is rarely measured. If the program is successful, it is implicitly assumed that replication would produce similar results, even if conducted in very different schools with different children and under different conditions. This would be true only if the program did not interact in significant ways with the implementation or the subjects.

The objective of educational research should be the precise specification of learning processes and their individual determinants among

[2] The classic design for educational programs is to assign children randomly to a study hour, often spent in the library, instead of participation in the educational program offered in the classroom. That the time so spent might be more educational than the curriculum variation is seldom considered.

children. Designing effective programs depends on knowledge of the mechanisms involved, not just their magnitude; if this requires broadening the scope of inquiry to include factors that operate outside the classroom, research should go in that direction. Assertions regarding the intimate relationship between home and school have become the platitudes of educational theory, yet evaluation studies remain locked into a simplistic format that attempts to randomize outside influences, rather than to understand or interpret them. Family conditions tend to be introduced as post hoc explanations for insignificant results, rather than as central causal factors or as interactive elements.

To be sure, quasi-experimental studies present problems. One can never be completely certain that all important variables have been included or that the unmeasured factors are not causally critical. The conclusions drawn from numerous studies suggest that programs are far less important than the differences among children in the same program; understanding this fact requires assessment of individual determinants. Studies of the learning context tend to obscure questions regarding the learning process. Nonexperimental studies that attempt, albeit imperfectly, to disentangle the individual influences can supplement and inform experimental studies that attempt to ascertain the unique impact of a program. The following section will attempt in an exploratory fashion to describe and quantify the effect of reading on summer learning and the role of public institutions in facilitating such behavior.

THE EFFECTS OF READING

The love of reading, it has been said, is caught, not taught. If such a reading germ exists, it apparently infects children from various backgrounds quite differently. Table 9.1 provides a summary of the relationship between family income and selected reading variables, separately by race. For both black and white children, there is a consistent and generally linear relationship between reading and family income. In Atlanta, black children reportedly spent more time reading, read more books, and used the library more regularly than did white children at the same income level. As the tables reveal, the average child read more than five books during the summer, while less than one-fifth read no books.[3]

[3] The data on reading are subject to many of the limitations mentioned earlier with respect to other unstructured activities. Parents, rather than children, supplied the infor-

TABLE 9.1
Distribution of Summer Reading and Use of Library by Family Income and Race, Sixth Grade

Race and family income	Hours spent reading	Mean books read	Used library regularly (in percentages)	Read no books during summer (in percentages)	*N*
White[a]	*.89*	*5.6*	*58*	*20.7*	*470*
Less than $4,000	.73	3.1	27	29.2	26
$4,000–8,999	.94	4.5	37	28.8	83
$9,000–14,999	.95	5.8	64	20.4	115
$15,000+	.85	6.5	73	11.6	124
η	.086	.232**	.316**	.092	
Black[a]	*1.12*	*5.2*	*59*	*14.7*	*1023*
Less than $4,000	.95	4.6	57	19.8	187
$4,000–8,999	1.14	4.9	55	15.9	325
$9,000–14,999	1.10	5.1	64	15.1	169
$15,000+	1.40	6.8	79	5.4	101
η	.128*	.167*	.160*	.137*	

[a] Total includes 122 white nonrespondents and 241 black nonrespondents on income.
* $p < .05$.
** $p < .01$.

Following the models introduced earlier, multiple regression analysis was used to estimate the effects of reading on summer achievement levels. Table 9.2 presents the results for all sixth-grade students in terms of books read and Table 9.3 the similar equations in terms of hours spent reading. The equations are presented in both standardized (b^*) and unstandardized (b) forms. The initial specification examines the degree to which reading is directly related to fall achievement scores when prior achievement is controlled; the second equation tests the degree to which this effect persists when the measures of parental status are entered.

mation, and such responses contain an unknown amount of error, wishful thinking, and sheer conjecture. The questions solicited information that could be easily quantified, but may not capture the true effects. The data refer to the actual distance in blocks to the library, rather than whether it was "close to home" or "too far to walk." Parents were asked whether the child used the library, not what he or she did there. Parents estimated the time spent reading or the number of books, not the quality of the experience. In the case of reading, there is some indirect evidence on the reliability of responses; the variables tend to be internally consistent and intercorrelated. Children whose parents reported that they read more books also spent more time reading ($r = 0.57$), even though some children may have concentrated on comics and hot-rod manuals. Children who used the library regularly read more books than those who did not ($r = 0.28$), even though some children may have used the library as a place to meet friends.

TABLE 9.2
Regression Coefficients of Fall Achievement Level, Word Knowledge, on Spring Achievement, Socioeconomic Background, and Books Read, Sixth-Grade Students, by Race

	Predetermined variables					
	Spring test	Family income (in thousands)	Parental education	Household size	Books read	R^2
White						
b	.8613[a]				.2711[a]	
(σ)	(.0231)				(.1309)	
b^*	.8602				.0612	.7738
b	.8173[a]	.1999[a]	.0660	−.2633	.2888[a]	
(σ)	(.0310)	(.0616)	(.1593)	(.2081)	(.1431)	
b^*	.8140	.0952	.0156	−.0336	.0656	.7841
Black						
b	.7386[a]				.2447[a]	
(σ)	(.0207)				(.0522)	
b^*	.7371				.1378	.6084
b	.6965[a]	.2218[a]	.2525[a]	−.1104[a]	.2381[a]	
(σ)	(.0240)	(.0524)	(.1191)	(.0272)	(.0771)	
b^*	.6941	.1118	.0601	−.1115	.1258	.6330

[a] Coefficients at least twice as large as their standard error.

The two measures of reading, number of books read and hours spent reading on a typical summer day, yield highly consistent estimates of the positive effects. Although reading is not independent of socioeconomic status, the data clearly indicate that the portion of variance causally related to summer learning operates independent of family origins. The unique effect of reading during the summer, or that portion of the gross relationship that is not explained by prior achievement, contributes an essentially additive increment for both black and white children. Insofar as reading is interpreted as a variable that mediates and transmits parental status, it does so only in conjunction with prior achievement level. For white children, the unique effect of reading is suppressed without the addition of background factors; when socioeconomic status is entered, the coefficient for reading increases, rather than declines in importance. For black children, reading mediates a small portion of the influence of family status, although most of the effect is due to the joint relationship with spring achievement. The magnitude of the direct effect tends to be roughly equivalent for both black and white children in unstandardized units, although read-

TABLE 9.3
Regression Coefficients of Fall Achievement Level, Work Knowledge, on Spring Achievement, Socioeconomic Background, and Hours Spent Reading, Sixth-Grade Students, by Race

	Predetermined variables					
	Spring test	Family income (in thousands)	Parental education	Household size	Hours spent reading	R^2
White						
b	.8795[a]				.7389[a]	
(σ)	(.0231)				(.3478)	
*b**	.8707				.0448	.7727
b	.8237[a]	.2014[a]	.0659	−.2610	.9145[a]	
(σ)	(.0313)	(.0738)	(.1592)	(.2031)	(.4343)	
*b**	.8155	.0965	.0153	−.0334	.0554	.7828
Black						
b	.7477[a]				1.1927[a]	
(σ)	(.0207)				(.2208)	
*b**	.7456				.1115	.6071
b	.6964[a]	.2346[a]	.2553[a]	−.1173[a]	1.0779[a]	
(σ)	(.0239)	(.0536)	(.1187)	(.0263)	(.2433)	
*b**	.6944	.1198	.0602	−.1198	.1008	.6320

[a] Coefficients at least twice as large as their standard error.

ing explains a larger portion of the variance in achievement among black students. The equations suggest that each additional hour spent reading on a typical day, or every four books completed over the summer, are worth an additional vocabulary word, irrespective of socioeconomic status, for both black and white children.

Decomposing the variance explained sheds some light on the relative impact of reading on summer achievement. Table 9.4 presents the variance explained by several combinations of variables. The largest influence is, not surprisingly, prior achievement level. The effects of both socioeconomic status and reading contribute only 1.3% or 3.8% to the variance for white and black students, respectively. The relative importance of reading as a proportion of the total increment in explained variance is larger for black children; the unique effect of socioeconomic status is perhaps three times as large as the reading effect for white children, while among black children, about one-third of the total increment in explanatory power is due to books read.

Assessing the effects of reading in raw score increments is satisfactory for a regression analysis; however, it does not provide a readily

TABLE 9.4
Summary of Variance Explained (R^2) in Fall Achievement by Selected Independent Variables, by Race

Independent variables	White	Black
Books read	.091	.103
Spring achievement	.771	.595
Spring achievement and books read	.774	.608
Spring achievement and SES (three measures)	.780	.622
Spring achievement, books read, and SES	.784	.633

interpretable metric. To do so, the patterns of learning in grade equivalent units may be compared.[4] Table 9.5 presents these results. To facilitate comparisons, the number of books read is dichotomized, and the comparisons are tabulated by income and race. Children in every income group who read six or more books during the summer consistently gained more than children who did not. The amount whites learned in months is quite consistent across income levels; both rich and poor children stood to gain over a month of summer achievement by reading, although a larger proportion of advantaged children read more than five books. The largest gains among black children tended to be in the most affluent groups, although children at every income level but the very lowest gained 2 or more months of achievement over those who read less.

How important are these results? In terms of explained variance, the results may not seem overwhelmingly impressive. A casual perusal of the equations presented earlier indicates that the effects are small in terms of absolute size and that most of the variance is inextricably related to prior achievement. Upward of 85% of the gross influence of books read on fall achievement is jointly determined with prior achievement level; the reading variables add less than 2% to the total explained variance. Although 1 or 2 months of achievement is not trivial, the standard errors of such estimates are close to the margin of acceptability.

I would contend that such results are important for three reasons. First, the effects are large in the context of what might be expected in the space of one summer. Second, the coefficients should not be taken solely at face value, but must be viewed as indicators of an achievement

[4] Grade equivalent gains, it should be recalled, do not lend themselves to linear models because the distribution of scores is skewed; transformations of such variables are possible, but would defeat the purpose, which is to present a readily interpretable metric.

TABLE 9.5
Mean Grade Equivalent Summer Gain, Word Knowledge, by Race, Family Income, and Number of Books Read, Sixth Grade

Race and family income	Read fewer than six books		Read six or more books		Total[a]	
	Mean	*N*	Mean	*N*	Mean	*N*
White[a]	*.17*	*268*	*.35*	*181*	*.24*	*449*
Less than $4,000	−.04	21	.08	4	−.02	25
$4,000–8,999	.00	52	.27	24	.09	76
$9,000–14,999	.12	63	.24	46	.17	109
$15,000+	.27	56	.38	63	.33	119
η	.1062		.0722		.1063	
Black[a]	*−.20*	*662*	*.05*	*324*	*−.12*	*986*
Less than $4,000	−.26	132	−.20	45	−.26	176
$4,000–8,999	−.18	222	.03	92	−.12	314
$9,000–14,999	−.15	112	.03	55	−.12	167
$15,000+	.00	44	.45	54	.23	99
η	.0581		.2162		.1388	

[a] Totals include the cases with missing data on the independent variables.

process that operates throughout the school career. Third, the available measures of learning are conservative and may well underestimate the degree of change observed.

First, 1 month's gain attributable to the summer reading of white children is not small relative to either an expected gain of 2.4 months or a time interval of only 5 months. The unique effect of books read is between one-fourth to one-third as large as the sum of the effects of family background on achievement during the same period of time. Comparing an increment of 1.3% to an estimated residual true score variance of less than 10% implies that the observed coefficients are not trivial.[5]

Second, the central concern of this study is not merely to derive an estimate of the amount of learning that occurred in Atlanta during a summer, but rather to examine the social factors that shape cognitive

[5] Assuming that the maximum amount of true score variance is equal to the reliability, and accepting estimates of reliability for the fall 1972 (KR-20) presented in Chapter 2, the multiple correlation between all independent variables and fall scores could not exceed .9315 for white and .8302 for black students. These values imply that once the observed prior score is entered into an equation predicting fall outcomes, only 9.7% of the true score variance remains for white students and 9.4% for black students.

growth throughout schooling. Although the empirical evidence is somewhat fragmentary, the patterns of learning observed during a single year can serve as benchmark estimates of the relative importance of influences that operate throughout a child's school career.[6] Any extrapolation of the effects, assuming they are cumulative through time, would heighten their importance.

Finally, the preponderant influence of prior achievement tests can hardly be debated. However, the magnitude of the correlation between pretest and posttest should not be allowed to obscure learning that does take place. Any growth process yields very high correlations over time. Economists interested in social accounting or prediction based on a time series would not argue that the importance of unemployment to the determination of Gross National Product (GNP) depended on how much variance was explained once the previous year's figure for GNP was included in the equation. Similar considerations should inform educational research. There are numerous reasons for supposing that tests are not ideal measures of cognitive growth; for one, the metrics are not sensitive to changes in the distribution of achievement. Any process that is exponential or interacts with individual attributes or experiences cannot be studied without assumptions about the distribution of true scores. Although there are reasons for supposing that true scores become more skewed over time and for anticipating that gains would not be independent of prior achievement, such notions have not been incorporated into measurement models.

These observations, coupled with the fact that isolating factors that shape cognitive development is far more important than demonstrating their stability, lead me to conclude that reading plays a critical role in the achievement process. Although the magnitude of the independent effect is not large, it is consistent for two distinct survey questions; the measured effects are significant for both white and black children. Such consistency would not be likely to occur if the relationship were spurious.

Although reading tends to be patterned by family circumstances, the increments to summer learning are largely independent of a child's social class background. Unlike the summer activities discussed in Chapter 8, reading tends to be beneficial irrespective of socioeconomic status and to exert a unique influence rather than mediate the effect of background. Although it seems likely that families differ in the degree to which they encourage or emphasize reading, the joint effects of reading and status operate entirely through earlier levels of achieve-

[6] See Chapter 4 and Appendix D for a discussion of the cumulative effects of education.

ment. This could be because families differ in the degree of intellectual support provided to children in ways untapped by the status measures or because reading habits established earlier in life have already had an impact on achievement. Whatever the reasons, the unique contribution of reading to summer learning suggests that increasing access to books and encouraging reading may well have substantial impact on achievement. The next section will explore the determinants of reading in greater detail.

CAUSES AND CORRELATES OF READING

Reading is both consequential and susceptible to nonfamilial influence. The major determinants of reading are, in order of importance, whether the child used the public library, the child's sex, his socioeconomic status, and the distance between a child's home and the library. Among white children, socioeconomic status was more important and sex less so. Girls read almost two books more than did boys during the summer, and this difference is even larger among black children. Insofar as library use influences summer learning, this effect operates entirely through reading. As one might surmise, library use is of little importance unless a child reads there. These relationships are documented in the regression equations presented in Tables 9.6 and 9.7. Table 9.6 presents the regression of fall achievement on spring achievement, socioeconomic status, and books read separately by sex, for the entire Atlanta sample. As these regressions clearly indicate, whether or not children used the library contributes little to the prediction of fall achievement once the amount of reading is controlled. For both males and females, reading is significantly related to fall achievement, when prior achievement and socioeconomic status are controlled. The direct effect of reading is larger among females, although it is significant for both; girls' reading seems to be less dependent on library use than is boys'.[7]

Table 9.7 presents the equations estimating the effects of parental status, sex, library use, and distance on the number of books read during the summer, for white and black students separately, and for the

[7] The equations also document the sex difference alluded to earlier; for females, the effects of parental status on achievement are larger than for males, irrespective of prior achievement. The general finding, that socioeconomic status is more important to the educational performance of females than to that of males, seems in this case to be supported. This relationship has been interpreted as due to the differential accuracy of children's reports; however, it seems to persist even when the respondents are parents.

TABLE 9.6
Regressions of Fall Achievement on Spring Achievement, Socioeconomic Status, Race, Books Read, and Library Usage by Sex, Total Sample, Sixth Grade

	Predetermined variables							
	Prior achievement	Family income (in thousands)	Parental education	Household size	Race	Books read	Library use	R^2
Males								
b	.766[a]	.139[a]	.121	−.110	3.636[a]	.204[a]		
(σ)	(.028)	(.063)	(.143)	(.149)	(.696)	(.075)		
b^*	.739	.066	.025	−.017	.131	.063		.7559
b	.763[a]	.136[a]	.094	−.101	3.753[a]	.181[a]	.954	
(σ)	(.028)	(.063)	(.144)	(.149)	(.699)	(.076)	(.604)	
b^*	.736	.065	.020	−.016	.136	.056	.037	.7571
Females								
b	.710[a]	.257[a]	.273[a]	−.165	2.851[a]	.290[a]		
(σ)	(.028)	(.063)	(.135)	(.150)	(.662)	(.067)		
b^*	.686	.124	.060	−.026	.109	.101		.7347
b	.709[a]	.257[a]	.270[a]	−.166	2.862[a]	.287[a]	.124	
(σ)	(.028)	(.063)	(.137)	(.150)	(.665)	(.069)	(.608)	
b^*	.685	.123	.059	−.026	.109	.100	.005	.7347

[a] Coefficients at least twice as large as their standard errors.

total sample. While it is clear that these variables do not begin to explain all of the variance among children in the number of books read, they do suggest an ordering of the relevant factors by magnitude of importance. For white children, the effects of library use and distance are very nearly equal to the combined effects of background; for black children, library use and proximity are more important determinants of reading than is socioeconomic status. Among whites, library use and distance add about 3% to the variance explained in reading, when background is controlled; background, in turn, adds perhaps 3% when distance and library use have been entered. For blacks, the unique variance attributable to parental status is 2%, contrasted with 5% due to library use and distance. Although parental status is related to reading, the measured effects of proximity and libraries rival the importance of class background as a determinant of reading. Such results imply that how much a child reads is due, to an important degree, to influences that lie outside of the immediate family.

The effects of distance are largely insignificant in the equations presented in Table 9.7. Although living within seven blocks of a public library adds between .6 and 1.1 books to the summer's accomplish-

TABLE 9.7
Regression Coefficients of Number of Books Read during the Summer on Social Class Background, Sex, Library Usage, and Number of Blocks to the Public Library, Sixth-Grade Students by Race

	Predetermined variables						
	Family income (in thousands)	Parental education	Household size	Sex	Library use	Distance	R^2
White							
b	.127[a]	.009	−.081	−1.179[a]	1.619[a]	−.080	
(σ)	(.054)	(.011)	(.481)	(.546)	(.232)	(.232)	
b^*	.182	.059	−.029	−.131	.178	−.019	.1063
b				−.997[a]	2.233[a]	.005	
(σ)				(.419)	(.445)	(.204)	
b^*				−.111	.246	.001	.0749
b	.147[a]	.080	−.084	−1.320[a]			
(σ)	(.055)	(.113)	(.151)	(.485)			
b^*	.208	.052	−.030	−.148			.0767
Black							
b	.064[a]	.134	−.022	−1.460[a]	1.851[a]	−.081	
(σ)	(.031)	(.071)	(.072)	(.285)	(.311)	(.126)	
b^*	.087	.084	−.011	−.181	.230	−.026	.1247
b				−1.388[a]	2.084[a]	−.091	
(σ)				(.258)	(.275)	(.105)	
b^*				−.173	.255	−.029	.1035
b	.076[a]	.193[a]	−.014	−1.549[a]			
(σ)	(.031)	(.073)	(.074)	(.293)			
b^*	.104	.121	−.008	−.193			.0722
Total sample							
b	.104[a]	.170[a]	.066	−1.476[a]			
(σ)	(.026)	(.060)	(.076)	(.252)			
b^*	.144	.109	.028	−.176			.0746
b				−1.263[a]	2.212[a]	.042	
(σ)				(.254)	(.056)	(.064)	
b^*				−.151	.260	.023	.0922
b	.095[a]	.078	.063		1.906	−.034	
(σ)	(.028)	(.064)	(.081)		(.287)	(.062)	
b^*	.133	.050	.026		.224	−.018	.0929
b	.095[a]	.104	.069	−1.367	1.809	−.040	
(σ)	(.028)	(.164)	(.079)	(.263)	(.283)	(.062)	
b^*	.134	.067	.029	−.163	.213	−.022	.1193

[a] Coefficients at least twice as large as their standard error.

ment, this gross relationship is almost entirely mediated by library use. As might be expected, the number of blocks to the nearest library influences reading primarily because increasing the accessibility of books and materials heightens the probability that a child will read. If a child does not use the library, the fact that it is conveniently located is irrelevant.

Distance tends to be a greater deterrent to library use for black children and for less economically advantaged children. Again, this is not surprising. Roughly one-fourth of the black children and one-seventh of the white children live within seven blocks of a branch library. Of these children, 80% or more used the library regularly, compared to barely half of the children living further away. Studies have shown that nearly 80% of the adult library clientele live within a 1-mile radius, the distance urban geographers have called the "catchment area" for library services; in low-income areas, library users are even more concentrated within walking distance (Levy, Meltsner, & Wildavsky, 1974). Although the rates of usage by adults and children in Atlanta cannot be compared, it seems likely that distance is an even more important factor in predicting utilization by children than by adults. The distribution of library services will be discussed more thoroughly in the subsequent section.

The relationship between using libraries and reading books is causally ambiguous. The previous regressions explicitly assumed that library use occurs at a point in time prior to reading and therefore causes children to read books. Instead, children may decide to go to the library because they want to read. Insofar as reading and library use are understood to have a reciprocal influence on each other, it makes sense to consider them as simultaneously caused by background factors and by each other; such a specification implies that the recursive models considered earlier are inadequate to account for the patterns. The relationships among the variables discussed suggest that it would be possible to estimate the mutual dependence of library use and reading by allowing distance and the child's sex to serve as instrumental variables. Distance, as we have seen, influences reading only through library use; although girls use the library more than boys, the partial relationship between sex and library use is essentially zero once reading is controlled. Assuming that distance influences reading through the use of the library and that sex influences going to the library only because of reading, one is able to obtain a unique solution for the model depicted in Figure 9.1 for black children. Library use is assumed to be determined by family income, parental education, reading, and distance to the library; reading is the result of family income, parental education,

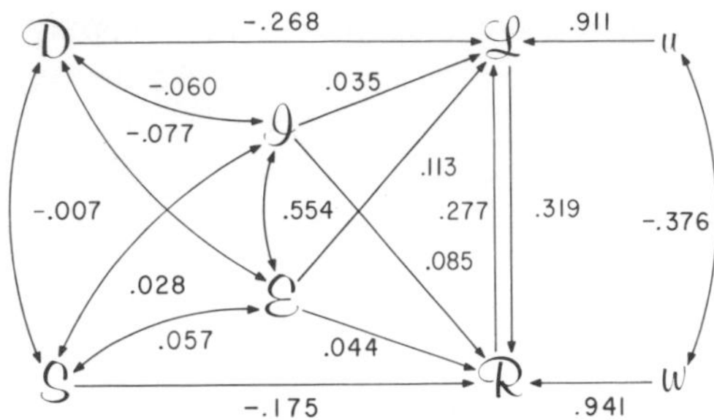

FIGURE 9.1. A simultaneous equation model for the determination of library use (*L*) and books read (*R*) by distance to the library (*D*), sex (*S*), income (*I*), and parental education (*E*), black sixth-grade sample.

sex, and library use. The disturbance terms are assumed to be uncorre-'ated with the predetermined variables, but not with each other. Accepting the model implies a fairly substantial negative correlation (−.376) between the residuals of the jointly dependent endogamous variables. Although somewhat troubling, such a relationship between residuals is common in nonrecursive models.

The model is presented to illustrate the pattern of effects under varying assumptions. The parameters, which were estimated by indirect least squares, imply that the reciprocal influences of reading and library use are stronger than the measured impact of any of the predetermined variables. Considered individually, the observed impacts of sex and distance to the library are more important than parental status measures. Reading is clearly influenced by social factors other than socioeconomic background. Given the observed relationships, it is tempting to conclude that libraries exert a more direct influence on reading than vice versa; this conclusion, however, is unfounded. The relative size of the paths linking the dependent variables to each other is a direct consequence of the fact that library use is more determined by other exogamous variables in the model than is reading.

The effects linking income and parents' education to reading and library use are intriguing. The model suggests that for black children, the indirect effect of parental education on reading, through library use, is almost as large as the direct effect. Libraries mediate the influence of income less directly, although, as we shall see, this is a consequence of the assumptions. Models that assume linear, additive relations among variables do not capture the relevant interactions. The distance to the library becomes a substantially more important variable in the nonrecursive model. Assuming that reading and library use are simultaneously determined leads to the conclusion that the distance in blocks to the library exerts an indirect impact on reading that is masked in the recursive models. Although it may seem obvious that access to a library is likely to increase reading, this result depends fundamentally on the causal assumptions and the analytic strategy employed.

The models I have discussed up to now attempted to depict and quantify the relations among variables that determine an individual child's summer reading. Although useful, this framework embodies a certain conceptual bias. The causal mechanisms that produce reading are likely to be interpreted as attributes or propensities originating in the individual, such as a desire to go to the library or a willingness to walk some distance. Within a community, however, the existence and distribution of libraries is institutionally determined and reflects numerous political decisions. The allocation of services to particular neighborhoods determines both the use by and the social composition of the constituency; distance determines the logistics of access to a large degree. The decisions and policies that affect the location, funding, and use of public institutions are therefore critical to educational outcomes. Although children differ in the degree to which they use the library, irrespective of its location, the ecology of public services is important and clearly relevant to policy.

THE IMPACT OF LIBRARIES

Libraries, as we have seen, facilitate reading and hence achievement. Libraries serve both as a repository of materials and as an educational resource for a community. Since libraries are publicly funded, the political decisions that influence access to books and the delivery of services are directly relevant to the formulation of educational policy. More than any other public institution, including the schools, the public library contributed to the intellectual growth of children during the summer. Moreover, unlike summer school programs, the library was used regularly by over half of the sample and attracted children from diverse backgrounds.

As we have seen, libraries have only an indirect influence on achievement, operating through the actual volume of reading children accomplished during the summer. Although both the proximity to a library and the fact that it was used regularly are correlates of achievement, the effects of these variables diminish precipitously when the number of books read or the time spent reading are controlled. The series of regression equations suggest quite forcefully that it is reading books that is causally instrumental, not libraries directly. Only when one assumes that reading and library use are mutually reinforcing do the effects of the public institution appear to be noteworthy. Since the propensity to read is governed by numerous individual traits and family influences, it seems reasonable to conclude that libraries have little impact once the more powerful individual-level determinants are controlled.

The fallacy of this reasoning is similar to that found in many policy analyses and educational evaluations. One assumes that the effects of an institution are explained by individual behavior when the individual characteristics prove to be powerful predictors of individual outcomes. The single criterion of importance too often becomes the unique contribution to variance, neglecting models that explicitly test for interactive effects. In the case of schools, I have argued that schooling must be contrasted with nonschooling in order to arrive at an appropriate model; schooling is critical for both status transmission and the patterns of learning of every child. Yet since socioeconomic status is a continuous influence in the achievement process, schooling does not equalize educational performance or attainment.

In the case of libraries, there are two major reasons for assuming that the institution plays a significant role in the achievement process. The first is that the ecology of public libraries shapes children's use in determinate ways, irrespective of the income or educational status of parents. Second, although library use is related to the socioeconomic status of both black and white children, the evidence suggests that libraries operate to transmit parental status in different ways in the two communities.

The first point is easily shown, both by the regression analysis presented earlier and by the data presented in Table 9.8. Children living near a library read more books than those who live beyond walking distance. Had all children lived within seven blocks, the aggregate amount of reading would have increased substantially. Although reading and library use are linked to socioeconomic status, the degree of access enjoyed by children is a critical factor for all socioeconomic groups. It would be possible to argue that families with an abiding concern for their children's reading behavior chose to live near libraries, but this seems unlikely. The alternative assertion, that the distribution of libraries shapes the patterns of use by socioeconomic status and race, is more plausible.

Libraries in Atlanta are used disproportionately by children of some affluence, yet family income is substantially more important as a determinant of use among white families than among black families. This is a direct consequence of residential housing patterns and the distribu-

TABLE 9.8
Mean Number of Books Read during the Summer by Race, Library Usage, and Distance to Library, Sixth Grade

	Uses library regularly		Does not use library		Total[a]	
Race and distance	Mean	*N*	Mean	*N*	Mean	*N*
White	*6.5*	*262*	*4.2*	*172*	*5.6*	*434*
Under seven blocks	6.8	55	4.6	20	6.2	75
Seven or more blocks	6.4	207	4.1	151	5.4	359
Black	*6.0*	*547*	*3.8*	*358*	*5.2*	*905*
Under seven blocks	6.0	241	3.9	55	5.6	296
Seven or more blocks	6.0	306	3.8	297	4.9	603

[a] Totals include nonresponse on library usage and distance to library, but exclude a small number who did not know how many books the child read.

tion of services. The ecology of public libraries in Atlanta, and perhaps in other cities as well, is the result of historical and demographic changes that have directly influenced access to public services. Urban services were traditionally concentrated in the central city—areas that are now largely black and relatively poor. For black families, there is an inverse relationship between family income and access to a library; the poorest children, living in the inner city, are those most likely to be near a library. Their rates of use are more than double that of poor white families. Relatively advantaged black families have tended to move to single-family dwellings in housing developments built after World War II. While these neighborhoods provide substantially more space, privacy, and the accoutrements of suburban living, the city services have not developed quickly. Parks, libraries, and other services tend to be some distance away.

In contrast, the availability of public services to white families reflects neighborhood income levels to a much greater extent. The wealthiest white areas in northeast Atlanta are built in a style of Antebellum opulence; the residents enjoy large, elegant homes as well as easy access to good schools, well-equipped libraries, meticulously maintained parks and gardens, and other amenities. Residents of these enclaves of privilege have little need to venture downtown. White families in more modest circumstances tend to have an intermediate degree of access; the average distance to the library is greater than for wealthy families or poor blacks, but they tend to live closer to services than do the black middle class. For whites, the correlation between distance to the library and income is negative.[8]

The spatial configuration of public libraries reflects the stratification system of another era. Viewing libraries as an object of public subsidy, it is clear that the allocation of services favors the most advantaged children from white families and the most disadvantaged blacks. Within a particular ecological unit, the library attracts disproportionate numbers of affluent children, yet the presence of a library increases the propensity to use it irrespective of parental influences and status. Had the libraries been allocated among black families in a manner similar to their allocation among whites, it seems reasonable to assume that use would have been considerably more unequal.

Black families tend to use libraries and other public services more heavily than white families, once income and the location of services are controlled. Low-income whites, even when living near the library, use the services somewhat less frequently than do similarly situated black children. This generalization applies not just to libraries but to summer schools, day camps, parks, and other public programs. Irrespective of their relative proximity, black children utilize public services in disproportionate numbers. White families rely to a much greater extent on private services and tend to restrict recreation and leisure to relatively exclusive and frequently all-white contexts. Whether this is caused by preferences or prejudices, the result is that during the summer many public institutions in Atlanta are primarily patronized by black children.

The most important observation to be made, however, is that the existence of public services and facilities for children are far more critical to black families than to whites. Without public schools and public libraries, black parents are seemingly unable to transmit social status to their children. This fact is dramatically evident in the pattern of relationships portrayed in Table 9.9. In both black and white families, there is a positive relationship between parental income and the number of books read during the summer. Yet for white children, differences in family income predict reading whether or not children used the library. Among those who do, there is more inequality in

[8] These patterns are somewhat obscured by the individual-level correlations. Ecological factors are less powerful than individual attributes and the correlation of coding decisions. Approximately 12% of the sample children used the bookmobile services of the library; these services were targeted to areas that otherwise would have been deprived. These children were coded as living within seven blocks of the library for purposes of operationalizing access, although their immediate neighbors who did not use such services were coded as living farther away.

TABLE 9.9
Mean Number of Books Read during the Summer by Race, Family Income, and Library Usage, Sixth Grade

	Uses library regularly		Does not use library		Total	
Race and family income	Mean	*N*	Mean	*N*	Mean	*N*
White	*6.5*	*262*	*4.2*	*172*	*5.6*	*434*
Less than $4,000	2.9	7	3.2	17	3.1	24
$4,000–8,999	5.7	29	3.8	44	4.5	73
$9,000–14,999	6.6	69	4.3	39	5.8	108
$15,000+	6.8	90	5.7	31	6.5	121
η	*.1803*		*.2021*		*.2320*	
Black	*6.0*	*547*	*3.8*	*358*	*5.2*	*905*
Less than $4,000	5.2	93	3.6	69	4.6	162
$4,000–8,999	5.9	166	3.6	129	4.9	295
$9,000–14,999	5.9	101	3.7	58	5.1	159
$15,000+	7.5	75	3.8	18	6.8	93
η	*.1744*		*.0164*		*.1669*	

outcomes, but reading is less directly dependent on parental income. Among blacks, however, family background is not at all predictive of the number of books read by children who did not use the library. The relationship between parental status and leisure reading is almost entirely mediated by the presence and use of a public library.

What factors could produce such a pattern of outcomes? One plausible explanation would be that the public provision of books is far more critical to families that do not or perhaps cannot purchase children's books or provide home libraries than for families that do. For white children, library books are a supplemental resource; since parents have the means to foster reading directly, outcomes are unequal whether or not children used the library. For children at every income level, access to the library promotes intellectual growth, but family circumstances such as economic resources and educational encouragement play the most significant role. Among black families, reading levels vary across income levels in the predictable way, yet the chief means of implementing parental influence seems to be through encouraging children to use the library, rather than by providing books in the home.[9] A good many

[9] An alternative explanation for the patterns of inequality in reading among black children could be constructed on the assumption that the farther one lives from a library, the greater must be the motivation to read to induce one to go there. Black children from relatively prosperous families tend to live further away; perhaps the larger returns to

families consider children's books an economic luxury and a cultural commodity foreign to their experience; libraries provide such families with a resource their children would not otherwise receive. Libraries transmit socioeconomic inequality, but they do so most decisively among families in which reading is crucially predicated on library use. Despite the fact that the allocation of public goods in the form of access to books is redistributive in the black community, with the poorest children having the most convenient access, the most advantaged children reap the greatest benefits. If libraries were not available, there would be greater equality of outcomes; however, black children would pay a considerably greater price for such equality than would white children. Libraries serve as a critical conduit of educational resources, but they are most critical to black families, or perhaps to all families whose aspirations for their children outstrip their ability to provide for them.

Educational institutions, including libraries, have been criticized repeatedly for perpetuating and perhaps exacerbating socioeconomic inequality. A germane assessment of the public library system in Oakland, California, argued that it was inefficient and that it tended to be used disproportionately by the most educated and affluent members of the community (Levy, Meltsner, & Wildavsky, 1974). Wildavsky raises the issue of whether it is in the public interest to provide books at public expense in direct competition with commercial booksellers or rental libraries, when the chief beneficiaries are the well-to-do. Oakland libraries apparently do not meet the minimal criteria of social equity. In the terms of welfare economics, social equity is met when a public good is equally distributed to all members of a community, or when equal benefits are realized per dollar cost to recipients. Libraries, as well as other educational institutions, typically meet neither criterion. In Oakland, the funds for new acquisitions are allocated to branch libraries based on their circulation, a practice that results in the most affluent neighborhoods receiving the most funds. Specialized collections and highly trained professionals are a major expense, and the central library received disproportionate amounts of each. "Subsidizing the rich and belaboring the poor to read," the authors argue, "requires

---

library use reflect the fact that users are self-selected by levels of motivation, rather than by family income. This explanation would be similar to that offered for the finding that achievement gains were largest among children who enrolled in a summer school program despite the fact that their own school was closed during the summer. However, even for the poorest children with the easiest access, libraries contributed to reading and achievement gains.

a more convincing rationale than it has yet received [Levy *et al.*, 1974, p. 168]."

A major difficulty with this line of reasoning is that the consumers of public goods are assumed to be equally able to exercise informed choice in the marketplace. If the alternative to public libraries involves returning funds to taxpayers, families with children would receive less than a proportionate share when based on use. Children currently constitute 50% or more of the library clientele, and there is no way to ensure that they would get equivalent services. For the young users, the library appears to be a critical source of materials; although young clients are also disproportionately drawn from the most advantaged classes, the children of the poor obtain benefits that would not be available in the absence of libraries.

Libraries, like schools, represent a commitment to educational opportunity; like schools, libraries effectively increase the achievement of children. Although outcomes are not equal, the major reason seems to be the influence of families, not institutional discrimination. Although it might be possible to increase access to poor children by instituting programs more responsive to their needs, educational institutions are unlikely ever to redress the prevalent patterns of inequality in society as a whole. Yet it does not follow that these institutions are ineffective for poor children or that poor children would be well served in their absence. This is the fundamental point.

10
Conclusions and Conjectures

Equality of educational opportunity occupies an eminent position in any description of American goals or aspirations. Historically, Americans have placed enormous faith in schools as equalizing institutions and as vital channels for upward mobility. Schools have been expected to inculcate democratic values, ensure social stability, and provide skills and opportunities to meet the aspirations of the underprivileged. Public education was considered a basic birthright for every American child, regardless of race, ethnic origin, or socioeconomic status. Although schooling was conceded to be an imperfect panacea (Perkinson, 1968) and the need for reform has been recognized, the American faith in education as the bulwark of a free and open society was largely unchallenged until the mid-1960s.

The conventional view of schools has been profoundly shaken since the mid-1960s by both public criticism and academic research. A raft of publications and educational program evaluations have demonstrated persuasively that we do not know, nor are we able to predict what educational contexts are most likely to produce increased achievement. Because there is no demonstrably effective educational program, it becomes exceedingly difficult to propose programs or policies aimed at improving education. The measured effects of the most successful preschool programs disappear before the third grade. Increased expenditures or the provision of additional educational resources do not lead to higher achievement for either the middle class or the poor. Even programs designed to increase retention or the rates of college attendance appear to be only marginally effective. Education has become a prime contender for the century's most "dismal science." The liberal promise of schooling seems no more than empty rhetoric.

The Atlanta study suggests that such conclusions are premature. Educational research results obtained thus far, I have argued, stem partly from the reliance on cross-sectional data, partly from a narrow focus on educational institutions, and partly from the inadequacies of the instruments available to measure learning or cognitive growth. Conceptually, research on schools is flawed by the assumption that one can operationalize the effects of education as differences among schools. Schooling should be measured as the cumulative impact of being in schools rather than out of them. The effects of education should include the total impact of all educational institutions, rather than the observed variability among them. As an institutional complex, the effects of schooling on achievement should be evaluated in terms of the degree of influence that is independent of socioeconomic status; this capacity, however, can only be measured relative to outcomes in the absence of schooling.

The explanatory paradigm adopted in the present study is based on three assumptions:

1. The socioeconomic background and general family conditions of children exert an influence on the achievement of children continuously, whether or not schools are in session.
2. Schooling exerts an influence as an intermittent causal factor, operating primarily during the period of time when schools are open.
3. Summertime constitutes a natural experiment for the evaluation of the relative importance of families and schools in the generation of achievement differentials.

The conceptual emphasis is temporal, rather than spatial. Achievement is presumed to be a process that should be analyzed longitudinally; the strength of the determinants at particular junctures can be used to assess the relative influence of concurrent factors. The effects of schooling can be measured by contrasting the achievement process during the school year with that operating when schools are closed.

Summer is a convenient but imperfect temporal construct for evaluating the effects of education. School vacations constitute breaks from a normal regimen, rather than a cessation of influence. Children may pursue interests and projects during the summer that were initiated during the school year, but without direct exposure to schooling. Summer is a relatively short period of time, and not devoid of academic influences; a sizable portion of students attend summer school or participate in other group activities that are structured much like school. Assuming that the influence of schooling is seasonally specific risks including all other influences that operate during the school year, but not the summer, with the effects of schooling. Although it seems intuitively plausible that children are more subject to familial influence during the summer, the sheer amount of time spent at home may be much the same whether school is open or not. The quality and intensity of parental contact are clearly more relevant than is the quantity, but these are not easily measured. My study faced the practical difficulty that testing intervals were not precisely congruent with the school calendar because achievement tests were administered in October and May, rather than in September and June.

Nevertheless, in a system of universal mass education, the summer constitutes the only time period in which the impact of schooling on achievement is not inextricably confounded with the effects of family. Presumably, all schools have some educational impact; conceptualizing the effects of education as differences between particular schools ignores the possibility of any common effect or any direct impact on the achievement process that might be relatively uniform across all schools. Short of designing an impractical experiment, the summer is the only period in which it is possible to distinguish the effects of families from the effects of educational institutions on achievement.

With these caveats in mind, the major findings can be summarized briefly. The data clearly support the contention that schooling makes a substantial contribution to cognitive growth. Schooling does not equalize outcomes in any absolute sense; during both the school year and the summer, relatively advantaged students learn at a faster rate than do less privileged pupils. Disadvantaged children, however, show a higher rate of relative achievement during the school years than during the summer. The gap between black and white children, and between low- and high-income children, widens disproportionately during the months when schools are not in session. Schooling apparently attenuates the influence of socioeconomic status on achievement and thereby reduces the direct dependence of outcomes on family background. The effect is common to every skill or subject tested, for either racial group, and persists irrespective of other controls. Although the magnitude of the direct effects of socioeconomic status or race on achievement may be reduced by including additional measures of individual achievement or intelligence, the differential importance of socioeconomic status on fall scores relative to spring scores remains. This differential impact is the basis for the conclusion that the effects of schooling on the achievement process are substantial.

Interpreting the schooling effect is somewhat problematic. It is not possible to discover, for example, whether relatively advantaged children learn more or forget less during the summer, or whether schooling promotes the absolute, as well as the relative, achievement of poor children. The most reasonable interpretation seems to be that the achievement of high-status children is not as dependent on the influence of schooling as is the achievement of the relatively disadvantaged. The rates of learning tend to remain fairly constant among children from affluent families, during both the summer and the school year. For less privileged children, the impact of schooling is more determinate; test scores tend to decline in absolute magnitude. For a number of children from lower socioeconomic backgrounds, schooling tends to boost spring achievement levels, whereas other factors less conducive to learning operate to reduce both test scores and the total variability in achievement by the fall.

Such patterns support the notion that to some degree schooling is a surrogate for the parental influences common in middle-class families. Education is a means for providing stimulation, encouragement, or perhaps a degree of intellectual coercion necessary for the acquisition of verbal skills. The role of schooling is supplemental and complementary to familial pressures; schooling does not operate strictly independently. Socioeconomic status exerts a continual impact on cognitive achievement through parental encouragement, resources, and values; education can offset influences in home life and compensate for certain deficiencies, but it does not equalize outcomes. If such a model is correct, it should come as no surprise that successful intervention programs do not have impressive long-term effects on the cognitive achievement of poor children.

This concept of schooling supports both popular folklore and liberal presumptions, but leaves many critical questions unanswered. What is it about schooling that promotes the relative equality of outcomes? Concluding that schooling is better than nonschooling for the achievement of poor children might be interpreted as an apology or a reprieve for public schools, which is neither intended nor justified. The more useful question for policy analysis is how schooling might become more effective. Would it be possible to structure a curriculum or an educational program that could increase the beneficial effects of schooling? Would year-round schooling increase general achievement levels or create greater equality of outcomes?

Such questions require a precise specification of the causal mechanisms operating to influence learning. Each of the 42 schools studied was different in the degree to which socioeconomic status declined in relative predictive power during the school year and in the degree to which achievement among low-income pupils was augmented. The differences among schools were not consistent across cohorts, however, and the degree of sampling variability prohibited an analysis of such differences. The patterns tend to support the contention that the schooling effect was a general phenomenon, rather than one tied to particular schools or programs. The effects of schooling seem to be at least partly the result of structures and programs common to all schools, irrespective of location, socioeconomic composition, or degree of racial integration.

The issue of year-round schooling cannot be resolved without making the untenable assumption that changing from a 9- to a 12-month calendar would involve no other changes in curriculum or student responses to school. The issue was pursued tentatively by scrutinizing the outcomes associated with summer school. The Atlanta school system sponsors a mammoth summer school program, enrolling nearly one-third of the sixth-grade students. The programs were targeted to schools in relatively poor, largely black areas; as a result, low-income and minority children were disproportionately likely to attend.

Summer school, however, had only a modest influence on the achievement levels of poor children; when socioeconomic status was controlled, the effects did not reach significance. Unlike the patterns found in regular schooling, summer school tended to increase the inequality of outcomes associated with the background of participants. The largest gains were invariably concentrated among children from the most affluent families.

Two issues are at stake: First, if the model of schooling is correct, why is the achievement of poor pupils not more positively influenced by summer school? Second, why are relative gains between participants and nonparticipants greater for relatively affluent students? The two most plausible explanations reduce to the characteristics of programs and the characteristics of students attending. Either schooling is not a similar experience in the context of summer programs, or the characteristics and motivation of students choosing to attend a voluntary program lead to patterns of outcomes different from those occurring during the year, or both.

Summer school programs are not, of course, entirely comparable to the regular school program in terms of curriculum, goals, or rigor. They are conducted in a relatively informal atmosphere, and the emphasis is clearly on nonacademic subjects. Summer school in Atlanta is not designed either to make up failing work or to permit acceleration to another grade; neither are cited as reasons for attending. The program has few requirements; attendance is not routinely taken. Although each school includes academic subjects and remedial courses, the curriculum is primarily devoted to subjects not normally taught, including library skills, typing, and recreational programs. The summer programs vary considerably in length of time, intensity of instruction, and effectiveness.

Summer school also differs from full-enrollment sessions in the composition of students. Since the program is voluntary, self-selection doubtless confounds the effects of attending. Summer school tends to attract children who particularly like school, who missed few days during the preceding year, and who might be expected to learn the most from the experience. Self-selection could explain the gains of the most advantaged children; however, it cannot explain the very small increments of achievement accruing to low-income children. One might argue that the minority of high-SES children attended because they were exceptionally motivated academically, while many of the low-income children were attracted for other reasons. This explanation, however, does not account for the fact that in every structured program, even those that attracted more high-income children, gains accrued disproportionately to the relatively affluent. There is no evidence to suggest that middle-class children gained substantially more from summer school than they did from attending camp or music lessons. Every structured program tended to present a similar pattern of outcomes by income level, whether or not academic motives were involved.

One might argue that peers constituted the critical influence on achievement and that the summer programs differed from the regular programs primarily in that children attending were denied contact with more advantaged classmates. This, however, does not accord with the observation that in each school studied, the summer school student body was on the average slightly more advantaged socioeconomically than the regular enrollment. Peer effects should have been even more effective during summer session than during the regular school year.

In short, the data provide few clues as to the nature of the schooling effect that could be generalized from the outcomes associated with summer school. A more rigorous program or a program that was compulsory for all children might yield effects similar to those of schooling; however, such conclusions are speculative. Increasing the amount of time spent in summer school beyond the half-day, 6-week program might enhance program effectiveness. The few schools with extended-day programs were not, however, more effective. Differences among summer programs were associated with sizable differences in rates of attendance, rather than achievement outcomes. Net of the socioeconomic composition of the programs, the summer programs did not substantially influence levels of achievement during the summer for participants more than for nonparticipants.

Much of the analysis has focused on the causal mechanisms that influence learning, on the actual behavior children engage in that produces achievement, and on the social context in which learning occurs. Since the data collected are specific to summer learning, identifying the mechanisms of schooling is inherently speculative. The one major activity that consistently influenced achievement, independent of socioeconomic class or race, was the amount children read. For both racial groups, for either sex, and irrespective of social class background, the number of books read and the amount of time spent reading consistently influenced summer achievement. Children attending summer school consistently read more books during the summer than children of similar income levels who did not attend; perhaps even more intriguing, the amount read by poor children was substantially greater among participants, while high-income children read much the same amount whether or not they attended. Although the differences in achievement outcomes were modest, summer school did tend to equalize reading behavior and to contribute differentially to the amount poor children read. It is plausible, although speculative, to infer that one mechanism for the effects of schooling is the provision of reading requirements. School influence might ensure that poor children read materials they would not otherwise read.

In any correlational analysis, the objective is to specify the relationships precisely and to deduce explanations from the available results. Such procedures have the advantage of reflecting what actually occurs, although without the control over outcomes and causal interpretations associated with experimental studies. In terms of policy analysis in education, the dominant paradigm has been the experimental method. This method has been used because of the intimate connections between education and the field of psychology and because experimental studies tend to be on a small scale and to involve the participation of school officials and administrative personnel. Experimental studies are far less threatening to administrators than are large-scale surveys, since the objectives are not to compare schools or districts, but to implement programs within schools or grades. Differences by socioeconomic level or race are seldom included in the research design, but are randomized by assignment to treatment groups. The statistical techniques that have a randomized design provide an elegant solution to the problem of causality, in that the differences among programs are unbiased estimates of program effects, irrespective of other influences.

This study has involved a natural experiment without the assumption that learning occurs in any particular context or because of a particular curriculum. My contention is that despite the causal ambiguity, such a design is more useful for policy analysis. If a particular program were to be implemented or the curriculum altered, it would be important to know how learning interacts with the program as well as what the other influences on achievement are; it would be important to assess which children profit most from the program and what the effects are likely to be if the program were implemented in a different environment. Each of the programs studied in Atlanta shows consistent interactions with socioeconomic status, in that the children who are more likely to benefit are disproportionately from the most advantaged backgrounds. Implementing programs during the summer involves choices about location and about the proportion of costs to be borne by the public sector. There is no way to ensure that participation is random in any program that is implemented on a large scale. The parameters estimated as program effects in an experimental study are never likely to be replicated in any real program, since there is no way to legislate attendance and no way to ensure that children in the control group, who were not exposed to the program, did nothing else to improve their achievement or cognitive skills in the absence of the program. In short, we do not have a placebo for participation; control groups are typically exposed to other influences or activities that may increase achievement independently. These factors lead directly to the conclusion that one must be able to identify the specific determinants of learning if one wishes to extend or broaden the scope of a particular program, or to evaluate outcomes.

A major portion of the analysis was devoted to looking at the activities and programs children were involved in during the summer and assessing their effects on achievement. Programs that were effective in raising cognitive achievement during the summer should perhaps be expanded to include other children or additional sites. The central question is which programs were effective in promoting cognitive growth during the summer, independent of parental background.

Among the available summer programs and organized group activities in Atlanta, a number seemed to increase learning; however, none had a significant effect on achievement independent of socioeconomic background. Structured programs of all sorts are more likely to enroll children from relatively well-to-do families, particularly programs that cost money and were sponsored by private organizations. Once the composition of the programs is taken into account, gains due to participation were not significant. Insofar as there are different outcomes, structured summer programs tend to promote the achievement of the most advantaged children to a greater extent than the achievement of low-income children. The differences are not great, but they are consistent for programs of many different types. Overnight camps and day camps, Little League and athletic lessons, music and dance classes, all present a similar pattern of effects. If the children in the program gained more than might be expected by chance, the reason was largely the propensity for the program or activity to enroll a disproportionate number of high-income children. Irrespective of the program content or composition, gains accrued primarily to the children who were most advantaged at the outset. Perhaps the structure of voluntary programs is sufficiently similar irrespective of curriculum to produce common patterns; perhaps children who dislike school do not respond well to any structured program. The conclusion would seem to be that programs and activities like those available to disadvantaged children in Atlanta are not likely to increase achievement. This conclusion must be qualified by the fact that attendance at any particular program is inversely related to attendance at some other program. Time is to some degree a zero-sum commodity; participation in particular programs rules out substantial involvement in other activities.

Although these conclusions do not brook much optimism about the potential of structured summer programs for increasing the achievement of poor pupils, the analysis revealed a large number of interactions between attendance and program effects. The logistics of attending, the location of programs, and the degree to which opportunities for participating differ by socioeconomic status suggest that these factors should be included in a policy analysis of outcomes. For poor children, the location of the program is a substantially more important determinant of attending than it is for children from high-status families. The distance to a library is more predictive of use among poor children, and library use does encourage reading. The relative cost of programs is a substantially more important factor among poor children than among the relatively advantaged. Such differences are crucial in assessing the impact of educational policies on children, and they are frequently overlooked in assessments of the outcomes. Equally, policy options tend to be narrowly defined in terms of both structure and desired outcomes. Broadening the conception of the role of public institutions in providing services and educational opportunities for children would necessarily include efforts to allow children similar experiences, even if such programs promoted an even greater degree of achievement for advantaged pupils.

If one poses the question of which activities contributed to the differential summer learning of high-income children, the answer is that most did. Each of the activities that seemed to influence achievement tended to attract and benefit children from relatively advantaged backgrounds more than children of the poor. Some activities seemed not to differentiate children by income level, such as the time spent playing at home, playing with friends, doing chores around the house, or playing alone. The amount of time spent in such activities is similar irrespective of socioeconomic level of families; it is also unrelated to cognitive growth during the summer.

Unstructured activities generally, such as vacations, trips, and other uses of leisure time that do not involve organized group activities, are quite differential with respect to background. Those that encourage differential summer learning, independent of socioeconomic status, seem likely to reflect a large number of unmeasured differences among families in socialization practices, values, or attitudes that are imperfectly correlated with socioeconomic status. For example, having a bicycle and visiting friends or relatives alone during the summer had consistent significant effects on summer achievement, when background was controlled. Equally, children attending a program further from home tended to benefit disproportionately from participation. Interpreting such effects literally obviously is illegitimate, since it would imply that buying a child a bicycle or sending him or her on a solitary trip would increase achievement. A more reasonable explanation is that such measures are indices of important differences among families that are not well specified by family income, parental education, or household size. Such factors could be characterized as a proxy for directed resources, or the willingness of a family to invest in children. The argument is that the actual amount of family resources available is imperfectly related to the underlying causal factor that influences achievement; a family that is child-centered and supportive of children's activities may spend additional funds on children irrespective of the total family income.

Equally, both taking a trip alone and having one's own source of transportation might reflect the degree of independence accorded to children. Perhaps such factors are behavioral indicators of a more general attitude toward childrearing that encourages the achievement of children. There is substantial support in the literature on socialization for the contention that parental values regarding independence differentiate families by socioeconomic level; such values may exert an independent influence on achievement levels as well.

Both interpretations have a common theme. There seem to be differences among families that influence the achievement of children but are not perfectly measured by socioeconomic status alone. The indicators of such differences in the present study are somewhat crude but suggestive. Bloom (1964) cites evidence that process variables, including attitudes toward education and the quality of parent-child interactions, are more important determinants of intelligence than family status variables taken alone. Several studies of stratification have posited a home environment variable operating independent of socioeconomic status, in order to explain the similarity of brothers' achievement that cannot be attributed to common class origins (Blau & Duncan, 1967; Jencks *et al.*, 1972).

A major conclusion of my analysis is that the role of families in the achievement process is ubiquitous; few educational outcomes can be unequivocally disassociated from parental influences. I have endeavored to specify possible causal mechanisms for this influence; however, my basic findings suggest that the linkages between school and family are intricate and complex.

In intellectual inquiry, attempting to find a rigorous answer to a particular question often forces one to acknowledge the limitations of asking the question in that way at all. In each chapter, the central issue posed was the degree to which public institutions and programs contribute to the cognitive growth of children, independent of family. Such a question assumes that disaggregating the effects of background and schooling is an important and a solvable problem. Yet, as we have seen, activities and programs reinforce rather than overcome the effect of family background.

In retrospect, the formulation of the problem that seems more correct was eloquently expressed by Davis and Havighurst (1946): "The pivotal meaning of social class to students of human development is that it defines and systematizes different learning environments for children of different classes [p. 698]." Perhaps the most fruitful task is to specify the mechanisms through which such influence takes place and to structure educational programs or activities so as to involve parents in the learning process of their children. This perspective seems more likely to lead to significant increments of knowledge about educational outcomes than is an attempt to separate effects, distinguishing the private and public spheres, with no effort to understand how the two interact in the lives of children.

APPENDIX A
A Primer on Test Score Construction and the Metrics of Learning

How much do children learn during the summer relative to the school year? The answer depends fundamentally on our ability to assess cognitive growth. The purpose of this appendix is to enumerate and explicate the assumptions implicit in utilizing standardized achievement tests to study learning. Since the bulk of this monograph has relied exclusively on these measures, it seems essential to examine the construction and measurement properties of these tests in some detail.[1]

In popular parlance, the term *achievement* connotes both a given level of performance and the process of attaining such a level. Tests of achievement, however, measure only the former. Standardized achievement tests, much like all tests of ability, are constructed to yield reliable measures of relative academic performance at a single point in time. Tests are normed relative to a population of children; they thus embody an age or grade-specific reference point, rather than a temporal one. The purpose of tests is to assess the performance of individuals relative to their peers, not relative to their own past performance.

The conventional critique of standardized tests as measures of educational outcomes is that they encompass too narrow a range of important skills and aptitudes, that they include many culturally biased items which handicap all but the white middle class, and that they are not particularly useful to teachers. Few educators have been trained to interpret test results correctly; their use for individual diagnosis or placement is a frequently cited abuse. The broad social consequences of testing have also been viewed with foreboding, and a number of commentators have expressed concern that standardized tests will replace all other methods and criteria for educational evaluation. Since norm-referenced tests are readily available and relatively easy to administer and quantify, they offer a seductively simple technique for complying with evaluation guidelines. Educational reports have increasingly relied on standardized measures, often presented with little or no analysis as an alternative to the more time-consuming process of setting goals and discussing how best to improve programs (Dyer, 1971; Friedenberg, 1969; Hoffmann, 1962; Lennon, 1971; Levine, 1976; Meier, 1973; Nash & Agne, 1972; Rivlin, 1971).

Analysts and critics have seldom recognized that standardized tests were not constructed to measure learning or cognitive growth. There is a long-standing division in psychology between test theory and learning theory. The former has been primarily concerned with the precise

[1] Portions of the argument to be presented in this appendix appeared in a different form in an article entitled "Education, Evaluation, and the Metrics of Learning," in *Journal for Teaching and Learning*, 1976, *2*, 2–16.

estimation of an individual's relative ability, and the latter has concentrated on the assessment of learning rates in experimental situations. Although psychometricians have noted with regret that two separate scientific disciplines exist with little contact (Cronbach, 1957), no consensus has yet emerged on the measurement of learning and change. Studies have consistently documented quite low correlations between ability levels and the rate of learning among children (Anderson, 1939; Atkinson & Paulson, 1972; Bloom, 1964; Cotton & Harris, 1973; Fleishman, 1965; Woodrow, 1946; Zeaman & House, 1967). Achievement tests are generally considered less heritable, and hence more unstable, than intelligence tests (Jensen, 1967), yet longitudinal comparisons reveal a substantial amount of stability over time. The techniques employed in the construction of achievement tests are similar to those used in developing other measures of ability. Achievement tests are routinely validated by comparing scores with measures of IQ. Ability tests are not designed to measure change; instead, concerted efforts are made to reduce the "contaminating" effects of development or age (Kohs, 1923).

The conceptual models and methodological assumptions employed in constructing both ability and achievement tests are similar to those used in a variety of forms of personality assessment in psychology. The model is adopted directly from the physical sciences, and textbooks abound with analogies between measuring heat and measuring intelligence. It is asserted that a construct exists that determines behavior, but that it is *not* directly measurable. The construct, whether self-esteem, anxiety, or intelligence, is presumed to inhere in individuals as a behavioral predisposition or an innate trait. The theoretical construct is related to observable behavior through epistemic (Torgerson, 1958) or semantic definitions (Lord & Novick, 1968). A variable is considered an indicator of the construct if the expected value varies systematically with respect to the construct. A variable is considered a measure if and only if the expected value of the indicator increases monotonically with respect to the construct. Achievement test scores are therefore valid measures of the latent, unobserved construct achievement if they increase monotonically with respect to increases in the construct.

Viewed in this manner, the intellectual problem is reduced to issues of measurement and validation. In assessing achievement, the problem is selecting the set of items that provide the best mapping from test scores to the construct achievement, or equivalently, that best differentiate persons having more or less of the postulated construct. The methods used in test construction are largely dictated by this conceptual framework. Pragmatic considerations predominate, rather than any theory of achievement or learning. Measures are compared in terms of face validity or predictive validity, since construct validity is considerably harder to demonstrate. To assess the empirical tools that result, it will be necessary to review briefly the specific methods employed in test construction and to discuss some rudimentary principles of measurement theory.

TEST CONSTRUCTION

The methods used in constructing standardized achievement tests differ from the methods that might be employed to construct a measure of learning primarily in the criteria used for selecting particular items. First, achievement is viewed as a trait that distinguishes individuals; the objective is to select items that consistently and reliably rank individuals in terms of the relative amount of achievement they possess. Although a stable rank ordering of individuals is not a necessary outcome of item selection, in practice it is difficult to distinguish between change and unreliability, between real learning and errors of measurement.

Second, items to be used on a sequential series of tests do not overlap. Each test to be administered to the same group of children at different points in time constitutes a unique set of questions. The rationale is that if the posttest consisted of material identical to that presented on the pretest, children might do better because of practice effects. The assumption is that if a child looks up an answer he or she did not know, such learning is illegitimate. Each item represents a host of skills or information, rather than an important piece of knowledge in its own right. Items are assigned to particular tests in order to generate equivalent forms, rather than identical ones. One must, therefore, assume that each form measures achievement with equal validity and reliability; in practice, this usually amounts to taking the test manufacturer's word for it.

Third, items are included because they cover a broad range of material an average student in a typical school at a particular grade might be expected to know. Since the tests are created with a national clientele in mind, the questions do not, and perhaps cannot, reflect what is taught or learned in any particular classroom. These procedures ensure that the tests are likely to measure general ability and aptitude levels more accurately than either specific skills or material unique to a particular curriculum.[2]

[2] The impetus for criterion-referenced tests stems from such issues. Teachers have

Fourth, the items are selected that best differentiate high- and low-scoring pupils on each test. This is justified as a way of refining the measure and increasing the predictive power of each item. It results, however, in selecting the most highly intercorrelated subset of items, which probably measure a common factor. Imagine, for example, that some skill is uniquely and universally learned in the fifth grade—let us say fractions. Imagine that at the beginning of the school year, not one child is able to multiply two fractions; but at the end of the year 90% can do so when the problem is clearly phrased. One might conclude that a considerable amount of actual learning, at least of fractions, had occurred. Yet items that clearly measured this skill would be unlikely to be included on a test of arithmetic achievement, since the items would have very little discriminatory power at either the beginning or the end of the year. The questions chosen would be those that could be answered by many bright students at the outset of the fifth grade without benefit of instruction, or those that were sufficiently ambiguous or tricky that a large number of students missed them at the end of the year despite their knowledge. Although it is doubtful that many skills are so directly related to a single year of school, the point is that the criterior of maximizing individual variability operates against including items that either very few or very many students have learned.

Fifth, although achievement tests typically consist of multiple choice questions, the scoring is based on a binary model. Correct responses are summed; incorrect answers receive no credit. The probability of a correct response, which is a measure of the relative difficulty of items, varies considerably. Children often make incorrect choices systematically (Sigel, 1963); disregarding the patterning of choices entails a loss of information. Several authors have suggested that empirical weighting schemes be used to account for differential difficulty (Davis & Fifer, 1959; Hendrikson, 1971; Reilly & Jackson, 1973: Sabers & White, 1969), such as weighting by expert judges (Patnaik & Traub,

---

argued that standardized achievement tests are infrequently updated and therefore do not correspond to advances in teaching methods and curricula and that they impose a relatively conservative bias on educational goals and objectives by limiting assessment to the skills taught in traditional, highly structured programs. The opposition of alternative schools to testing is based on the perception that any nationally standardized test will narrow educational goals and provide little incentive for innovation (Sartore, 1975). Schools have changed more than tests in the 1970s, but updating standardized tests or substituting alternative measures does not seem to me to be an answer. Tests that do not permit comparisons between classrooms and schools are of little use for educational accountability; tests that do will have a tendency to dictate educational goals and subject matter, thereby reducing teacher autonomy.

1973), or that tests be designed that would require students to indicate their degree of confidence in the chosen response (Hambleton, Roberts, & Traub, 1970). Test manufacturers have not yet incorporated such suggestions into the scoring procedures, nor, to my knowledge, have these criticisms been linked to issues of measurement.

Sixth, many achievement tests are timed; this also is a means of increasing the amount of individual variation in scores, since not all students can complete the test. To some degree, the total score is determined by how quickly one can read and respond, rather than by how much one knows. Being able to work rapidly may well be a virtue, but it is not one many educators claim to teach.

Such considerations are problematic to an unknown degree. Most secondary analysis cannot adequately document item selection procedures or precisely assess the validity of measures. My presumption is that the high relationship between measures of achievement and measures of aptitude or ability stems from the similar concepts and techniques used in the construction of the two kinds of tests. It has been argued that the use of tests designed to maximize individual differences is unwarranted for studying the effects of schools or educational programs (Carver, 1975). Yet standardized tests remain the most reliable existing measure for assessing academic performance relative to other students, at a single point in time. Tests measure a variety of skills neither taught nor learned in schools, yet such skills are seemingly quite predictive of later attainments. The question that remains central to the present study is the degree to which it is possible to infer learning or cognitive growth from changes in relative position as measured by standardized tests. This question requires an examination of the measurement properties of tests.

LEVELS OF MEASUREMENT

The most important set of assumptions required to utilize standardized achievement tests to assess learning are assumptions about levels of measurement and the interval properties of tests. Numerical relations must be established in order to infer cognitive growth based on test scores; without interval measurement or an ordered-metric scale (Coombs, 1964), growth rates in time or across groups of students cannot be compared. A level of measurement is distinguished by the relative complexity of the mathematical system with which it is associated; theoretically, levels admit only certain kinds of transformations and operations that may be performed meaningfully within the system (Guilford, 1956; Kerlinger, 1964; Krantz, Luce, & Suppes, 1971; Lord & Novick, 1968; Stevens, 1951; Torgerson, 1958). A brief review of basic issues seems in order.

First, nominal measurement is used only to classify objects into mutually exclusive subsets. In order to do so, one must be able to apply the identity and the equality functions.

$$a = b \text{ or } a \neq b \ldots$$
$$\text{If } a = b \text{ and } b = c, \text{ then } \ldots$$

Strictly speaking, a nominal category is not measurement, since a numerical label can be attached only for the purpose of classification, without any assumption of order or magnitude.

The second level of measurement presupposes nominal properties but in addition allows observations to be ordered in varying degrees of magnitude. Ordinal measurement requires the transitivity postulate, or

$$\text{If} \quad a > b \quad \text{and} \quad b > c, \quad \text{then} \quad a > c.$$

The capacity to order subsets meaningfully is thus permitted, and any scale that yields the same relative order is an admissible transformation.

Third, interval measurement is the level commonly used in achievement tests or other tests of ability. An interval scale specifies a linear mapping between behavioral elements and the real number system; the zero point is arbitrary, but intervals are equal at different points on the scale. The importance of interval measurement is that the scales can be subject to any linear transformation, such as addition or subtraction. It is possible, for example, to assert that the difference between students scoring 6 and 8 is equal to the difference between students scoring 2 and 4, or 4 and 6. Interval measurement permits the comparison of students at different points on a scale, or the comparison of differing amounts of gain in two or more time intervals.

A fourth level of measurement, ratio scales, allows for multiplicative transformations because the existence of a zero point is fixed. A ratio scale permits the assertion that the achievement of a student scoring 20 is twice as great as the achievement of a student scoring 10, for example. Ratio measurement is seldom used for psychometric tests, although the literature abounds with assertions that, strictly speaking, assume it.

Achievement tests, just like other tests of ability, are constructed to provide ordinal relationships, but scaled to yield intervals. The rationale for imputing intervals is distributional. It is assumed that the true values of the underlying construct are normally distributed. The observed scores are scaled in terms of population percentiles, and scores are normalized by imposing the standard scores corresponding to the percentiles attained. The distributional assumption is convenient and is justified by the empirical fit of measures and ultimately by the central limit theorem. Several authors have suggested the desirability of assuming some other distribution (Gardner, 1947, 1950), or of choosing scales so as to provide additivity of effects (Abelson & Tukey, 1959). Acceptance of such proposals, however, has not been widespread.

Learning, then, must be defined as a change in the relative position of students. If every individual in a norming sample improved his score by a constant amount, no change would be detected in relative position, nor could it be inferred that learning had occurred as distinct from the relative difficulty of the test instrument. Imagine that a highly reliable pretest is given and Student A scores 50, while Student B scores 40 points. The question of whether A's achievement is higher than B's is one of the validity and the reliability of the test. Imagine that a parallel form posttest is administered, under identical conditions, and that Students A and B scored 55 and 50, respectively. How would one determine which student learned the most? The interval (50, 55) is less than the interval (40, 50); if the intervals were equal, the intuitive response that Student B had learned the most would be correct, provided the assumptions about test validity and reliability were correct.

On most achievement tests, however, the answer is at best equivocal, even if the test instrument is perfect. Test manufacturers provide a series of transformations for raw scores, which allow the classroom teacher or the social scientist to compare scores in terms of standardized values, stanines or percentiles, and grade equivalent scores.[3] These measures are not linear transformations of each other, nor do they necessarily yield the same answer to the question which student learned the most across different metrics. In the above example, if the gains of Students A and B are compared in terms of normalized standard scores, the gains are about equal, at approximately 1.4 standard deviations. In grade equivalent scores, however, the intuitive answer is reversed; Student A will be shown to have gained 1.3 years, while Student B gained only .8 of a year. Such disparities are not uncommon in comparing metrics of achievement.

To understand better the difficulties inherent in using test scores to infer cognitive growth, it is useful to compare test results across the several available metrics. Table A.1 presents the mean scores and gains

[3] Grade equivalent scores are constructed by interpolating points between median scores obtained by students at particular grade levels.

TABLE A.1
Comparisons of Scores and Gains in the Intermediate Battery, Metropolitan Achievement Subtest, Word Knowledge, for the Fifth and Sixth Grades. National Averages and Scores by Grade for Atlanta: 1970–1972[a]

Sample and scores on word knowledge	Test scores				Gains		
	Fifth grade		Sixth grade		School year (5.1–5.8)	Summer (5.1–6.1)	School year (6.1–6.8)
	Fall	Spring	Fall	Spring			
National sample							
Raw score	25.0	31.5	33.8	37.7	6.5	2.3	3.9
Standard score	44.0	48.0	49.5	52.7	4.0	1.5	3.2
Grade equivalent	5.1	5.8	6.1	6.8	.7	.3	.7
Atlanta: White students only, sixth grade							
Raw score	22.9	28.4	30.7	n.a.	5.5	2.3	
Standard score	42.8	46.0	47.8	n.a.	3.2	1.8	
Grade equivalent	4.89	5.74	5.82	n.a.	.85	.08	
Atlanta: White students only, seventh grade							
Raw score	23.9	30.3	32.2	35.8	6.4	1.9	3.6
Standard score	43.2	47.2	48.1	50.6	4.0	.9	2.5
Grade equivalent	4.91	5.99	6.16	6.90	1.08	.17	.74

[a]The means presented above are taken from the test history files and include 592 sixth-grade students with matched test score data at the relevant three points in time, and 513 seventh-grade students with the same four test periods. Since a number of the students did not have completed survey forms, the *N*s are not the same as those reported in substantive chapters.

on the Metropolitan Achievement Test in vocabulary skills, for the nation and for the white students in the Atlanta sample, by three common metrics. The raw scores are the actual number of correct responses given by the students at each point in time. Standard scores are normalized and then scaled to have a mean of 50 and a standard deviation of 10 points. The national averages are those reported by the test publisher, Harcourt Brace Jovanovich. The scores used in the example are from the most reliable subtest, word knowledge; the Atlanta sample consists of only those students for whom there were test scores at each time period. The time periods encompass the complete intermediate battery, which is normed for fifth- and sixth-grade students. The four tests within each battery are reported to be equivalent forms; that is, the expected number of correct responses is the same for each form. Grade equivalents are those provided by the publisher; the grade equivalent scores are customarily interpreted as months, even though they are constructed by dividing the school year in tenths, rather than twelfths, and assuming a gain of a single month during the summer. The national averages for grade equivalent scores are arbitrary, since they are determined by the date of the test administration and constructed to reflect the scores achieved at each date.

The question posed at the outset, "How much do children learn during the summer?", can most effectively be addressed with reference to Table A.1. The first point is that neither raw scores nor standardized scores are linear with respect to time. The average child in the nation as well as in Atlanta added more words to his or her vocabulary during the fifth grade than the sixth. The differential is substantial in raw scores, and somewhat less dramatic in a comparison of standard scores. If one wishes to infer that the summer represents a certain portion of the annual increment in learning, the answer would clearly depend on which grade was chosen for comparison, the fifth or the sixth.

Second, the three metrics do not have equal intervals during particular time periods. Raw scores in both the nation and the sixth-grade Atlanta sample increased by 2.3 words during the summer. A gain of 2.3 words translates into a larger gain in grade equivalent units in the nation than in Atlanta, however; the difference is just the opposite in standardized score gains,with the return to 2.3 words being greater in Atlanta. This occurs because the distance between two positions on a scale is not constant across metrics. Five additional words of vocabulary are worth progressively more in grade equivalent units the higher up the scale one moves. In Table A.1, the means for the Atlanta sample are computed by summing the individual scores, which have first been converted to standardized scores and grade equivalents. If the raw score means were transformed into grade equivalents *after* averaging, the scores and gains would be systematically lower. From the Metropolitan Achievement Test manual, raw scores of 23.9, 30.3, 32.2, and 35.8 are equivalent to the scores earned at grades 4.9, 5.7, 5.8, and 6.3. The discrepancy between these scores and those reported in Table A.1 is due to unequal intervals at different points on the scale.

Such results are not peculiar to this subtest, nor do they reflect a ceiling or threshold in the test score data. The rate of learning vocabulary words does not fall off dramatically between the fifth and sixth grades—or rather if it does, then so does every other skill assessed by the Metropolitan battery. For each subtest, the rate of learning tends to decline with movement through time, or to a higher position on the scale, on each metric except grade equivalent scores. If one were to construct a learning curve to fit the raw data, one would posit a decelerating function and interpolate between points that were scaled to give equal intervals in terms of time. The resulting values would be artificial, would vary considerably across subtests, and would have an unknown relationship to actual learning. Such procedures would, however, approximate those used in constructing grade equivalent scores at present.

The major difficulty in utilizing grade equivalent scores for research is that they are relatively crude, derived measures that involve an unknown amount of smoothing prior to publication. Grade equivalents assume a single learning curve, based on the median scores of successive cohorts; tests have not been normed on a longitudinal sample. To the degree that grade cohorts are noncomparable, in terms of background or ability, additional error is introduced. Grade equivalent scores are typically extrapolated below and beyond the norming population, a practice that invites error at both extremes of the scale. Grade equivalents have one major advantage over other measures, however; they link each score earned to the point in time at which the average child attained that level of achievement. The metric can be interpreted longitudinally, not just relative to other students.

The nonlinear relationship between grade equivalent scores and other measures of achievement has been noted in the literature (Coleman & Karweit, 1972; Fennessey, 1973). Campbell (1971) has described the fan spread phenomenon of grade equivalent scores through time. Coleman *et al.* (1966) documented the fact that although the gap between black and white children was very nearly constant across grades at one standard deviation, the gap in grade equivalents widened substantially at each successive grade. McNemar (1942) discussed the problem of interval measurement in an investigation of the potential for using the Stanford–Binet to study learning; however, the argument was not extended to other tests of either ability or achievement. Most work on both test theory and evaluation seems to have ignored the problem altogether, or to have arrived at no consensus about what measures of change are most reasonable, if any (Coleman & Karweit, 1972; Cronbach & Furby, 1970; Lindquist & Hieronymus, 1964; Tallmadge & Horst, 1974). Although many analysts have argued that better measurement tools are essential for evaluating educational outcomes, such recommendations are often appended to many pages of carefully documented null findings; it is not surprising that the issue of measurement has attracted little attention.

The implications of unequal intervals are enormous for both educational evaluation and research on learning. Ordinal measurement, strictly speaking, cannot be used to assess rates of learning, since the true distance between two numerically equidistant points will not necessarily be constant at all points on the scale. This fact confounds efforts to determine whether the amount learned in the sixth grade is less, more, or equal to the amount learned in the preceding year. Equally, without assumptions about which metric is correct, it is not possible to surmise whether rich or poor children learned the most during any particular time period. As I have shown elsewhere (Heyns, 1976a), raw scores indicate that children from high-status families appear to learn less than children from low-status backgrounds, while the relative improvement measured in grade equivalents consistently favors the advantaged children. Such patterns are often interpreted as regression effects; however, a more plausible explanation of the patterns can be deduced by comparing metrics in a longitudinal context.

The most common tactic for dealing with ordinal measurement in test scores is to assume that the true scores are normally distributed. Such an assumption is tantamount to imposing a metric, based on the proportions of students falling about the mean. The assumption that ability is normally distributed has not been seriously disputed since Galton published *Hereditary Genius* in 1869. Galton believed that physical characteristics and natural abilities were distributed according to the Gaussian law of error (cf. Mincer, 1958; Staehle, 1943). The theoretical standing of this assumption has with time very nearly attained the status of a scientific truth. Empirically, the observed distribution of correct responses tends to fit a normal curve quite closely, on a large number of tests; moreover, this distribution has numerous advantages for statistical analysis.

Grade equivalent scores are not normally distributed, however. The observed distribution is instead very close to log normal, with a substantial skew to the right. One plausible explanation for the discrepancy between raw scores and grade equivalents is suggested by the empirical relationship between them. The items on an achievement test are not equally difficult, yet the score attained is the sum of correct responses. Each item on a well-constructed test is presumed to be a mini-test of the students' total skill; however, since questions vary considerably in difficulty, each correct answer cannot reflect an equal amount of knowledge. It seems likely that the amount of information or skill reflected in the tenth item a student gets correct is less than the amount needed to answer the twentieth question correctly. The student who improves a score by five relatively easy items, at the lower end of the scale, would have learned less of whatever the test was measuring than the student who improved by 5 points on somewhat more difficult items. On a well-designed test the average student correctly answers slightly over half of the available questions, and virtually no one gets everything right. The more esoteric or abstruse the question, the more likely it seems that a correct response reflects a substantially greater body of general knowledge or ability than would be the case for an easier item. If above average scores represented progressively larger amounts of skill, one would expect them to be worth more in grade equivalent units; it would take longer for most students to achieve a given increment. If the learning process depicted by test scores consists of adding points on progressively more difficult questions, one would not expect the total number of correct responses to have a distribution mirroring that of the true scores on the construct achievement. The true distribution of ability or achievement should be skewed to the right, rather than being normal.

The implicit model of intelligence assumed by classical test theory is that measured ability is a constant, determined by true ability level and a random shock or disturbance. If the distribution of true ability were log normal, the causal process generating the distribution could be described by Gibrat's law of proportionate effect (Kalecki, 1945). That is, the strength of the disturbance is proportional to the score, rather than being independent of the level of achievement. A skewed distribution lends credence to the notion that a process is operating, that learning is cumulative and builds on previous knowledge, and that test scores tap a dimension of human learning rather than just reflecting an innate attribute, measured with a certain amount of error. A skewed distribution that becomes increasingly skewed, such as grade equivalent scores, suggests that learning is not a linear process, but might be better modeled as a logistic equation, similar to other equations representing learning (Hamblin *et al.*, 1971; Stevens & Savin, 1962). Such reasoning is, of course, highly speculative. In the absence of a widely accepted, empirically grounded theory of learning, it has the merit of at least being consistent with the evidence.[4]

[4] A theory of testing that claimed that the true distribution of achievement was log normal, rather than normal, might also contribute an interesting resolution to the long-standing debate about why ability and income have distinct forms (Staehle, 1943), as well as contributing to theoretical formulations about learning. For an interesting discussion of the analogies between distribution and process in the case of income, see Mincer (1958).

When issues of measurement are raised in intellectual circles the response is often boredom among older academics and shock among those somewhat younger. Standardized tests are among the most widely accepted and frequently used measures in social science and certainly are among the most reliable. Measures of differential ability have been described as "the most important technical contribution psychology has made to the guidance of human affairs [Cronbach, 1970, p. 197]." Yet tests were not designed to measure learning, and using them for research or evaluation in which the central questions involve change invites misinterpretations. The logic of ordinal measurement leads to the conclusion that a large number of distributions, from normal to highly skewed, are compatible with the observed ranking of students. Ordinal measurement allows any transformation that preserves the relative magnitude of scores; it can easily be shown that a host of transformations have this property, while wildly influencing the observed means. Ordinal measurement implies that an additive model cannot be compared to a number of multiplicative formulations, since it is possible to transform the scales to fit the observations without changing the order (Wilson, 1971). In its strongest terms, measurement theory implies that without equal intervals, the mathematical operations of addition and subtraction, much less multiplication and division, are meaningless and illegitimate. Such a stricture neatly rules out almost all statistical treatment of data (Anderson, 1961; Lord, 1953; Stevens, 1951).

The position taken in the present study is that the metric assumptions utilized should depend on the objectives. Insofar as the observed distributions yield distinct interpretations or implications for a model of learning, this should be documented. Although it is possible to fit a model to the data precisely, such a tactic implies that only prior scores influence present ones. Without an empirically validated theory of learning, test score data must necessarily remain descriptive; curve-fitting is an exercise in applied mathematics, rather than hypothesis-testing. The analytic rationale employed in this study is to utilize standardized raw scores for all regression analyses and to present grade equivalent scores for descriptive purposes as measures of the amount of learning. The subtest used, and the findings reported, are fairly robust with respect to test score metrics; however, I suspect that the definitive study of learning patterns over time must await the development of valid measures that are designed for the study of cognitive growth.

APPENDIX B
The Sampling Design and Data Collection Procedures

The purpose of this appendix is to outline the procedures utilized and the pitfalls encountered in the process of collecting the data. The initial section will detail the sampling and design issues and attempt to justify the various decisions made at particular junctures. Then I will turn to the testing program within the schools. Finally, the survey results will be assessed, in terms of both results and the assumptions imposed. Throughout the various stages of design, data collection, and analysis, the staff of the Atlanta public schools was enormously cooperative and willing to go to great lengths to further the aims of the study. Without such assistance from all levels, it is quite doubtful that the coordination of diverse data collection procedures would have been possible.[1]

The Atlanta public school system is a large and heterogeneous district, including 129 elementary schools and some 63,000 pupils in the fall of 1972. Initially, I planned to sample students in Grades 1–6 randomly within schools for the parental survey, and to utilize all of the available longitudinal test score data. This proved impractical for several reasons. During the spring of 1972, Atlanta voted to discontinue citywide testing, as of the fall of 1972; obviously, this decision seriously jeopardized the study. Since the planning for the parental survey and the data collection phase were well under way, the school board relented and agreed to support a limited amount of testing in a subsample of schools provided that the principals were willing. This decision, plus general considerations of cost and administrative efficiency, necessitated using schools as the sampling unit, rather than individuals.

In order to minimize the disruption caused by fall testing, it was necessary to limit both the sample of schools and the number of grades involved. Since the project was contingent on the approval of each and every principal in sample schools, it seemed advisable to restrict the number of schools to fewer than 50 and the number of grades to no more than 2 in order to increase the likelihood of cooperation and support. Limiting the composition of the sample to two grades ensured obtaining a sufficient number of students for whom both socioeconomic status and longitudinal data on testing were available. Ultimately, every principal asked agreed to cooperate, and the sample included all students enrolled in these schools.

Statewide testing in Georgia, which was intended to replace the biannual testing program given by the district, involved only fourth-

[1] Without the cooperation and encouragement of John Letson, then superintendent of schools, Jarvis Barnes, director of research and development, and Tom McConnell, director of the Atlanta public schools computer center, this study would not have been approved by the Board of Education, nor could the design and data collection have been so successfully implemented.

and eighth-grade pupils in the fall of each year. The Iowa Test of Basic Skills was used rather than the Metropolitan Achievement Tests. Including fourth-grade students in this study would have entailed an unconscionable amount of fall testing, so this grade cohort was eliminated. Metropolitan Achievement Tests for the fifth-grade students, were not available for the fall of 1971; since it seemed unwise to attempt a study of learning rates using test forms drawn from disparate instruments, the fifth grade was not included. For the primary grades (1–3), the testing procedures required teachers to handscore booklets rather than use the more reliable machine-readable forms. These factors dictated restricting the grade composition to students who were in the sixth or seventh grades in the fall of 1972.

A sample of schools was chosen, with the following basic objectives:

1. The total enrollment of the schools should yield a sample of approximately 4800 students, divided equally between the sixth and seventh grades; all students in the sample schools would be included in fall testing and in the parental survey.
2. The racial composition of the sample should be roughly balanced. This would involve disproportionate representation of majority–white schools, since the district enrolled nearly 72% black children.
3. The sample should be heterogeneous with respect to socioeconomic background; in order to ensure a sufficient number of children from advantaged and disadvantaged backgrounds, schools were stratified by socioeconomic level and race.

SAMPLING PROCEDURES

The total number of 129 schools was limited at the outset for administrative and practical reasons to 101 schools. Two elementary schools were strictly primary, with no students older than third grade. Two schools were middle schools with only seventh- and eighth-grade pupils. Eight schools had no seventh grade, and 7 schools had neither a sixth nor a seventh grade, presumably feeding into either a junior high school or a middle school. Two schools had no sixth grade because of shared space arrangements. Seven additional schools were eliminated from the target group because the assistant superintendent of research and development anticipated their closing prior to the fall of 1972. Two schools were eliminated because they had been used as sites for pretesting the survey instrument in June 1972.

The remaining 101 elementary schools were designated as the sample universe. These schools were then stratified by race and a crude measure of social class composition. The indicator of school socioeconomic status available was the proportion of students receiving a free lunch. This variable was dichotomized, with roughly half of the schools having 46% or more of the student body reportedly eligible for the free lunch program. Additionally, schools were divided by racial composition; white schools were defined as those in which less than half of the students registered were nonwhite. This schema produced the fourfold classification summarized in Table B.1.

The objective was to select approximately equal numbers of students from each of the cells shown in Table B.1. The number of schools actually chosen would depend on the average size of the schools within quadrants, and the corresponding number of students required to reach a target of 1200 students per cell. Schools were rank-ordered within quadrants by enrollment level, thus ensuring diversity in school size while permitting some control over the number of schools selected. Sampling probabilities were assigned to each school, based on the socioeconomic and racial composition; the objective was to select disproportionate numbers of schools located at the extremes of the distributions within cells.

The distribution of cumulative probabilities was divided into *N* equal intervals, where *N* was equal to the number of schools to be selected. By adding the interval length to a randomly selected entry point systematically, exactly *N* schools were selected. For example, in the upper right quadrant, the objective was to pick predominantly high socioeconomic

TABLE B.1
Composition of Atlanta Schools by Race and Percentage Paid or Free Lunch, Spring 1972[a]

Predominant race of schools	46%+ Free lunch (low SES)	54% Paid lunch (high SES)
Black (50%+)	44 schools enrolling 5941 students Grades 6–7	17 schools enrolling 2491 students Grades 6–7
White (50%+)	8 schools enrolling 1158 students Grades 6–7	32 schools enrolling 3247 students Grades 6–7

[a]The measure of school socioeconomic status available was the proportion of children eligible for free lunches; eligibility was determined, at least in theory, by family income and family size, and was limited to children who fell below the poverty line for urban areas.

status (SES) black schools. For each of the 17 schools in this quadrant, the product of the proportion black and the proportion of all lunches paid was computed. It was deemed necessary to select 10 schools to achieve a minimum of 1200 in the sample, since the mean size of the sixth and seventh grades combined was equal to 131 students. A table of random numbers was consulted for the starting point in the complete distribution of cumulative product terms. The next 9 schools were selected from the upper right quadrant by systematically adding the mean interval width to the point of entry and selecting the schools in which these probability values occurred.

In the example chosen, the 10 schools selected enrolled 1352 students in Grades 6 and 7. The mean proportion black was 93.5% compared to an average of 89.4% for the quadrant. The mean proportion paid lunch was 78.2% compared to 74.8% for the total group of 17 schools. The procedures yielded a sample that was more likely to be black and more likely to have paid lunches than the average of all high SES black schools in Atlanta.

In retrospect, the sampling design was an elegant solution to the administrative and intellectual requirements of the study. The small number of low-income white schools did not seem a serious problem since it was expected that the overall distribution by individual socioeconomic status would yield sufficient students for a comparison. The total sample of black students chosen by this procedure was larger than a perfectly balanced design would dictate; yet since it was assumed that completing interviews in the black community would be more difficult than in the white community, the sample seemed reasonable.

Initially, some consideration was given to other criteria for stratifying the sample. One might have wished equal numbers of stable schools, or of integrated schools, for purposes of control. The logic of doing so would have been to overrepresent schools most likely to have cases that could be matched by achievement across time. Additional integrated schools would have had to be selected to compensate for the sampling procedures, which tended to overrepresent segregated schools. In Atlanta, however, the stable schools were rarely integrated. To attempt stratifying by both conditions would merely balance their impact. To choose schools randomly without taking such differences into account seemed the wisest course. The procedures that were adopted tended to overrepresent both the stable and the most segregated elementary schools. Since the possibilities of selection were determined in advance, the possibility existed of weighting the selected schools to yield a sample representative of the universe. Since it was imperative to select schools during the early months of the study in order to provide sufficient lead time to plan and implement fall testing, simplified procedures seemed preferable.[2]

TESTING: FALL 1972

The sample of students selected for the study was, therefore, all pupils enrolled in 1 of the 42 sample schools as of September 1972. The Atlanta Public Schools Computer Center assumed the responsibility for providing student names, addresses, telephone numbers, and other information on the sample children to the survey team and principal investigator. The information was provided in two forms:

1. A listing by school and grade of each child enrolled in a sample school, followed by the student's identification number, address, telephone number, and race.
2. The same information on gummed labels that could be affixed to the survey instrument. A total of 4866 students were enrolled in the sample schools as of September 1972, and these students constituted the basic sample.

The racial composition of this sample was unbalanced, relative to the study design. Fully 65% of the children were black, when the expected proportion was barely 55%. This imbalance was largely the result of substantial "white flight" in the face of an incipient integration crisis, plus a concerted effort by black parents to integrate the remaining all-white schools in Atlanta. The integration policy in operation at the time of the study design was voluntary and being challenged in the courts. The school system ultimately lost the case early in the fall of 1972, and a more extensive, nonvoluntary program was negotiated. The voluntary program allowed any student in the Atlanta system to transfer from a school in which he or she was in the racial majority to one in which he or she was in the racial minority, provided the new school had sufficient space and the student could arrange for personal transportation. During the summer of 1972, extensive and organized efforts were made by the black community to use this voluntary "Majority-to-Minority" plan to promote racial balance. The all-white schools, located primarily in the affluent northeastern sections of Atlanta, were prime

[2] The sampling techniques were adopted in consultation with Reuben Cohen, the staff of Response Analysis Corporation in Princeton, New Jersey, and the staff of the Center for Educational Policy Research, Harvard University, in Cambridge, Massachusetts.

targets for organized car pools and minibusing. These efforts did achieve more racial balance within Atlanta, but they tended to unbalance the sample population markedly. The reduced size of the white sample was an unforeseen difficulty; however, it was possible to obtain a data base sufficient for the purposes of the study.

The testing program, which took place during the first week of October 1972, was conducted in the sixth and seventh grades in each of the 42 sample schools. The objective was to replicate as far as possible the normal conditions that had pertained during test administration in previous years. Each of the principals was contacted, informed of the objectives of the study, and asked to cooperate with both the testing and the parental survey. Since Atlanta had engaged in an extensive testing program for several years, only new teachers needed to be trained, and the individual school principals or a designated test coordinator in the school agreed to assume this task. The test booklets and answer sheets were distributed and collected with the assistance of the Instructional Services Division of the Atlanta public schools. The testing was concentrated in two successive mornings and followed the guidelines recommended by the test manufacturer. Answer sheets were preprinted with students names and identification numbers to reduce errors in transcribing. Teachers checked all forms for extraneous marks or invalid responses prior to returning them to the computer center. All forms were processed on IBM scanning equipment, and raw scores were tabulated for each student on each subtest. With the assistance of the programming staff, the test score data were merged with all available information on the child, including all prior tests that had been taken in any school in the Atlanta system. The capacity to trace children even though they had enrolled in another school within Atlanta significantly reduced sample loss due to short-distance residential mobility. The merged data constituted the complete test history and student information file on every child in the 42 sample schools for the complete time they had been in any school in Atlanta. In addition, the student information file coded the school number in which the achievement test was taken at each date, thus allowing comparison of those students who had moved within Atlanta and those who had not. The student information file was the source of exact age of the child, attendance data during the year 1971–1972, IQ, and demographic data on families that were useful for comparing the responses of parents to the survey. Test score data were merged for all students completing the Metropolitan Achievement batteries, even if they had enrolled in a sample school after the date the survey addresses were printed. Data on a total of 4908 children were compiled in this manner and formed one of the two central data files for this study. The test history file included all information for the 4866 students involved in the parental survey, even though some of the children were absent or had moved prior to the fall testing date in 1972. A total of 63 students had moved into one of the sample school districts in Atlanta and took the fall tests, and 21 students did not take the tests. Table B.2 presents the summary, by grade and race, of the Atlanta sample and the degree of attrition due to incomplete survey results or to incomplete matching test histories over time. The total proportion of students in either grade or racial category with results from three phases of consecutive testing as well as a completed parental survey was never below 60% for any category, a figure that compares favorably with other longitudinal studies. Equally important, attrition was random with respect to both race and grade, and seemed to be due in equal numbers to incomplete test histories or to incomplete survey results.

THE SURVEY

Designing and pretesting of the survey instrument proceeded concurrently with the plans for fall testing. The basic objective was to obtain detailed and specific information from the parents of sample children regarding both socioeconomic background and summer activities. The survey instrument included questions regarding both the demographic composition of the household and the education, occupations, and family income of respondents, framed in such a way as to replicate census queries. The questions regarding summer activities of children covered a large range, including vacations, camps, day programs, summer school experiences, and other structured programs and activities, as well as questions on the unstructured, informal activities of children. The questionnaire used in the study is reproduced in Appendix C.

Since the majority of respondents were to be interviewed by telephone, the length of the questionnaire was set to take an average of 20 minutes. Personal interviews were mandated for households in which there were no telephones and for a random sample of nonrespondents. The personal interview protocols were identical to those used in the telephone interviews, and no attempt was made to collect more detailed information. A total of 500 personal interviews were contracted for, to be assigned randomly and in equal numbers from two groups: (1) those without telephones and (2) those who could not be reached by telephone or who refused to be interviewed. The survey instrument was pretested

TABLE B.2
Summary of Metropolitan Achievement Test Scores and Student Information Files Available for Forty-Two Sample Schools, Attrition by Source for Each Grade and Racial Group

Grade and race	Total number of cases enrolled in schools and taking MATs, Fall 1972	Total not included in survey sample, or not available for interviews	Total merged cases with some test data and parental interview	Percentage of students enrolled with survey data	Total cases with test scores, three points in time	Percentage of those enrolled
Sixth grade	*2474*	*523*	*1951*	*78.9*	*1493*	*60.3*
Black	1698	363	1335	78.6	1023	60.2
White	776	160	616	79.4	470	60.6
Seventh grade	*2434*	*480*	*1954*	*80.3*	*1485*	*61.0*
Black	1570	332	1238	78.9	959	61.1
White	864	148	716	82.9	526	60.9
Total	*4908*	*1003*	*3905*	*79.6*	*2978*	*60.7*
Black	3268	695	2573	78.7	1982	60.6
White	1640	308	1332	81.2	996	60.7

in June on a small, racially mixed sample of parents of sixth-grade students in Atlanta.[3] The final questionnaire was printed and precoded by the survey staff.

The survey was scheduled to begin in the first week of October and to last for 3 weeks. A letter was sent to every parent in the survey sample the week prior to being contacted by the interviewer. The letters were signed by the principal of each child's school, explaining the purposes of the survey and asking for the parents' cooperation.[4]

During the fall of 1972, a considerable amount of upheaval and political discontent overtook the Atlanta schools. The central administration lost the court case on the constitutionality of the extant voluntary integration plan, and large-scale busing was viewed as imminent. The Atlanta school system was under attack from civil rights groups and from both black and white parents. The criticism was directed primarily at the central administration, however, and rarely toward the local school. Parents tended to regard their schools and school staff as on their side. In retrospect, it was fortuitous that the letters were not sent from the central administration, and that they were seen as largely independent of the prevalent conflicts.

In general, the concern with integration did not seem to affect the survey adversely; in fact, the salience of school politics and issues may have increased parents' desires to discuss the educational experiences and summer activities of their children. Several of the interviewers reported that the respondents were disappointed that the survey did not explicitly ask about their feelings and attitudes toward integration. Quite a few parents insisted on augmenting the basic interview with unsolicited opinions on the subject.

The original survey design called for matching respondents and interviewers by race for both telephone and personal contacts; because of the large excess of black parents in the sample, this was not possible in every case. The large majority of telephone interviews and all personals were completed by interviewers of the same race as the respondent. The most problematic interviews were, somewhat surprisingly, those in

[3] Marilyn F. Jackson Associates supplied two experienced interviewers for the pretesting; the candid comments of these interviewers as well as the tabulations from the pretest were enormously helpful in delineating the particular questions that were irrelevant or unclear to Atlanta parents and in tailoring questions on sponsorship of activities to the actual availability of programs in Atlanta.

[4] The letters were quite important to large numbers of parents, and they substantially increased response rates and level of cooperation. These letters were sent out in waves corresponding to the order of interviewing; the Atlanta City Schools Print Shop was responsible for duplicating the letters.

affluent all-white areas; these interviews were typically conducted by only the older, more experienced interviewers. All telephone interviews were initiated from a centralized telephone bank and were under constant supervision.

The sample of names provided by the school system was initially divided into two groups—those with and those without telephones. The pool of students for whom no current telephone number was listed on school records was then assigned for personal interviews. However, in the first week of the survey substantial problems arose. The telephone listings on central records were almost invariably inaccurate. More than half of the students in the first set of schools could not be reached at the numbers provided. Two tactics were adopted: First, telephone directories by street were used to correct listings; and, second, individual schools were contacted directly for corrections and current information. The individual elementary school proved to be a much more productive source of corrected numbers, and each school was ultimately asked to check the entire list of telephone numbers for the sixth and seventh grades. This procedure was quite time-consuming and depended heavily on the cooperation of school officials. Several principals asked teachers for updated telephone numbers, and in at least one instance a child was summoned from class.

The policies with respect to the assignment of personal interviews were also changed. The corrected telephone listings indicated a much smaller proportion of persons without a telephone, thereby increasing that interview pool considerably. Since the original contract had specified three callbacks, and since a large number of wrong numbers were found, some adjustments were deemed essential. As there were many more black respondents than anticipated, a random sample of 10% of the cases were pulled, and no attempts were made to reach these parents. Second, all wrong numbers were regarded as "no attempt" and corrected; updated listings were considered as part of the actual sample. This meant that far more attempts were made for each respondent than had been originally contracted; a considerably higher response rate resulted, however.

The correction procedure unearthed another dilemma for the survey team. A substantial number of children had at least one sibling in the sample pool, attending the same school. The solution was to match children by household addresses and common surnames so that a single interview could be attempted. Interviews with parents who had more than one child or boarder in either the sixth or seventh grade were paired to minimize both the length of the interview and the likelihood of exhausting parental goodwill. The quesionnaires were administered in random order of siblings; these interviews were carefully assigned to the more experienced interviewers. The procedure was to administer the entire survey form for the first child and to ask only the questions on summer programs and activities for the second child, excluding demographic data and family socioeconomic status. Although some difficulty had been anticipated because of the longer interview schedule, the response rates were similar to those obtained in single-child interviews. The final sample of students included 263 seventh graders and 298 sixth graders who had a sibling or boarder living in the same household and part of the sample.

The telephone interviews that were not completed after four or more attempts to a corrected telephone number were placed in the personal interview pool. A random half of these students were assigned for personal interviews, including multiple interviews for siblings as in the telephone contacts. The total response rates were high, for both telephone and personal interviews. Excluding 115 households in which the family had recently moved, the proportion of completed telephone interviews was 80.6% of the sample attempted. For personal interviews, which included the most difficult and evasive cases, the total proportion of completed interviews was 81.6% of the assigned pool, excluding families that had moved. Taken together, the total proportion of interviews completed from the pool was 87.3% of the sample. Over two-thirds of the personal interviews were with nonrespondents from the telephone phase of the interviewing.

The completion rates for the interviews were thus higher than expected in every respect. Table B.3 presents the summary of noncompleted interviews and reasons for attrition by race and provides a comparison with the subsample of respondents merged with the test history file. The relative proportions compare favorably with the best longitudinal studies of students available.

Comparisons between those students who could or could not be matched over time are suggestive of the changes experienced by the Atlanta student body during the interim, although such differences are not comparable to differential rates of attrition in a longitudinal study. The nonmatched sample was almost equally distributed between white and black students, despite the increase in the proportion of blacks in the sample schools. Black entrants to the sample tended more often to come from Atlanta schools and therefore matching data were available. White students, however, tended to move outside the system limits, and not to be in the sample.

The preferred respondent for every interview was the child's mother. In all, 89.1% of the completed interviews were with the female head of

TABLE B.3
Noncompleted Survey Interviews for Children Reported as Enrolled in a Sample School, September 1972, by Race and Reason for Noncompletion

Reason for noncompletion	White	Black	Total
Total noncompleted	*308*	*695*	*1003*
Interview not attempted	*2*	*367*	*369*
New enrollees	2	40	42
Withheld	0	327	327
Not reached by telephone	*477*	*495*	*972*
No phone number available	143	128	271
Moved, phone disconnected	67	48	115
Not reached after four attempts	238	310	548
Refused	29	9	38
Assigned to personal interview pool and attempted	*245*	*254*	*499*
Completed	147	191	338
Moved	58	27	85
Not home after three attempts	40	36	76

the household; the remaining were almost invariably with the male head. The response rates differed slightly between male and female respondents, in that the mothers were more likely to know what activities the child had engaged in during the summer and were more likely to complete an interview once begun. The differences were small, however, and not of substantial importance. Nor did the presence of a sibling in the sample alter the relationships observed in any other variable examined, once socioeconomic status was controlled. Families that had two or more children in the sample were likely to have larger households and to be poorer than average. However, no evidence of differential validity or reliability of responses to paired interview schedules was discovered.

The single most difficult item on the questionnaire, as anticipated, was family income. The response rate for this question was lower than for any other. The proportion of black parents responding to the income question was 77% and 80% for the sixth and seventh grades, respectively, and for all white parents in the matched sample was 74% and 78%. In general, there was an inverse relationship between socioeconomic status and response rates on family income. Response rates by grade and race for the matched sample are given in Appendix F, Table F.8.

The Atlanta sample schools were differentially affected by the integration crisis and were not equally responsive to the study or to the continuation of testing. Biases introduced by differential cooperation of school personnel were anticipated, however, in no case were they severe. Differences in response rates and sampling by school were explored in a variety of ways. The rate of completion compared to the enrollment level by race and grade was quite stable across schools, averaging approximately 60%. The differences among schools in attrition of the sample resulted primarily from differences in the stability of enrollment, and were not related to cooperation with the study. The distribution of tests available for the fall of 1972 is quite close to the enrollment figures presented, and the slight variance observed could easily be due to differential absenteeism. Moreover, the observed differences in response rates by school are consistent both for racial groups and across grade levels. It is unlikely that the characteristics of schools influenced either the attrition rates or the patterns of nonresponse.

In conclusion, this appendix has reviewed the data collection procedures and described the sample in considerable detail. The schools and children selected were not a random sample of any particular universe, including that of the Atlanta city schools. The objectives of the study were not to limit generalizations to Atlanta, but rather to explore the relative achievement of children from different socioeconomic levels during the school year and the summer. The social context was defined by the schools, programs, and people residing in one urban location; the implications, however, are more broadly defined. Throughout this report, references are made to characteristics of Atlanta that might affect the results. Until the study is replicated with a larger sample, the conclusions must remain tentative. However, it seems fair to assume that the students are representative of black and white American children from diverse backgrounds and that the results do not depend on the particular school system or city involved.

APPENDIX C
The Survey Questionnaire

SURVEY OF ATLANTA PARENTS

CALL RECORD, TELEPHONE SURVEY

NO TELEPHONE: X

CALL #	DATE	TIME	INTERVIEWER	CODE FOR RESULT*
1				
2				
3				
4				

TOTAL NUMBER OF CALLS: 0 1 2 3 4

*CODE FOR RESULT OF CALL:

1 - Interview completed
2 - Not at home
3 - Too busy. Call back at:_______________
4 - Refused
5 - Partially complete (terminated)
6 - Disconnected; wrong number
7 - Moved
8 - Other. Explain on bottom of this page.

CALL RECORD, HOME INTERVIEW

CALL #	DATE	TIME	INTERVIEWER	CODE FOR RESULT*
1				
2				
3				

TOTAL NUMBER OF CALLS: 0 1 2 3

ATLANTA SCHOOLS

Hello, my name is _________ and I'm working on a survey sponsored by the Atlanta school system.

ASK TO SPEAK TO MOTHER OR FEMALE GUARDIAN OF CHILD NAMED ON LABEL. IF MOTHER OR FEMALE GUARDIAN IS NOT AT HOME, INTERVIEW FATHER OR MALE GUARDIAN.

VERIFY CHILD'S NAME, SCHOOL, AND GRADE. THEN EXPLAIN THAT THE INTERVIEW WILL REFER TO THAT CHILD ONLY.

TIME BEGAN:__________

Person Number	1. What is the name of each person living in your household?	2. How is this person related to (sample child)? 1 Father or male guardian; 2 Mother or female guardian; 3 Sibling; 4 Grandparent; 5 Other relative; 6 Nonrelative; 7 Sample child	3. Age (Actual number)	4. Sex 1 Male; 2 Female	5. Marital status 1 Married; 2 Separated, divorced; 3 Widowed; 4 Never married
1	____________________	1 2 3 4 5 6 7	_____	1 2	1 2 3 4
2	____________________	1 2 3 4 5 6 7	_____	1 2	1 2 3 4
3	____________________	1 2 3 4 5 6 7	_____	1 2	1 2 3 4
4	____________________	1 2 3 4 5 6 7	_____	1 2	1 2 3 4
5	____________________	1 2 3 4 5 6 7	_____	1 2	1 2 3 4
6	____________________	1 2 3 4 5 6 7	_____	1 2	1 2 3 4
7	____________________	1 2 3 4 5 6 7	_____	1 2	1 2 3 4
8	____________________	1 2 3 4 5 6 7	_____	1 2	1 2 3 4
9	____________________	1 2 3 4 5 6 7	_____	1 2	1 2 3 4
10	____________________	1 2 3 4 5 6 7	_____	1 2	1 2 3 4

INTERVIEWER: FILL IN

6. Respondent is person number: _________

7. There are how many persons living in this household? ________

To begin with, we would like to ask about your family's summer activities, especially those (child's name) was involved in this last year.

8a. Did (child's name) stay at least one night with relatives or friends?

1 YES
2 NO → SKIP TO Q. 9a

IF "YES" ON Q. 8a, ASK:

8b. Who did (child's name) stay with? Any others?

13

Q. 8b	Q. 8c	Q. 8d	Q. 8e
1 GRANDPARENTS	1 ALONE 2 MOTHER 3 FATHER 4 BOTH PARENTS 5 SIBLINGS 6 OTHER	1 2 DAYS OR LESS 2 3 DAYS - 1 WEEK 3 8 DAYS - 2 WEEKS 4 15 DAYS - 4 WEEKS 5 1 MONTH OR MORE 6 DON'T KNOW	1 IN ATLANTA 2 OUTSIDE ATLANTA (URBAN) 3 OUTSIDE ATLANTA (SUBURBAN) 4 OUTSIDE ATLANTA (RURAL)
2 AUNT OR UNCLE	1 ALONE 2 MOTHER 3 FATHER 4 BOTH PARENTS 5 SIBLINGS 6 OTHER	1 2 DAYS OR LESS 2 3 DAYS - 1 WEEK 3 8 DAYS - 2 WEEKS 4 15 DAYS - 4 WEEKS 5 1 MONTH OR MORE 6 DON'T KNOW	1 IN ATLANTA 2 OUTSIDE ATLANTA (URBAN) 3 OUTSIDE ATLANTA (SUBURBAN) 4 OUTSIDE ATLANTA (RURAL)
3 FRIENDS	1 ALONE 2 MOTHER 3 FATHER 4 BOTH PARENTS 5 SIBLINGS 6 OTHER	1 2 DAYS OR LESS 2 3 DAYS - 1 WEEK 3 8 DAYS - 2 WEEKS 4 15 DAYS - 4 WEEKS 5 1 MONTH OR MORE 6 DON'T KNOW	1 IN ATLANTA 2 OUTSIDE ATLANTA (URBAN) 3 OUTSIDE ATLANTA (SUBURBAN) 4 OUTSIDE ATLANTA (RURAL)
4 OTHER (SPECIFY RELATIONSHIP): ____________	1 ALONE 2 MOTHER 3 FATHER 4 BOTH PARENTS 5 SIBLINGS 6 OTHER	1 2 DAYS OR LESS 2 3 DAYS - 1 WEEK 3 8 DAYS - 2 WEEKS 4 15 DAYS - 4 WEEKS 5 1 MONTH OR MORE 6 DON'T KNOW	1 IN ATLANTA 2 OUTSIDE ATLANTA (URBAN) 3 OUTSIDE ATLANTA (SUBURBAN) 4 OUTSIDE ATLANTA (RURAL)
5 OTHER (SPECIFY RELATIONSHIP): ____________	1 ALONE 2 MOTHER 3 FATHER 4 BOTH PARENTS 5 SIBLINGS 6 OTHER	1 2 DAYS OR LESS 2 3 DAYS - 1 WEEK 3 8 DAYS - 2 WEEKS 4 15 DAYS - 4 WEEKS 5 1 MONTH OR MORE 6 DON'T KNOW	1 IN ATLANTA 2 OUTSIDE ATLANTA (URBAN) 3 OUTSIDE ATLANTA (SUBURBAN) 4 OUTSIDE ATLANTA (RURAL)

ASK FOR EACH PERSON STAYED WITH ON Q. 8b:

8c. Did (child's name) visit (person stayed with) alone, or did someone else go with him/her? (IF SOMEONE ELSE, ASK: Who was that?)

8d. How many days or weeks did (child's name) visit with (person stayed with)?

8e. Do they live in Atlanta, or in another community? (IF OTHER COMMUNITY, ASK: Is that an urban, suburban, or rural area?)

9a. Did your family take any (other) vacation together outside of Atlanta this past summer? (PROBE: Who went?)

1 YES: → 1 MOTHER
2 FATHER
3 CHILD
4 OTHER CHILDREN
5 OTHER FAMILY MEMBER: ________

____

2 NO → SKIP TO Q. 10a

IF "YES" ON Q. 9a, ASK:

9b. How long was the vacation?

1 ONE OR MORE WEEKENDS
2 THREE DAYS - ONE WEEK
3 BETWEEN ONE - TWO WEEKS
4 BETWEEN TWO - FOUR WEEKS
5 MORE THAN A MONTH
6 DON'T KNOW

10a. Did (child's name) attend summer school or take part in a program run by the public schools last summer? (PROBE FOR SUMMER SCHOOL OR OTHER PROGRAM.)

1 YES, SUMMER SCHOOL
2 YES, OTHER PROGRAM
3 NO → SKIP TO Q. 11a

IF "YES" ON Q. 10a, ASK:

10b. Which school did (child's name) go to for the summer program?

____

____

10c. Was this mainly an academic program -- that is, one in which (child's name) studied regular school subjects?

1 YES (Which subjects) → 1 READING/ENGLISH/SPELLING
2 ARITHMETIC
3 FOREIGN LANGUAGE
4 MUSIC/ART
5 SCIENCE
6 SOCIAL STUDIES/HISTORY
7 TYPING/CLERICAL
8 PHYS ED/GYM
9 SEWING/HOME ECONOMICS
0 OTHER: ________________ (specify)
X DON'T KNOW

2 NO (What activities were offered? What kinds of things did child do?) → 1 SPORTS, GAMES
2 ARTS AND CRAFTS
3 SAW PLAYS, MOVIES, SHOWS
4 OTHER: ________________ (specify)
5 DON'T KNOW

3 DON'T KNOW

10d. Whose idea was it that (child's name) should go to the summer school program?

1 PARENT
2 TEACHER
3 CHILD'S OWN IDEA
4 OTHER: ________________ (specify)
5 DON'T KNOW

10e. On the average, how many hours per day

1 2 OR LESS
2 3 - 4
3 5 - 6
4 7 - 8
5 DON'T KNOW

10f. How many weeks did the child go?

1 LESS THAN ONE
2 ONE
3 TWO
4 THREE
5 FOUR TO FIVE
6 SIX
7 SEVEN OR MORE
8 DON'T KNOW

11a. Did (child's name) attend a daily summer program, such as a day camp or other organized activity? That is, one where he or she did not sleep overnight.

1 YES
2 NO → SKIP TO Q. 12a

IF "YES" ON Q. 11a, ASK:

11b. Was this a day camp, or was it some other program?

1 DAY CAMP
2 OTHER PROGRAM
3 DON'T KNOW

11c. Was the program run by a church, the Scouts, or who?

1 CHURCH
2 SCOUTS
3 CITY PARK DEPARTMENT
4 YMCA OR YWCA
5 COMMUNITY CENTER
6 BOYS/GIRLS CLUB
7 PRIVATE GROUP
8 OTHER: ____________________
(specify)
9 DON'T KNOW

11d. Whose idea was it that (child's name) attend the day camp or program?

1 MOTHER
2 FATHER
3 OTHER ADULT: ____________________
(specify)
4 CHILD'S IDEA
5 NOT SURE

11e. What kinds of activities did (child's name) take part in at this program? What kinds of things did (child) do in this program?

1 SPORTS, GAMES
2 ARTS AND CRAFTS
3 SAW PLAYS, MOVIES, SHOWS
4 OTHER: ____________________
(specify)
5 DON'T KNOW

11f. On the average, how many hours per day did (child's name) spend at this program?

1 TWO OR LESS
2 THREE - FOUR
3 FIVE - SIX
4 SEVEN - EIGHT
5 DON'T KNOW

11g. How many weeks did (child's name) go to this day program?

1 LESS THAN ONE
2 ONE
3 TWO
4 THREE
5 FOUR TO FIVE
6 SIX
7 SEVEN OR MORE
8 DON'T KNOW

11h. How was the day program financed? That is, did you pay, or was it free for everyone, did the child have a scholarship, or what? (IF SCHOLARSHIP, PROBE: Was that a partial or a complete scholarship?)

1 FREE FOR EVERYONE
2 PARTIAL SCHOLARSHIP
3 COMPLETE SCHOLARSHIP
4 PARENTS PAID FEES
5 OTHER: ____________________
(specify)
6 DON'T KNOW

12a. Did (child's name) go away to a camp where he/she stayed overnight?

1 YES
2 NO → SKIP TO Q. 13a

IF "YES" ON Q. 12a, ASK:

12b. Was this a private camp or sponsored by a group, or what?

1 PRIVATE

2 GROUP → 1 FEDERAL (MODEL CITIES)
2 CITY/COUNTY
3 SCOUTS
4 YMCA OR YWCA
5 GIRLS/BOYS CLUB
6 OTHER: ________________ (specify)

3 OTHER: ________________ (specify)

4 NOT SURE

12c. Whose idea was it that (child's name) go away to camp?

1 MOTHER
2 FATHER
3 OTHER ADULT: ________________ (specify)
4 CHILD'S IDEA
5 NOT SURE

12d. How many weeks did (child's name) spend there?

1 LESS THAN ONE
2 ONE
3 TWO
4 THREE
5 FOUR TO FIVE
6 SIX
7 SEVEN OR MORE
8 DON'T KNOW

12e. How was this camp financed? That is, did you pay, or was it free for everyone, did the child have a scholarship, or what? (IF SCHOLARSHIP, PROBE: Was that a partial or a complete scholarship?)

1 FREE FOR EVERYONE
2 PARTIAL SCHOLARSHIP
3 COMPLETE SCHOLARSHIP
4 PARENTS PAID FEES
5 OTHER: ________________ (specify)
6 DON'T KNOW

13a. Besides these programs we just talked about, were there any other things that (child's name) participated in last summer? (PROBE: Any music or sports lessons, Little League or other organized sports?)

1 YES
2 NO → SKIP TO Q. 14

IF "YES" ON Q. 13a, ASK:

13b. What were those activities?

1 LITTLE LEAGUE OR OTHER ORGANIZED TEAM SPORTS
2 MUSIC LESSONS
3 SPORTS LESSONS
4 DANCING OR DANCE LESSONS
5 ORGANIZED TRIPS
6 SCOUTING ACTIVITIES
7 REGULAR CHURCH ACTIVITIES (NOT SUNDAY SERVICES) SUCH AS CHOIR
8 OTHER: ____________________ (specify)
9 DON'T KNOW

ASK FOR EACH ACTIVITY CIRCLED IN Q. 13b:

13c. What organization sponsored this activity?

Activity: ____________________

Q. 13c	Q. 13d	Q. 13e
1 CHURCH	1 2 OR LESS	1 LESS THAN ONE
2 CITY/COUNTY	2 3 - 4	2 ONE
3 NEIGHBORHOOD CLUBS	3 5 - 6	3 TWO
4 SCOUTS	4 7 - 8	4 THREE
5 YMCA OR YWCA	5 DON'T KNOW	5 FOUR TO FIVE
6 GIRLS/BOYS CLUB		6 SIX
7 COMMUNITY CENTER		7 SEVEN OR MORE
8 EXTENDED DAY PROGRAM		8 ALL SUMMER
9 PARENTS PAID		9 DON'T KNOW
0 OTHER: ________		
X NOT SURE		

Activity: ____________________

Q. 13c	Q. 13d	Q. 13e
1 CHURCH	1 2 OR LESS	1 LESS THAN ONE
2 CITY/COUNTY	2 3 - 4	2 ONE
3 NEIGHBORHOOD CLUBS	3 5 - 6	3 TWO
4 SCOUTS	4 7 - 8	4 THREE
5 YMCA OR YWCA	5 DON'T KNOW	5 FOUR TO FIVE
6 GIRLS/BOYS CLUB		6 SIX
7 COMMUNITY CENTER		7 SEVEN OR MORE
8 EXTENDED DAY PROGRAM		8 ALL SUMMER
9 PARENTS PAID		9 DON'T KNOW
0 OTHER: ________		
X NOT SURE		

Activity: ____________________

Q. 13c	Q. 13d	Q. 13e
1 CHURCH	1 2 OR LESS	1 LESS THAN ONE
2 CITY/COUNTY	2 3 - 4	2 ONE
3 NEIGHBORHOOD CLUBS	3 5 - 6	3 TWO
4 SCOUTS	4 7 - 8	4 THREE
5 YMCA OR YWCA	5 DON'T KNOW	5 FOUR TO FIVE
6 GIRLS/BOYS CLUB		6 SIX
7 COMMUNITY CENTER		7 SEVEN OR MORE
8 EXTENDED DAY PROGRAM		8 ALL SUMMER
9 PARENTS PAID		9 DON'T KNOW
0 OTHER: ________		
X NOT SURE		

13d. How many hours per day did (child's name) spend at these activities?

13e. How many weeks did the child go to these activities during the summer?

We are also interested in the kinds of things (child's name) did around home during the summer, when not in school or visiting.

14. Tell me, on a typical day during last summer, how much time would you say (child's name) spent watching TV? (RECORD ANSWER, GO ON TO NEXT AREA. WHEN YOU HAVE ASKED ABOUT EACH AREA, PROBE: Are there any other kinds of things (child) did on a typical day last summer? How much time did (child) spend doing this?)

	None	Less than 1 hour	1-2 hours	2-3 hours	3-5 hours	6+ hours	Not applicable
a. Watching TV	1	2	3	4	5	6	7
b. Playing with friends or brothers or sisters at your home	1	2	3	4	5	6	7
c. Playing with friends outside or at their homes	1	2	3	4	5	6	7
d. Reading	1	2	3	4	5	6	7
e. Working on hobbies	1	2	3	4	5	6	7
f. Playing alone	1	2	3	4	5	6	7
g. Other (specify):							
______________________	1	2	3	4	5	6	7
______________________	1	2	3	4	5	6	7

15. About how many books did (child's name) read over the summer?

1 NONE
2 1 - 5
3 5 - 10
4 OVER 10
5 DON'T KNOW

16a. Is there a park or playground near your home?

1 YES
2 NO → SKIP TO Q. 17

IF "YES" ON Q. 16a, ASK:

16b. How many blocks away from your home would you say it is?

1 LESS THAN ONE BLOCK
2 1 - 2 BLOCKS
3 3 - 4 BLOCKS
4 5 - 6 BLOCKS
5 7 OR MORE BLOCKS
6 DON'T KNOW

16c. What kind of park or playground is this, a school playground, a city park, or what?

1 SCHOOL PLAYGROUND
2 CITY PARK
3 OTHER: ______________________

____
(specify)

4 DON'T KNOW

16d. How often during the summer would you say (child's name) played there?

1 DAILY OR ALMOST DAILY
2 2 OR 3 TIMES A WEEK
3 ONCE A WEEK OR LESS
4 2 OR 3 TIMES A MONTH
5 ONCE A MONTH OR LESS
6 HARDLY EVER
7 DON'T KNOW

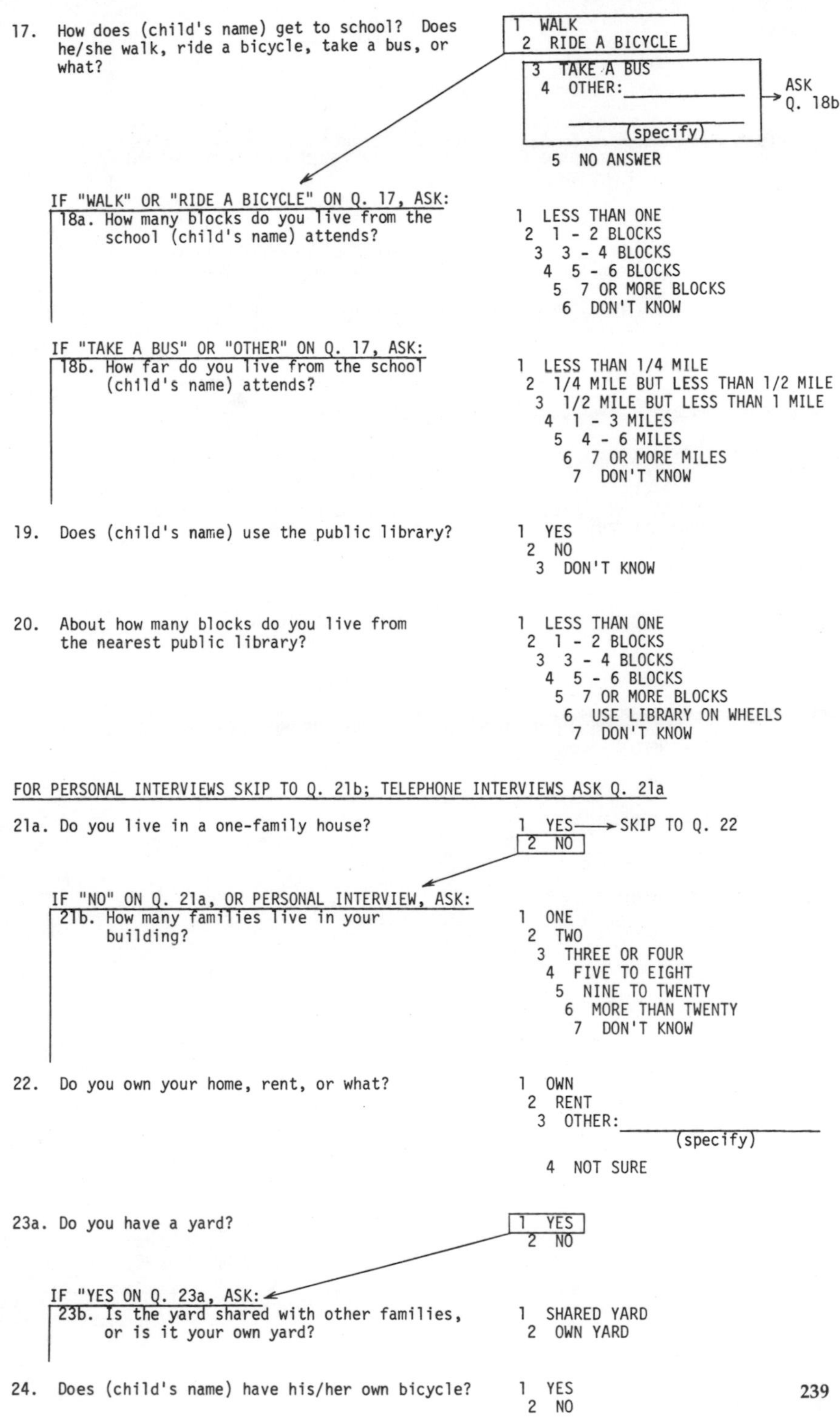

17. How does (child's name) get to school? Does he/she walk, ride a bicycle, take a bus, or what?

1 WALK
2 RIDE A BICYCLE
3 TAKE A BUS
4 OTHER: ______ (specify) → ASK Q. 18b
5 NO ANSWER

IF "WALK" OR "RIDE A BICYCLE" ON Q. 17, ASK:

18a. How many blocks do you live from the school (child's name) attends?

1 LESS THAN ONE
2 1 - 2 BLOCKS
3 3 - 4 BLOCKS
4 5 - 6 BLOCKS
5 7 OR MORE BLOCKS
6 DON'T KNOW

IF "TAKE A BUS" OR "OTHER" ON Q. 17, ASK:

18b. How far do you live from the school (child's name) attends?

1 LESS THAN 1/4 MILE
2 1/4 MILE BUT LESS THAN 1/2 MILE
3 1/2 MILE BUT LESS THAN 1 MILE
4 1 - 3 MILES
5 4 - 6 MILES
6 7 OR MORE MILES
7 DON'T KNOW

19. Does (child's name) use the public library?

1 YES
2 NO
3 DON'T KNOW

20. About how many blocks do you live from the nearest public library?

1 LESS THAN ONE
2 1 - 2 BLOCKS
3 3 - 4 BLOCKS
4 5 - 6 BLOCKS
5 7 OR MORE BLOCKS
6 USE LIBRARY ON WHEELS
7 DON'T KNOW

FOR PERSONAL INTERVIEWS SKIP TO Q. 21b; TELEPHONE INTERVIEWS ASK Q. 21a

21a. Do you live in a one-family house?

1 YES → SKIP TO Q. 22
2 NO

IF "NO" ON Q. 21a, OR PERSONAL INTERVIEW, ASK:

21b. How many families live in your building?

1 ONE
2 TWO
3 THREE OR FOUR
4 FIVE TO EIGHT
5 NINE TO TWENTY
6 MORE THAN TWENTY
7 DON'T KNOW

22. Do you own your home, rent, or what?

1 OWN
2 RENT
3 OTHER: ______ (specify)
4 NOT SURE

23a. Do you have a yard?

1 YES
2 NO

IF "YES ON Q. 23a, ASK:

23b. Is the yard shared with other families, or is it your own yard?

1 SHARED YARD
2 OWN YARD

24. Does (child's name) have his/her own bicycle?

1 YES
2 NO

PART II

25. Please tell me what state (you were/child's father was) born in. (INTERVIEWER: ASK ABOUT CHILD'S FATHER OR MALE GUARDIAN IF LIVING IN HOUSEHOLD. IF NOT, ASK ABOUT MALE HEAD OF HOUSEHOLD.)

    1 GEORGIA

    2 SOUTH ATLANTIC - not Georgia (includes: District of Columbia, Florida, North Carolina, South Carolina, Virginia, West Virginia)

    3 MIDDLE ATLANTIC AND NEW ENGLAND - (includes: Connecticut, Delaware, Maryland, New Jersey, New York, Pennsylvania, Maine, Massachusetts, New Hampshire, Rhode Island, Vermont)

    4 NORTH CENTRAL - (includes: Illinois, Indiana, Iowa, Kansas, Michigan, Minnesota, Missouri, Nebraska, North Dakota, Ohio, South Dakota, Wisconsin)

    5 SOUTH CENTRAL - (includes: Alabama, Arkansas, Kentucky, Louisiana, Mississippi, Oklahoma, Tennessee, Texas)

    6 MOUNTAIN AND PACIFIC - (includes: Alaska, Arizona, California, Colorado, Hawaii, Idaho, Montana, Nevada, New Mexico, Oregon, Utah, Washington, Wyoming)

    7 FOREIGN BORN

    8 NO FATHER, MALE GUARDIAN, OR MALE HEAD OF HOUSEHOLD PRESENT

    9 DON'T KNOW

26. And where (were you/was child's mother) born? (INTERVIEWER: ASK ABOUT CHILD'S MOTHER OR FEMALE GUARDIAN IF LIVING IN HOUSEHOLD. IF NOT, ASK ABOUT FEMALE HEAD OF HOUSEHOLD.)

    1 GEORGIA

    2 SOUTH ATLANTIC

    3 MIDDLE ATLANTIC AND NEW ENGLAND

    4 NORTH CENTRAL

    5 SOUTH CENTRAL

    6 MOUNTAIN AND PACIFIC

    7 FOREIGN BORN

    8 NO MOTHER, FEMALE GUARDIAN, OR FEMALE HEAD OF HOUSEHOLD PRESENT

    9 DON'T KNOW

INTERVIEWER: REFER BACK TO Q. 2. IF THERE IS A MALE HEAD OF HOUSEHOLD, ASK Q. 27 - 29.

27. What is the highest grade which the male head of household completed?

    1 8TH GRADE OR LESS
    2 HIGH SCHOOL INCOMPLETE
    3 HIGH SCHOOL GRADUATE
    4 COLLEGE INCOMPLETE
    5 COLLEGE GRADUATE
    6 GRADUATE WORK
    7 OTHER: ____________________

    ____________________ (specify)

    8 DON'T KNOW

28a. Does the male head of the household work at a job for pay?

1 YES
2 NO → SKIP TO Q. 29

IF "YES" ON Q. 28a, ASK:

28b. What is the job? What exactly does he do?

____

____

28c. What kind of business is that in? (What do they make or do?)

____

____

PLEASE CIRCLE:

1 OWNS BUSINESS: HIRES OTHERS
2 SELF-EMPLOYED: HIRES NOBODY
3 WORKS FOR SOMEONE ELSE
4 OTHER:____________________

28d. Is that full time or part time work?

1 FULL TIME
2 PART TIME
3 DON'T KNOW

28e. Does he work all year long, or only part of the year?

1 ALL YEAR
2 PART OF THE YEAR
3 DON'T KNOW

IF "NO" ON Q. 28a, ASK:

29. Is he looking for a job, retired, or what?

1 LOOKING FOR A JOB
2 RETIRED
3 OTHER:________________

____
(specify)

4 DON'T KNOW

INTERVIEWER NOTE: FOR QUESTIONS 30 - 32, ASK ABOUT CHILD'S MOTHER OR FEMALE GUARDIAN, IF LIVING IN HOUSEHOLD. IF NOT, ASK ABOUT FEMALE HEAD OF HOUSEHOLD.

30. What is the highest grade which (you/child's mother) completed in school?

1 8TH GRADE OR LESS
2 HIGH SCHOOL INCOMPLETE
3 HIGH SCHOOL GRADUATE
4 COLLEGE INCOMPLETE
5 COLLEGE GRADUATE
6 GRADUATE WORK
7 OTHER:________________

____
(specify)

8 DON'T KNOW

31a. Do you (Does child's mother) now work at a job for pay?

1 YES
2 NO → SKIP TO Q. 32

IF "YES" ON Q. 31a, ASK:

31b. What is your job? What exactly do you do?

____

____

31c. What kind of business is that in? (What do they make or do?)

____

____

PLEASE CIRCLE:

1 OWNS BUSINESS: HIRES OTHERS
2 SELF-EMPLOYED: HIRES NOBODY
3 WORKS FOR SOMEONE ELSE
4 OTHER:____________________

31d. Is that full time or part time work?

1 FULL TIME
2 PART TIME
3 DON'T KNOW

31e. Do you work all year long, or only part of the year?

1 ALL YEAR
2 PART OF THE YEAR
3 DON'T KNOW

IF "NO" ON Q. 31a, ASK:

32. Are you a full time housewife, looking for a job, retired, or what?

1 FULL TIME HOUSEWIFE
2 LOOKING FOR A JOB
3 RETIRED
4 OTHER:____________________

____

5 DON'T KNOW

33. How many people living in your household work at jobs for pay?

1 NONE
2 ONE
3 TWO
4 THREE OR MORE
5 NOT SURE

34. Considering all sources of income and all salaries, what was the approximate total family income for 1971, before deductions for taxes or anything? (IF "DON'T KNOW" PROBE BY ASKING EACH RANGE INDIVIDUALLY: Well, would you say it was . . .?)

1 LESS THAN $4,000 ($0 - $76 A WEEK)
2 $4,000 - $5,999 ($76 - $115 A WEEK)
3 $6,000 - $8,999 ($115 - $173 A WEEK)
4 $9,000 - $11,999 ($173 - $230 A WEEK)
5 $12,000 - $14,999 ($230 - $288 A WEEK)
6 $15,000 AND OVER ($288 AND OVER)
7 DON'T KNOW
8 REFUSED

35a. Did you or anyone in your household have any income from the County, State, or Federal Government?

1 YES
2 NO
3 NOT SURE

IF "YES" ON Q. 35a, ASK:

35b. What kind of income was that?

1 SOCIAL SECURITY
2 WELFARE
3 AFDC
4 UNEMPLOYMENT COMPENSATION
5 V.A. PENSION
6 OTHER:________________

____
(specify)

7 DON'T KNOW

THANK YOU VERY MUCH FOR YOUR TIME

INTERVIEWER: RECORD:

TIME (END OF INTERVIEW):____________

TOTAL INTERVIEW TIME:________ MINUTES

INTERVIEWER'S NAME:____

DATE:____________

APPENDIX D

Notes on Achievement and the Transmission of Parental Status through Education: Comparisons by Grade Level

The correlations reported in this study differ in magnitude from those found in the literature. The correlations between IQ and achievement are quite high, although they are not unlike those reported for longitudinal data in the literature on psychological testing. I have also argued that academic achievement and learning are substantially more dependent on the socioeconomic status of parents than previously believed. The models of cognitive growth elaborated thus controvert much of the conventional social science wisdom on the subject. This appendix is intended both to compare the results in Atlanta with those from several other studies and to justify these conclusions. I will argue that the bulk of the evidence supports the contention that the effects of parental status on early achievement are larger than sociologists have typically inferred and that these effects decline during the course of schooling.

Considering the importance of the questions concerning the relationship between academic achievement and socioeconomic status, surprisingly few studies have gathered data on large or representative samples of children. To my knowledge, no study exists giving longitudinal data on the relationship between IQ or ability and parental socioeconomic status for the duration of schooling. Following psychologists, sociologists have implicitly assumed that this relationship is stable over the life cycle. Correlations observed among high school students are therefore taken to represent the relationship, rather than a measure taken near the completion of schooling. This has resulted in a consensus among quantitative sociologists that ability exerts a substantial unmediated influence on schooling, and through schooling, on later attainments; and that ability is only modestly related to socioeconomic background. As Duncan (1968a) states: "In view of the loose relationship between IQ and social class . . . it seems that . . . ability measured by intelligence tests . . . serves as a kind of springboard, launching many men into achievements removing them considerable distances from the social class of their birth [p. 11]."

Throughout this book, I have argued that schooling exerts a substantial unmediated influence on achievement and that schooling attenuates a fairly strong relationship between socioeconomic status and ability observed in the elementary grades. Definitive studies of change or the patterning of change in the relationship between class background and academic achievement have been hampered by the paucity of longitudinal data and by disciplinary boundaries. The conclusion widely accepted among sociologists, summarized by the quotation taken from Duncan, depends exclusively on fragmentary data and problematic samples. The most extensive and careful data sets have been collected for high school students; most analysts have projected such results into the early grades by making assumptions about the stability of test scores and the observed relationship between socioeconomic status and ability among high school students. Models of the socioeconomic attainment process, such as that described by Duncan (1968a) pertain to mature cohorts. Duncan's model, for example, is relevant to men aged 25–34; the correlations at issue, those between academic achievement and origin status, are either imputed from the model or drawn from high school samples. Duncan disregards substantially larger relationships found in studies of younger children. These studies are typically based on small unrepresentative samples of students, in sharp contrast to the best sociological surveys. The coding and analysis of social class variables are seldom systematic, and the relationships appear to be quite different than those reported for older students. Since sociologists have traditionally been most concerned with schooling as a mechanism for the intergenerational transmission of status, they have tended to ignore data collected on younger students, particularly when the results were not strictly comparable, when the samples were questionable, and when the pattern of results appeared inexplicable. Duncan (1968a) borrows an estimate of the relationship between IQ and the number of siblings from a review by Anastasi (1956) of −.25, which seems much closer to the true value than the other estimates of the correlation between early intelligence and father's education (.27) or father's occupation (.28) inferred from models of status attainment. Neff (1938), for example, reviews a number of early studies and reports correlations between intelligence tests and socioeconomic status between .21 and .53.

The most common source of data has been the Equality of Educational Opportunity Survey (Coleman *et al.*, 1966); that survey has been extensively used to estimate the relationship between early achievement and socioeconomic status (Jencks *et al.*, 1972). Although the Coleman survey represents by far the largest and most comprehensive sample, it contains inherent problems. The respondents were children, and the best evidence suggests that for conventional estimates of parental status, the responses of children are quite unreliable (Mason *et al.*, 1976). The total variance in verbal achievement explained by all available indices of parental status approximates the size of correlations reported in other studies; however, such measures confound home environments or aspirations with more conventional measures of socioeconomic status.

Table D.1 summarizes the correlations between ability and socioeconomic status reported for elementary school children in five studies. These studies support the general argument that the Atlanta results are not seriously exaggerated and that the relationships between ability and socioeconomic background tend to be generally larger for younger students than for those calculated on older cohorts. The range of correlations reported for father's occupational prestige are between .40 and .43, while the Atlanta values are .44 to .45. There is less consensus about parental educational attainments, with the correlations ranging from .27 to .41, compared to the Atlanta estimates of .37 to .42. The smallest correlations between achievement and parental education, found in the Kerckhoff (1974) data, would be considerably higher (.50) if based solely on parents' responses (Mason *et al.*, 1976). The correlations between the number of siblings or children in the family range from −.18 to −.31, with the Atlanta data yielding the most conservative figures. Family income data are available for only one other study (Williams, 1976b), based on 58 cases, and I suspect that the correlations for Atlanta are more accurate. In sum, these values suggest substantial collinearity between socioeconomic background and ability, and larger correlations than most analysts have assumed. The average correlation between ability on verbal score and father's occupation is .43; for parental education, the figure is .36 for fathers and .34 for mothers. The mean relationship for siblings or family size is −.23, which is still larger than the data on sixth-grade students in the Equality of Educational Opportunity Survey would suggest.

Table D.2 summarizes the relationships between tested ability and socioeconomic origins for those studies of high school students that published results. There tends to be substantially more agreement among studies about the magnitude of the correlation between parental status and ability for older students; this is, of course, what one would expect if the responses were considerably more reliable at this age. The correlations of father's occupation with ability are between .18 and .31, with a mean score of .241. Father's education varies between .22 and .34, with a mean of .248. Mother's education has an average correlation of .226 and a range of .20 to .25. A comparison of the 49 correlations between these three aspects of parental status and ability for both groups shows only a single instance in which the largest value reported for high school students is as large as the smallest estimate for sixth-grade students reported in Table D.1.[1] This constitutes prima facie

[1] The correlation between father's education for males (.341) reported in the Explorations in Equality of Opportunity (Alexander & Eckland, 1973) is larger than this correlation (.266) in Fort Wayne, Indiana (Kerckhoff, 1974). The EEO sample is not strictly comparable to the other studies in several ways; the original survey interviewed sophomores and then relocated them at age 30. Parental status measures were drawn from the second wave of interviews rather than the first; also, the male and female correlations are unaccountably different. The Fort Wayne data for both estimates of parental education are highly unreliable in the sixth grade, and I suspect they are too low when based on sons' reports.

TABLE D.1
Summary of Correlations between Socioeconomic Variables and Academic Ability for Elementary School Cohorts, Five Studies

Date of study	Sample description	Measure of academic ability (1)	Status variables[a] (2)	Correlation (1 × 2)
1972	Atlanta sample, sixth grade (N = 1493)	IQ	Father's occupational prestige	.454
			Mother's education	.390
			Father's education	.408
			Mean parental education	.421
			Family income	.457
			Number of siblings	−.226
			Race	.359
1972	Atlanta sample, sixth grade (N = 1493)	MAT test, word knowledge	Father's occupational prestige	.439
			Mother's education	.368
			Father's education	.391
			Mean parental education	.404
			Family income	.422
			Number of siblings	−.181
			Race	.367
1969	Fort Wayne, Indiana,[b] sixth-grade white males (N = 249)	IQ	Father's occupational prestige	.427
			Mother's education	.273
			Father's education	.266
			Number of siblings	−.314
1969	City in western Canada,[c] white males, fourth grade (N = 100 except for income, for which N = 58)	Verbal ability factor scores, calculated from Wechsler Intelligence Scales	Father's occupational prestige	.40
			Mother's education	.34
			Father's education	.39
			Family income	.25
			Family size	−.19
		Nonverbal ability factor scores, calculated from Wechsler Intelligence Scales	Father's occupational prestige	.42
			Mother's education	.29
			Father's education	.41
			Family income	.34
			Family size	−.24

1965	Equality of Educational Opportunity survey, Northern whites, sixth grade[d]	Verbal test	Parents' education[e]	.28
			Items in home[f]	.22
			Reading material[g]	.23
			Number of siblings[h]	.13
			Structural integrity of family[i]	.11
			Urbanism[j]	−.10
	Northern blacks, sixth grade[d]	Verbal test	Parents' education[e]	.17
			Items in home[f]	.23
			Reading material[g]	.21
			Number of siblings[b]	.12
			Structural integrity of family[i]	.09
			Urbanism[j]	.02
1965	Equality of Educational Opportunity Survey[k]	Verbal test		
	Northern white, sixth grade		Six measures[l]	.375
			Eight measures[l]	.395
	Northern black, sixth grade		Six measures	.308
			Eight measures	.320
	Southern white, sixth grade[m]		Six measures	.426
			Eight measures	.446
	Southern black, sixth grade[m]		Six measures	.383
			Eight measures	.393
1957	Berkeley Growth Study[n]	IQ Stanford–Binet, 1937 Revision		
	Aged 10 (N = 197)		Mother's education	.34
			Father's education	.34
	Aged 12–13 (N = 192)		Mother's education	.38
			Father's education	.39
	Aged 14–15 (N = 168)		Mother's education	.35
			Father's education	.37

Footnotes appear on page 252

TABLE D.1 (*continued*)

[a] Unless otherwise noted, the status variables were coded in comparable ways. Father's occupational prestige was scored using Duncan's socioeconomic index (1961); educational levels represent years of schooling; family income is given in dollars earned for the previous year; and the number of siblings or family size is coded in actual numbers. Race, when used, is coded as a dichotomous variable, with 1 being the designation for whites.

[b] Source: Kerckhoff (1974, Table 6.3, p. 69). Subsamples of these data have been used for several other analyses. Mason *et al.* (1976) report on 130 cases (80 white students and 50 blacks) for whom information was gathered from both the students and their parents. The correlations reported by Kerckhoff are based on student responses only. Correlations presented by Mason and his colleagues (1976, Table 15.3, p. 450) suggest that parental responses on educational attainment for whites are more highly correlated with IQ than are responses of students. For parental responses the correlation is .50, while sons' responses correlate .27 and .35 with fathers' and mothers' education, respectively. The correlations for blacks are even more drastically attenuated.

[c] Source: Williams (1976b, Table 3.5, pp. 76–77). Williams's data were sampled from the extremes of the socioeconomic status distribution within this community. He reports that the distribution of parental status measures is roughly rectangular.

[d] Source: Smith (1972 , Tables G and H, pp. 331–332).

[e] Smith (1972) reports that this variable is actually father's education, due to a coding error in the original data.

[f] Includes the possession of six items: TV, phone, vacuum cleaner, record player, refrigerator, and automobile.

[g] Includes three kinds of reading material: dictionary, encyclopedia, and newspaper.

[h] This variable is the total of questions regarding the number of brothers and the number of sisters, coded so that fewer children have higher values.

[i] This variable was constructed from two questions relating to the presence of the child's real mother and real father.

[j] This is perhaps more properly considered a migration variable, since it was constructed from two items pertaining to the child's birthplace (weighted twice) and the birthplace of the child's mother.

[k] Source: Coleman *et al.* (1966, Table 3.221.3, p. 330).

[l] The six items include all of the variables studied by Smith (1972). Two additional variables consist of an index of parental interest in the child's schooling and whether or not the child was read to when small, and an index of parent's educational desires for child, or how good a student the mother and father expect the child to be. The "correlation" in this case is the multiple correlation coefficient, computed from the reported variance in the verbal test explained by the relevant background variables.

[m] The larger correlations between status and achievement in the South are curious. Smith (1972) argued that this was due to the greater between-school variance in social class prevalent among the sampled Southern schools, rather than due to a larger relationship. He also questions the finding reported by Coleman *et al.*, (1966) that school resources are more important in the South than in the North, since the unstandardized coefficients are uniformly lower in the South.

[n] Source: Honzik (1957, Tables 1 and 2, pp. 216–221). Bowles and Nelson (1974) report an unpublished corrected correlation provided by the California Guidance Study between parental income and early childhood IQ of .299. Based on their estimates of unreliability, this would imply an uncorrected value equal to .226.

evidence for the proposition that intelligence is substantially more related to background characteristics among elementary than among high school students.[2]

None of the correlations presented in Tables D.1 or D.2 are corrected for measurement error. Estimates of the reliability of student responses by grade have been published; however, such calculations serve to enhance the discrepancy between grades rather than to explain it. My presumption is that the pattern of differences is already sufficiently large to warrant explanation without enlarging the differences. I do not think the patterns result from either sampling biases or measurement error; rather, I think there is a substantial decline in the effect of parental status on the cognitive abilities of children between the sixth and the twelfth grades. Furthermore, the diminishment of these relationships, irrespective of measures used, is precisely the pattern one would expect if education had a pronounced equalizing effect on the achievement of children and if this effect were cumulative over time.

Alternative explanations are possible. The studies cited are based on relatively large samples, but tend to be specific to a given region. Cross-sectional data may be inappropriate for studying change, yet longitudinal data on achievement patterns do not exist in a form permitting the relevant comparisons. The tests for ability are diverse; no two studies of the high school population used identical instruments. The majority of studies relied on students' responses about parental status, and measurement error of an unknown amount is doubtless prevalent.

One explanation, which cannot be ruled out, is that the measures of ability available for the younger cohorts are more reliable than those available for older students. The high school studies have relied on

[2] Perhaps a word is in order regarding the methodology of comparisons employed herein. Schoenberg (1972) and others have cautioned against comparing standardized coefficients across samples that may differ substantially in observed variances. For most purposes, the point is well taken. Ability, however, as commonly measured, does not have an intrinsic metric, short of accepting intervals based on normal distributions. Differences in variances tend to be meaningless and misleading when different tests are compared. Parental status measures have common coding schemes, although I doubt that anyone would argue very hard that the units of measurement are inherently meaningful. Conceptually, stratification is a relative phenomenon; it is not a year of schooling or an increment of occupational prestige per se that produces a given ability score in children; it is the relative advantage parents possess within a particular community at a particular point in time that should be related to the relative performance of their children. Restrictions of range and measurement error do, of course, influence the estimation of effects whether one is dealing with standardized or unstandardized parameters. Comparisons across grades are hazardous for this reason; one risks confounding attenuation due to selective social processes, such as dropping out, with a diminished real effect. The relationships presented seem to me sufficiently robust to withstand such criticism.

TABLE D.2
Summary of Correlations between Socioeconomic Variables and Academic Achievement in High School

Date of study	Sample description[a]	Measure of academic ability (1)	Status variables[b] (2)	Correlation (1 × 2)
1955	Explorations in Equality of Opportunity, national sample of high school sophomores, reinterviewed in 1970 (males, N = 947, females, N = 1130)[c]	Academic aptitude[d] (20 items, weighting vocabulary and arithmetic reasoning equally)	Males	
			Father's occupation	.314
			Mother's education	.209
			Father's education[e]	.341
			Number of siblings[f]	−.190
			Acquisitions[g]	.287
			Females	
			Father's occupation	.232
			Mother's education	.227
			Father's education[e]	.237
			Number of siblings[f]	−.170
			Acquisitions[g]	.177
1957	Lenawee County, Michigan, high schools, 17-year-old males, reinterviewed in 1972 (N = 340)[h]	Cattell IPAT Test of G Culture-Free Scale	Father's occupation	.227
			Mother's education	.254
			Father's education	.220
1957	Male Wisconsin high school graduates (N = 3427)[i]	Score on Henmon–Nelson Test, 11th grade	Father's occupational prestige[j]	.212
			Mother's education	.230
			Father's education	.244
			Parental income[j]	.203
1957	Male Wisconsin high school graduates employed in 1964 with nonzero earnings (N = 1789)[k]	Score on Henmon–Nelson Test, 11th grade	Father's occupational prestige[j]	.181
			Mother's education	.205
			Father's education	.246
			Parental income[j]	.178
1959	Toronto high school students, third year (males, N = 5458, females, N = 5072)[l]	Factor Loadings on CAAT I, CAAT II, and CAAT III tests	Males	
			Father's occupation	.21
			Mother's education	.20
			Father's education	.22

			Females	
			Father's occupation	.24
			Mother's education	.24
			Father's education	.25
1960	Project Talent,[m] eleventh-grade older brothers in families with two or more children[n]	Verbal knowledge factor scores	Father's occupation	.293
			Father's education	.216
1964	CPS Veterans Sample, males, aged 21–34 (N = 1454)[o]	AFQT test	Father's occupation	.242
			Father's education	.229
			Race	.174
1966	Parnes Survey, males, 18–24[p] (N = 669)[q]	Mental ability, pooled across standardized tests	Father's occupation	.24
			Family education[r]	.18
			Literature in home[s]	.25
			Race	.40
1969	Fort Wayne, Indiana, twelfth-grade males (N = 757)[t]	IQ	Father's occupation	.258
			Mother's education	.237
			Father's education	.274
			Number of siblings	−.093
1972	Panel Study of Income Dynamics, males, 18–30[u] (N = 353)[v]	Lorge-Thorndike Sentence Completion Test	Mother's education	.32
			Father's education	.32
			Family income[w]	.21
			Number of siblings	−.21
	National Longitudinal Study (NCES), twelfth grade whites (males, N = 4758; females, N = 4887)[x]	Linear composite of standardized subtests in math, vocabulary, letter groups, and reading	Males	
			Father's occupation	.239
			Mother's education	.279
			Father's education	.312
			Household items index	.145
			Females	
			Father's occupation	.209
			Mother's education	.280
			Father's education	.279
			Household items index	.127

Footnotes appear on pages 256–257

TABLE D.2 (*continued*)

[a] The Equality of Educational Opportunity Survey (Coleman *et al.*, 1966) also gathered data on the socioeconomic background and achievement of high school students that have not been included in this summary. These correlations are slightly in excess of those reported for the sixth grade, but still of somewhat dubious quality. In an earlier work (Heyns, 1974), I endeavored to code and analyze these data in a manner consistent with the stratification literature; however, I suspect the results underestimate the impact of socioeconomic status. I argued, for example, that high school track placement was a consequence of ability and only minimally related to ascribed characteristics. Replications based on the Wisconsin longitudinal study (Hauser *et al.*, 1976) and on a sample of schools studied by Alexander and McDill (1976) have found substantially greater influence of parental socioeconomic status on curriculum. The differences stem in part from less reliable measures of ability; however, I suspect the largest difference is due to the relatively inaccurate data available on parental status.

[b] All data were based solely on student reports, except for the income data in the Wisconsin samples. Unless otherwise noted, status variables were coded as follows: Father's occupation: Duncan's SEI Scale of Occupation. Mother's and father's education: years of schooling. Number of siblings: actual number.

[c] Source: Alexander & Eckland (1973, Appendix tables). These correlations are very slightly lower (+.002–.013) than the published figures for males (cf. Alexander & Eckland, 1973, Tables 6.5, p. 115, and 7.2, p. 135). All the status variables are based on the 1970 interviews, with the exception of the number of siblings and the household acquisitions index, which were taken from the 1955 responses.

[d] This scale was normed for twelfth-grade students and is believed to have been quite difficult for the tenth-grade students. The mean score reported was 7.8, with a standard error of 4.03; it is possible that the reported correlations are attenuated for this reason.

[e] Father's education was asked in both 1955 and 1970. The zero-order correlations between the responses in high school and at age 30 were .82 for males and .85 for females (Alexander & Eckland, 1973, p. 73).

[f] Data on siblings are based on 1955 responses (cf. Table 3.10, p. 65, and Table 3.11, p. 67, in the report).

[g] The Acquisition Index is based on a factor analysis of 13 possessions found in the high school family household. The items were (1) a telephone; (2) a second phone; (3) a set of encyclopedias; (4) more than 50 books; (5) more than 200 books; (6) more than one car; (7) a typewriter; (8) a bathtub; (9) more than 10 phonograph records; (10) more than one bathroom; (11) a daily newspaper; (12) a magazine subscription; (13) a map or globe of the world.

[h] Source: Otto (1976, Table 1, p. 1368).

[i] Source: Hauser (1973, Table 1, p. 261).

[j] Parents' average income was obtained from the Wisconsin state tax return for the years 1957–1960. Father's occupational status was from the tax reports in 1956 or the closest year, or in a few cases from student questionnaires.

[k] Source: Sewell & Hauser (1975, Table 4.1, p. 93).

[l] Source: Williams (1976a, Table 1, p. 229).

[m] These correlations are somewhat higher than those reported for younger brothers; the verbal scores were constructed to be orthogonal to a math component and may therefore be underestimated. Porter (1976, Table 1, p. 26) reports a correlation between Duncan's SEI for father's occupation and a composite score based on several Project Talent aptitude instruments of .290 for whites.

[n] Source: Jencks *et al.* (1972, Table B-4, p. 348).

[o] Source: Griliches & Mason (1973, Table 2, p. 294).

[p] National survey of males aged 18–24 who were not enrolled in school in 1966, but who had completed at least 1 year of high school.

[q] Source: Kohen (1971, Table 3).

[r] Family education is defined as the number of family members who ever attended college, excluding the respondent.

[s] The literature variable is the presence of newspapers, magazines, and a library card.

[t] Source: Kerckhoff (1974, Table 6.3, p. 69).

[u] The correlations are based on the children of sample respondents who were living at home in the initial wave, but who had left home by 1972, the fifth wave. All of the family status measures were collected from the parents, rather than children.

[v] Source: Morgan *et al*. (1974, Table A7-1, p. 328).

[w] Family income is the 5-year average during the course of the study.

[x] Source: Thomas (1977, Table VI and Table VII).

diverse measures of achievement or ability and have not scrutinized their measurement as closely as is typically done in smaller studies. Three of the five studies of sixth-grade students used either IQ scores or factor scales derived from IQ tests (Honzik, 1957; Kerckhoff, 1974; Williams, 1976b). It could be argued that the more reliable measures of ability at younger ages systematically inflate the relationships observed. As the Atlanta results demonstrate, IQ is more highly related to socioeconomic background than is the achievement score recorded during the fall of 1972. Perhaps the values estimated for high school seniors are understated, due to measurement error in the achievement variable, rather than indicating any temporal process related to schooling.

The only high school sample that used IQ as the ability measure was the Fort Wayne study, which also collected data for the sixth and ninth grades (Kerckhoff, 1974). Mason *et al*. (1976) undertook an extensive analysis of measurement error on this data set, which permits a comparison of the reports of parents with those of sons. Table D.3 summarizes the results from regressions of IQ on father's education, occupational prestige, and mother's education, separately by whether the respondent was the parent or the son, by grade and race. The sample sizes are small, since only those cases with complete data were included; however, the pattern is unmistakable. When parents' responses are compared, the explanatory power of background decreases routinely across grades; the reports of sons are considerably more ambiguous. When results are based on comparable measures of ability, and when socioeconomic status is collected directly from parents and coded in systematic ways, the measured effects of parental status are clearly attenuated between the sixth and the twelfth grades.

TABLE D.3
Summary of Explained Variance (R^2) in IQ by Father's Occupation, Father's Education, and Mother's Education by Grade and Race[a]

Race and education	Sixth grade	Ninth grade	Twelfth grade
White			
Parents	.29	.23	.18
Sons	.19	.21	.18
Black			
Parents	.13	.03	.02
Sons	.05	.02	.05

[a] Source: Mason *et al*. (1976, compiled from Tables 15.8, 15.11, 15.14, 15.17, 15.20, and 15.24, pp. 468, 473, 477, 482, 485, and 491).

In my opinion the most compelling alternative explanation is that the cross-sectional comparisons between the sixth and the twelfth grades are systematically biased due to differential retention rates. Samples of school populations must be based on students currently enrolled; students leaving a system at age 16 do not appear in the studies of high school seniors or graduates. Moreover, dropouts are not a random subsample, but tend to cluster at the lower end of the distributions, thus attenuating the observed relationships.

There is no completely satisfactory method of testing this possibility, short of collecting longitudinal data. One unpublished study, however, is highly suggestive. Hauser (1968) reanalyzed data collected on Davidson County, Tennessee, and presented grade- and sex-specific correlations for all students between the seventh and the twelfth grades. Although cross-sectional, the data are at least specific to one area and embody comparable measures of parental status and intelligence across grades. The socioeconomic background information was systematically collected by student questionnaires anonymously administered in homerooms for 41 schools. Table D.4 presents the correlations for the total Nashville Standard Metropolitan Statistical Area (SMSA), by grade and sex presented by Hauser[3] and the total variance explained, computed from the original matrices.

The pattern of correlations suggests that the impact of parental status declines across cohorts, although perhaps not as dramatically as might be expected from other cross-sectional data. Five out of the six correlations observed for the seventh grade are significantly larger than those calculated for the twelfth grade, and two exceed the twelfth-grade value by more than .10. If one accepts the plausible assumption that responses of seventh graders are less reliable than those of older children, the differences would be larger. It seems reasonable to assume that the number of siblings is the most reliable measure, since it requires less detailed knowledge than either of the other measures of paternal status; the declines are most consistent for this variable for the entire SMSA as well as for the two subsamples.

The data also suggest that the attenuation of relationships tends to occur at critical junctures, such as between tenth and eleventh grades, when one might expect the largest exodus. Could these patterns be the result of selective retention?

Tentatively, the answer is no. Lord and Novick (1968) have described a formula for correcting correlations between a predictor and a criterion when a subsample is selected, as in admission to selective schools. If

[3] Hauser (1968) also reports correlations between and within schools and matrices separately for the city of Nashville and for the Davidson County ring.

TABLE D.4
Correlations between Socioeconomic Status and IQ[a] by Sex and Grade, Nashville SMSA, 1957[b]

	Grade in school					
	7	8	9	10	11	12
White males						
Father's occupation	.331	.346	.335	.303	.306	.364
Father's education	.375	.357	.362	.341	.324	.294
Number of siblings	−.286	−.272	−.254	−.163	−.189	−.095
$R^2_{Q \cdot OES}$	.187	.178	.178	.137	.131	.144
N	1780	1823	1627	1294	918	783
White females						
Father's occupation	.367	.396	.366	.365	.281	.267
Father's education	.410	.384	.391	.325	.312	.287
Number of siblings	−.263	−.271	−.267	−.257	−.150	−.194
$R^2_{Q \cdot OES}$	.207	.200	.203	.179	.118	.110
N	1775	1861	1649	1446	1012	925

[a] IQ tests were either the Otis or the Kuhlman-Anderson group tests, administered in odd-numbered grades.
[b] Source: Hauser (1968, Table A.1, pp. 375–386). R^2 computed from matrices provided.

one were to assume that the twelfth-grade sample was identical to the seventh grade sample, except for an explicit selection process that reduced the observed variance and correlation and that the relationship between IQ and the family background measure was linear, with uncorrelated errors, one could calculate the true relationship. The formula is

$$\rho^2_{QS} = \left[1 + \frac{\delta^2_{S_*}}{\delta^2_S}\left(\frac{1}{\rho^2_{Q_*S_*}} - 1\right)\right]^{-1}$$

where Q is the intelligence measure, S is the measure of status, and the selected group is designated by an asterisk (Lord & Novick, 1968, p. 145).

Applying this formula to the data for number of siblings presented by Hauser yields the estimated true correlations separately for Davidson County and Nashville, by sex. The model assumes that family size was an explicit, rather than an incidental, basis for dropping out; the results are therefore likely to be undercorrected. The expected amount of decrease is greatest for explicit selection.

The results are presented in Table D.5. In all cases the corrected coefficients are less than those observed in the seventh grade. If one can assume that the only difference between the two grades was that children from large families dropped out first, one would expect a correla-

TABLE D.5
Predicted and Observed Correlations for Nashville City and Davidson County Ring of Intelligence (*Q*) and Number of Siblings (*S*) in the Seventh Grade, Based on the Twelfth-Grade Scores[a]

	Standard deviations		Observed correlations		Predicted correlations
Sex and residence	Twelfth grade	Seventh grade	Twelfth grade	Seventh grade	Seventh grade
Males					
City	1.937	2.202	−.048	−.287	−.055
County	1.951	2.066	−.111	−.255	−.117
Females					
City	2.133	2.245	−.144	−.259	−.151
County	1.927	1.963	−.219	−.238	−.223

[a]Source: Calculated from standard deviations and correlations reported by Hauser (1968).

tion between family size and IQ score to be larger by about .01 or less. Clearly, this difference is not sufficient to account for the observed diminution of effect.

Lord and Novick caution that relatively little empirical work has been done to assess the accuracy of the selection formulas. In the present case, the ratio of standard deviations implies that between 95 and 98% of the cases were selected, whereas the decline in students suggests a far higher dropout rate. Similar calculations for the other status variables yield similar results, however. Although the assumption that the two groups are identical except for selection by family size is problematic, the correction factors suggest that selection is unlikely to be sufficiently powerful to account for the observed decline. If one assumes that the twelfth-grade correlation is equal to .24, for example, the ratio of variances must be 4:1 in order to produce a seventh-grade correlation of .44.[4]

To argue that the observed patterns result from the impact of schooling on cognitive development is perhaps premature. Buttressed by the results of the Atlanta study, however, this conclusion seems more reasonable than the alternative—that test scores are unaffected by education. The conventional wisdom regarding tests of intelligence has

[4] The values of .24 and .44 were chosen because they represent the mean correlation between father's occupation and achievement computed from the five elementary school studies and the nine studies for which data have been published at the high school level.

been that scores are quite stable after the age of 8. Bloom (1964) concludes on the basis of a detailed summary of empirical studies that repeated tests, corrected for unreliability, tend to produce correlations between .8 and 1.0 . Such results are not incompatible with the inferences I have drawn, at least not if one accepts a value less than unity. The Metropolitan Achievement Test for vocabulary, uncorrected by measurement error, has been shown to correlate between .80 and .90 with prior vocabulary achievement based on parallel forms, while still producing significant differences in learning. Admittedly, correlations of this magnitude give pause when one considers studying learning, particularly when accustomed to the models prevalent in sociology. Yet there is certainly room for measurable effects and consistent patterns of the sort inferred, even when dealing with highly reliable and hence stable measurements based on conventional instruments. Learning can be shown to depend systematically on environmental conditions over time, despite a highly stable relative position.

In sum, the best evidence suggests that it is possible, indeed likely, that cognitive abilities are relatively more dependent on family background in the early grades than later in the educational career. The stability of test scores, as well as the change, are due to measurable environmental influences, such as socioeconomic status and schooling. Although schooling does not dramatically alter patterns of relative achievement, the progressive influence of education seems to attenuate the relationship between achievement and social class. This conclusion emerges from numerous studies of young children and high school students and is supported in broad outline by the results presented for the Atlanta sample. The assertion that such patterns are the direct result of schooling is somewhat speculative; however, pending a more tenable conclusion, the bulk of the evidence clearly supports such an inference.

APPENDIX E
Correlation Matrices

TABLE E.1
Correlation Matrix of Test Scores by Metric in Longitudinal Perspective, Seventh-Grade Matched Sample (N = 739)

Scores	(1)	(2)	(3)	(4)	(5)	(6)	(7)	(8)
Raw scores								
(1) Fall 1970	1.0							
(2) Spring 1971	.8113	1.0						
(3) Fall 1971	.8263	.8453	1.0					
(4) Spring 1972	.8054	.8487	.8900	1.0				
Grade equivalent scores								
(5) Fall 1970	.9755	.7906	.8066	.7749	1.0			
(6) Spring 1971	.7944	.9740	.8047	.8090	.8023	1.0		
(7) Fall 1971	.8451	.8362	.9724	.8609	.8494	.8248	1.0	
(8) Spring 1972	.8301	.8544	.8857	.9766	.8145	.8354	.8838	1.0
Mean	17.29	21.91	22.82	26.44	4.30	4.91	4.89	5.55
Standard deviation	11.26	12.49	12.81	13.52	1.45	1.78	1.84	2.04

TABLE E.2
Correlation Matrix of Matched Sample with Test Score Data at Four Points in Time, Seventh Grade (N = 739)

	(1)	(2)	(3)	(4)	(5)	(6)	(7)	(8)
(1) Test scores, Fall 1970	1.0							
(2) Test scores, Spring 1971	.8113	1.0						
(3) Test scores, Fall 1971	.8263	.8453	1.0					
(4) Test scores, Spring 1972	.8054	.8487	.8900	1.0				
(5) Family income	.4696	.4540	.5397	.5432	1.0			
(6) Parental education	.4256	.4129	.4661	.4551	.5491	1.0		
(7) Race	.4668	.4898	.5188	.5137	.4380	.2386	1.0	
(8) IQ	.7447	.7659	.7919	.7976	.5277	.4485	.4541	1.0
Mean	17.29	21.91	22.82	26.44	$13,256	11.43	.371	94.11
Standard deviation	11.26	12.49	12.81	13.52	$5,522	2.73	.483	17.44

TABLE E.3
Correlation Matrix for Sixth-Grade Matched Sample, White Students (N = 470)

	(1)	(2)	(3)	(4)	(5)	(6)	(7)	(8)
(1) Test scores, Fall 1972	1.0							
(2) Test scores, Spring 1972	.8779	1.0						
(3) Test scores, Fall 1971	.8570	.8700	1.0					
(4) Sex	.0149	−.0201	.0105	1.0				
(5) Family income	.4669	.4405	.4676	.0867	1.0			
(6) Parental education	.5021	.5115	.5470	.1249	.6735	1.0		
(7) Household size	−.1149	−.0933	−.0672	−.0578	−.0489	−.1019	1.0	
(8) IQ	.8144	.7951	.7832	.0070	.4976	.5290	−.1056	1.0
Mean	30.69	28.40	22.91	.48	$12,855	12.09	5.11	104.32
Standard deviation	12.53	12.40	11.48	.50	$6,002	2.91	1.60	16.78

TABLE E.4
Correlation Matrix for Sixth-Grade Matched Sample, Black Students (N = 1023)

	(1)	(2)	(3)	(4)	(5)	(6)	(7)	(8)
(1) Test scores, Fall 1972	1.0							
(2) Test scores, Spring 1972	.7716	1.0						
(3) Test scores, Fall 1971	.7813	.7238	1.0					
(4) Sex	−.0865	−.1045	−.0883	1.0				
(5) Family income	.3603	.2775	.2657	.0276	1.0			
(6) Parental education	.3465	.2900	.2592	.0571	.5540	1.0		
(7) Household size	−.1523	−.1336	−.1321	−.0043	−.1099	−.2992	1.0	
(8) IQ	.6732	.6378	.7271	−.1083	.3262	.3127	−.1418	1.0
Mean	18.99	18.67	14.53	.49	$8445	11.11	5.91	91.36
Standard deviation	10.71	10.68	9.05	.50	$5468	2.52	2.07	15.11

TABLE E.5
Correlation Matrix of Background Variables and Test Scores for Sixth-Grade Matched Sample (N = 1493)

	(1)	(2)	(3)	(4)	(5)	(6)	(7)
(1) Test scores, Fall 1972	1.0						
(2) Test scores, Spring 1972	.8404	1.0					
(3) Test scores, Fall 1971	.8389	.8114	1.0				
(4) Family income	.4830	.4228	.4218	1.0			
(5) Parental education	.4334	.4067	.4042	.6081	1.0		
(6) Household size	−.2423	−.2142	−.1812	−.2853	−.3095	1.0	
(7) Race	.4325	.3732	.3671	.3391	.1699	−.2200	1.0
Mean	22.65	21.73	17.18	$9803	11.42	5.65	.32
Standard deviation	12.54	12.12	10.62	$5992	2.69	1.96	.46

TABLE E.6
Correlation Matrix for Seventh-Grade Matched Sample, White Students (N = 526)

	(1)	(2)	(3)	(4)	(5)	(6)	(7)	(8)
(1) Test scores, Spring 1972	1.0							
(2) Test scores, Fall 1971	.8764	1.0						
(3) Test scores, Spring 1971	.8524	.8218	1.0					
(4) Sex	−.0573	−.0737	−.0946	1.0				
(5) Family income	.4017	.4059	.3010	.0071	1.0			
(6) Parental education	.5284	.5436	.4814	−.0128	.5853	1.0		
(7) Household size	−.2172	−.2435	−.2076	−.0083	−.0198	−.2075	1.0	
(8) IQ	.8069	.8107	.7674	−.0778	.4278	.5507	−.2069	1.0
Mean	35.76	32.24	30.26	.53	$13,800	12.41	5.07	105.94
Standard deviation	12.46	12.40	11.84	.50	$6,103	2.86	1.66	16.41

TABLE E.7
Correlation Matrix for Seventh-Grade Matched Sample, Black Students (N = 959)

	(1)	(2)	(3)	(4)	(5)	(6)	(7)	(8)
(1) Test scores, Spring 1972	1.0							
(2) Test scores, Fall 1971	.8592	1.0						
(3) Test scores, Spring 1971	.7809	.8247	1.0					
(4) Sex	−.1218	−.0978	−.1037	1.0				
(5) Family income	.3807	.3944	.3113	.0191	1.0			
(6) Parental education	.3516	.3596	.2934	.0143	.5235	1.0		
(7) Household size	−.2065	−.1972	−.1460	−.0029	−.0778	−.2523	1.0	
(8) IQ	.7441	.7376	.7088	−.1212	.3618	.3338	−.1923	1.0
Mean	22.27	18.84	17.85	.45	$8360	11.13	5.97	89.07
Standard deviation	11.88	10.69	10.08	.50	$5432	2.49	2.11	15.37

TABLE E.8
Correlation Matrix of Background Variables and Test Scores, with Means and Standard Deviations Used in the Analysis, for Matched Samples, Seventh-Grade Cohort (N = 1485)

	(1)	(2)	(3)	(4)	(5)	(6)	(7)
(1) Test scores, Spring 1972	1.0						
(2) Test scores, Fall 1971	.8954	1.0					
(3) Test scores, Spring 1971	.8497	.8587	1.0				
(4) Family income	.5096	.5216	.4438	1.0			
(5) Parental education	.4663	.4816	.4291	.5810	1.0		
(6) Household size	−.3170	−.3219	−.2772	−.2859	−.3156	1.0	
(7) Race	.4785	.4928	.4758	.4159	.2260	−.2535	1.0
Mean	27.08	23.57	22.24	\$10,260	11.56	5.43	.35
Standard deviation	13.51	13.01	12.48	\$6,240	2.69	1.99	.48

TABLE E.9
Correlation Matrix for Sixth-Grade Males, Matched Sample (N = 728)

	(1)	(2)	(3)	(4)	(5)	(6)	(7)
(1) Test scores, Fall 1972	1.0						
(2) Test scores, Spring 1972	.8526	1.0					
(3) Test scores, Fall 1971	.8434	.8366	1.0				
(4) Family income	.4625	.4261	.3954	1.0			
(5) Parental education	.4444	.4520	.4136	.6214	1.0		
(6) Household size	−.2064	−.1916	−.1645	−.1581	−.2531	1.0	
(7) Race	.4627	.3980	.4011	.3620	.2099	−.2055	1.0
Mean	22.05	20.86	16.64	$10,072	11.64	5.62	.31
Standard deviation	12.80	12.40	10.80	$6,112	2.68	1.99	.46

TABLE E.10
Correlation Matrix for Sixth-Grade Females, Matched Sample (N = 765)

	(1)	(2)	(3)	(4)	(5)	(6)	(7)
(1) Test scores, Fall 1972	1.0						
(2) Test scores, Spring 1972	.8269	1.0					
(3) Test scores, Fall 1971	.8335	.7845	1.0				
(4) Family income	.5068	.4257	.4519	1.0			
(5) Parental education	.4342	.3780	.4603	.5938	1.0		
(6) Household size	−.1955	−.1689	−.1716	−.1203	−.2695	1.0	
(7) Race	.4032	.3503	.3344	.3193	.1333	−.1710	1.0
Mean	23.23	22.56	17.70	$9550	11.22	5.69	.316
Standard deviation	12.21	11.80	10.44	$5870	2.69	1.95	.470

TABLE E.11
Correlations for Interactive Model of Schooling with List-Wise Deletions of Missing Cases, Sixth Grade, White Students (N = 326)

	(1)	(2)	(3)	(4)	(5)	(6)	(7)
(1) Posttest	1.0						
(2) Pretest	.8698	1.0					
(3) Family income	.4488	.4391	1.0				
(4) Parental education	.4995	.5083	.6667	1.0			
(5) Household size	−.1309	−.1134	−.0618	−.1468	1.0		
(6) IQ	.7882	.7559	.4586	.4939	−.1560	1.0	
(7) Schooling	−.0801	−.2329	0.0	0.0	0.0	0.0	1.0
Mean	29.74	25.88	$12,923	12.19	5.21	105.14	.5
Standard deviation	12.44	12.31	$6,020	2.85	1.65	18.05	.5

TABLE E.12
Correlations for Interactive Model of Schooling with List-Wise Deletions of Missing Cases, Sixth Grade, Black Students (N = 745)

	(1)	(2)	(3)	(4)	(5)	(6)	(7)
(1) Posttest	1.0						
(2) Pretest	.7386	1.0					
(3) Family income	.3175	.2691	1.0				
(4) Parental education	.3266	.2797	.5554	1.0			
(5) Household size	−.1497	−.1328	−.0980	−.2752	1.0		
(6) IQ	.6256	.5836	.2955	.2669	−.0950	1.0	
(7) Schooling	−.0143	−.2026	0.0	0.0	1.0	0.0	1.0
Mean	19.02	16.67	$8574	11.26	5.84	92.67	.5
Standard deviation	10.69	10.17	$5486	2.58	2.06	15.89	.5

TABLE E.13
Correlations for Interactive Model of Schooling with List-Wise Deletions of Missing Cases, Sixth Grade, Total Sample (N = 1071)

	(1)	(2)	(3)	(4)	(5)	(6)	(7)	(8)
(1) Posttest	1.0							
(2) Pretest	.8187	1.0						
(3) Family income	.4487	.4121	1.0					
(4) Parental education	.4150	.3920	.6056	1.0				
(5) Household size	−.1881	−.1687	−.1305	−.2546	1.0			
(6) Race	.4051	.3633	.3339	.1579	−.1478	1.0		
(7) IQ	.7244	.6894	.4237	.3758	−.1521	.3274	1.0	
(8) Schooling	−.0328	−.1972	0.0	0.0	0.0	0.0	0.0	1.0
Mean	22.29	19.48	$9898	11.54	5.65	.305	96.47	.5
Standard deviation	12.29	11.66	$5996	2.70	1.96	.46	17.54	.5

TABLE E.14
Correlation Matrix for Selected Summer Activities, Sixth Grade, Blacks, Students, Matched Sample (N = 1023)

	(6)	(7)	(8)	(9)	(10)	(11)	(12)	(13)	(14)
(1) Fall 1972	.053	−.263	.286	.189	.321	−.048	.157	.054	.093
(2) Spring 1971	.032	−.147	.233	.161	.254	−.057	.092	.019	.045
(3) Sex	−.011	.219	−.183	−.042	−.183	−.007	−.076	−.049	.026
(4) Family income	.051	−.013	.119	.160	.165	−.060	.249	.096	.097
(5) Parental education	−.005	.186	.118	.199	.166	−.077	.223	.173	.104
(6) Hours TV	1.000	−.261	−.061	−.017	−.038	.020	.006	−.041	.031
(7) Hours sports		1.000	−.368	−.012	−.188	−.122	−.172	−.199	−.041
(8) Hours reading			1.000	.167	.479	−.115	.030	.003	−.026
(9) Uses library				1.000	.271	−.308	.059	.050	.020
(10) Number books read					1.000	−.106	.001	.020	.015
(11) Blocks to library						1.000	.066	.008	.049
(12) Bike							1.000	.090	.074
(13) Trip alone								1.000	.612
(14) Outside Atlanta alone									1.000
Mean	2.93	1.69	1.05	.59	5.20	4.94	.74	.14	.05
Standard deviation	1.84	1.70	.94	.49	4.0	1.23	.44	.35	.22

APPENDIX **F**
Supplementary Tables

TABLE F.1
Mean Raw Scores on Metropolitan Achievement Test, Word Knowledge, by Race and Family Income, Sixth Grade

Race and income	Fall 1971	Spring 1972	Fall 1972	*N*
White				
Less than $9000	17.1	22.5	24.0	109
$9000–14,999	21.5	27.7	29.7	115
$15,000+	29.7	35.2	37.5	124
Black				
Less than $4000	12.0	15.3	14.6	185
$4000–8999	13.7	18.0	18.3	325
$9000–14,999	15.9	20.4	21.0	169
$15,000+	19.8	24.7	27.3	101

TABLE F.2
Standard Deviations of Raw Scores, Word Knowledge, Metropolitan Achievement Test, by Race, Family Income, and Test Date, Sixth Grade

Race and income	Fall 1971	Spring 1972	Fall 1972	*N*
White				
Less than $9000	9.3	10.2	10.6	109
$9000–14,999	10.9	12.5	12.8	115
$15,000+	10.7	10.8	10.0	124
Black				
Less than $4000	7.8	10.1	8.6	184
$4000–8999	8.3	10.1	10.1	325
$9000–14,999	9.4	10.6	10.5	169
$15,000+	10.7	10.5	10.7	101

TABLE F.3
Standard Deviations of Grade Equivalent Scores, Word Knowledge, Metropolitan Achievement Test, by Race, Family Income, and Test Date, Sixth Grade

Race and income	Fall 1971	Spring 1972	Fall 1972	*N*
White				
Less than $9000	1.11	1.36	1.45	109
$9000–14,999	1.36	2.01	2.09	115
$15,000+	1.59	1.91	1.91	124
Black				
Less than $4000	.96	1.38	1.07	187
$4000–8999	.97	1.34	1.28	325
$9000–14,999	1.09	1.50	1.43	169
$15,000+	1.44	1.47	1.58	101

TABLE F.4
Median Grade Equivalent Test Scores by Race and Family Income for Each Test Date, Sixth Grade

Race and income	Fall 1971	Spring 1972	Fall 1972
White			
Less than $9000	3.8	4.5	4.0
$9000–14,999	4.0	4.9	4.9
$15,000+	5.8	6.9	7.1
Black			
Less than $4000	3.2	3.6	3.3
$4000–8999	3.6	4.0	3.8
$9000–14,999	3.8	4.3	4.3
$15,000+	4.3	4.9	5.1

TABLE F.5
Proportion of Students with an Absolute Decline in Correct Responses during the School Year and the Summer, by Race and Family Income, Sixth Grade[a]

Race and income	School year (Fall 1971–Spring 1972, in percentages)	Summer (Spring 1972–Fall 1972, in percentages)	*N*
White[b]	*13.7*	*30.1*	*459*
Less than $4000	15.4	32.0	26
$4000–8999	10.0	38.2	80
$9000–14,999	15.2	29.4	112
$15,000+	9.9	30.3	121
Black	*22.1*	*39.1*	*986*
Less than $4000	24.6	42.6	176
$4000–8999	21.8	38.2	314
$9000–14,999	19.5	42.5	167
$15,000+	16.2	26.3	99

[a]Includes only students with matched test scores.
[b]Totals include students without family income data.

TABLE F.6
Mean Grade Equivalent Scores, Word Knowledge, by Race, Family Income, and Test Date, Seventh Grade[a]

Race and income	Fall 1970	Spring 1971	Fall 1971	Spring 1972	*N*
White					
Less than $9000	4.48	5.61	5.21	6.14	51
$9000–14,999	5.04	5.74	5.98	6.53	54
$15,000+	5.57	6.57	6.82	7.82	89
Black					
Less than $4000	3.52	3.82	3.72	3.99	84
$4000–8999	3.63	4.04	4.01	4.42	133
$9000–14,999	3.94	4.50	4.45	5.05	66
$15,000+	4.61	5.10	5.51	6.26	36
Total[b]	*4.30*	*4.91*	*4.89*	*5.55*	*739*

[a]Includes only those students with test scores for every date.
[b]Includes students for whom family income was missing.

TABLE F.7
Standard Deviations of Grade Equivalent Scores, Word Knowledge, by Race, Family Income, and Test Date, Seventh Grade[a]

Race and income	Fall 1970	Spring 1971	Fall 1971	Spring 1972	*N*
White					
Less than $9000	1.43	2.15	2.04	1.95	51
$9000–14,999	1.52	1.93	1.83	1.86	54
$15,000+	1.73	2.08	2.05	2.00	89
Black					
Less than $4000	.72	1.09	.98	1.65	84
$4000–8999	.74	1.36	.99	1.19	133
$9000–14,999	1.11	1.21	1.33	1.50	66
$15,000+	1.39	1.72	1.68	2.17	36
Total[b]	1.45	1.78	1.84	2.04	739

[a]Includes only those students with test scores for all four test dates.
[b]Includes students without parental income data.

TABLE F.8
Nonresponse by Race and Grade for Selected Socioeconomic Items

	Proportion not responding included in matched sample[a] (in percentages)			
	Sixth grade		Seventh grade	
Variables	Black	White	Black	White
Child's age[b]	99.5	100.0	99.9	99.6
Child's IQ[b]	99.1	98.7	99.5	100.0
Father's occupation[c]	55.6	79.1	56.0	80.0
Mother's education	97.6	98.1	97.0	97.0
Father's education[c]	63.0	86.2	64.2	87.3
Household size	100.0	100.0	100.0	100.0
Family income	76.4	74.0	79.4	77.8
Number of siblings	92.2	88.5	91.1	88.6
Mean parents' education	98.9	98.1	98.5	99.0
N	1023	470	959	526

[a]Matched sample are those respondents with data available for three or more consecutive tests and a completed parental survey.
[b]Data from school records; in all other cases, the data were obtained from parental interviews.
[c]These data were obtained only for those households with an adult male present at the time of the survey, and pertain to this person, whether he was the father or the guardian.

TABLE F.9

Comparison of Coefficients Estimated for the Effects of Socioeconomic Status and Prior Achievement on Fall Achievement Level 1972, by Race, Sixth Grade

	Predetermined variables								
Sample	Spring 1972	Family income (in thousands)	Parental education	Household size	Father's occupational prestige	Mother's education	Number of siblings	Mother works	R^2
White									
b	.836	.191	.061	−.249					
(σ)	(.031)	(.074)	(.160)	(.204)					
b^*	.828	.091	.014	−.032					.780
b	.836	.237	−.466	−.492	−.017	.642	.318	−.698	
(σ)	(.034)	(.094)	(.377)	(.599)	(.022)	(.340)	(.725)	(.743)	
b^*	.828	.114	−.108	−.063	−.034	.145	.034	−.028	.7838
Black									
b	.713	.243	.267	−.126					
(σ)	(.024)	(.053)	(.120)	(.122)					
b^*	.716	.124	.063	−.024					.6224
b	.720	.268	.134	−.363	−.044	.313	.271	.285	
(σ)	(.031)	(.077)	(.383)	(.384)	(.021)	(.346)	(.433)	(.685)	
b^*	.718	.137	.032	−.070	−.080	.076	.047	.013	.6283

Bibliography

Abelson, Robert P., and Tukey, John W.

1959 "Efficient Conversion of Non-Metric Information Into Metric Information." In *Proceedings of the Social Statistics Section,* Chapter 14. Washington, D.C.: American Statistical Association, pp. 226–230.

Acland, Henry

1973 "Social Determinants of Educational Achievement: An Evaluation and Criticism of Research." Ph.D. dissertation, Oxford University.

1975 "Parents Love School?" *Interchange,* 6:1–10.

Alexander, C. Norman, and Campbell, Ernest Q.

1964 "Peer Influence on Adolescent Aspirations and Attainments." *American Sociological Review* 29 (August):568–575.

Alexander, Karl, and Eckland, Bruce K.

1964 "Sex Differences in the Educational Attainment Process." *American Sociological Review* 39 (October):668–682.

1973 *Effects of Education on the Social Mobility of High School Sophomores Fifteen Years Later (1955–1970).* Final Report, Project no. 10202, National Institute of Education. Chapel Hill, N.C.: University of North Carolina.

Alexander, Karl L., Eckland, Bruce K., and Griffin, Larry S.

1975 "The Wisconsin Model of Socioeconomic Achievement: A Replication." *American Journal of Sociology* 81 (September):324–342.

Alexander, Karl L., and McDill, Edward L.

1976 "Selection and Allocation Within Schools: Some Causes and Consequences of Curriculum Placement." *American Sociological Review* 41 (December):963–980.

Allen, Donna

1964 *Fringe Benefits: Wages or Social Obligation.* Ithaca, N.Y.: Cornell University Press.

Alwin, Duane
1976 "Assessing School Effects: Some Identities." *Sociology of Education* 49 (October):294–303.

Alwin, Duane F., and Hauser, Robert M.
1975 "The Decomposition of Effects in Path Analysis." *American Sociological Review* 40 (February):37–47.

Anastasi, Anne
1956 "Intelligence and Family Size." *Psychological Bulletin* 53:187–209.

Anderson, B. Robert
1972 " 'Four Quarter' Makes a Whole Year in Atlanta." *School Management*, June, pp. 7–11.

Anderson, C. A.; Brown, J. C.; and Bowman, M. J.
1952 "Intelligence and Occupational Mobility." *Journal of Political Economy* 60:218–239.

Anderson, J. E.
1939 "The Limitations of Infant and Preschool Tests in the Measurement of Intelligence." *Journal of Psychology* 8:351–379.

Anderson, Loren W.
1973 "Time and School Learning." Ph.D. dissertation, University of Chicago.

Anderson, Norman H.
1961 "Scales and Statistics: Parametric and Nonparametric." *Psychological Bulletin* 58:305–316.

Anderson, Richard
1967 "Individual Differences and Problem Solving." In *Learning and Individual Differences*, edited by Robert M. Gagné. Columbus, Ohio: Merrill.

Angoff, William H.
1971 "Scales, Norms, and Equivalent Scores." In *Educational Measurement*, 2nd ed., edited by Robert L. Thorndike, pp. 508–600. Washington, D.C.: American Council on Education.

Armor, David J.
1972 "The Evidence on Busing." *The Public Interest* 28 (Summer):90–126.
1974 "Toward a Unified Theory of Reliability for Social Measurement." Santa Monica: Rand Corp., mimeographed, P-5264, July.

Ashline, Nelson F., Pezzullo, Thomas R., and Norris, Charles I., eds.
1976 *Education, Inequality and National Policy*. Lexington, Mass.: D. C. Heath.

Astin, Alexander W.
1971 "Open Admissions and Programs for the Disadvantaged." *Journal of Higher Education* 42 (November):629–647.
1974 "The Intermediate Effects of Inequality: Differences in Access and Utilization of Educational Resources," *American Educational Research Journal* 11:155–159.

Atkinson, John W.
1974 "Motivational Determinants of Intellective Performance and Cumulative Achievement." In *Motivation and Achievement*, edited by John W. Atkinson and J. O. Raynor, pp. 389–410. Washington, D.C.: Winston.

Atkinson, John W., Lens, Willy, and O'Malley, P. M.
1976 "Motivation and Ability: Interactive Psychological Determinants of Intellective Performance, Educational Achievement, and Each Other." In *Schooling and Achievement in American Society*, edited by William H. Sewell, Robert M. Hauser, and David L. Featherman. New York: Academic Press.

Atkinson, R. C., and Paulson, J. A.
1972 "An Approach to the Psychology of Instruction." *Psychological Bulletin* 78:49–61.

Austin, G., Rogers, B., and Walbesser, H. M., Jr.
1972 "The Effectiveness of Summer Compensatory Education: A Review of the Research." *Review of Educational Research* 42 (Spring):171–181.

Austin, Mary C., and Morrison, Coleman
1963 *The First R: The Harvard Report on Reading in Elementary Schools.* New York: Macmillan.

Averch, Harvey A., Carrol, Stephen J., Donaldson, Theodore S., Kiesling, Herbert J., and Pincus, John
1975 "How Effective Is Schooling? A Critical Review and Synthesis of Research Findings." In *The "Inequality" Controversy: Schooling and Distributive Justice,* edited by Donald Levine and Mary Jo Bane. New York: Basic Books.

Bagdikian, Ben
1971 *The Information Machine.* New York: Harper and Row.

Baker, Frank B.
1977 "Advances in Item Analysis." *Review of Educational Research* 47 (Winter):151–178.

Bane, Mary Jo
1972 "The Effects of Structure: A Study of First Grade Children in Open and Traditional Classrooms." Ed.D. dissertation, Harvard University.

Becker, Gary S.
1964 *Human Capital.* New York: Columbia University Press.
1965 "A Theory of the Allocation of Time." *The Economic Journal* 75 (September):493–517.

Beggs, D. L., and Hieronymus, A. N.
1968 "Uniformity of Growth in the Basic Skills Throughout the School Year and During the Summer." *Journal of Educational Measurement* 5:91–97.

Bell, Daniel
1972 "On Meritocracy and Equality." *Public Interest* 29 (Fall):29–68.

Bellingham, Ann R.
1972 *Leisure Survey (5–14 Year-Olds).* London: Inner London Education Authority.

Bereiter, Carl
1963 "Some Persisting Dilemmas in the Measurement of Change." In *Problems in Measuring Change,* edited by C. W. Harris. Madison: University of Wisconsin Press.
1969 "The Future of Individual Differences." *Harvard Educational Review* 39:310–318.

Berg, Ivan
1970 *Education and Jobs: The Great Training Robbery.* New York: Wiley.

Bidwell, Charles E., and Kasarda, John D.
1975 "School District Organization and Student Achievement." *American Sociological Review* 40 (February):55–70.
1977 "Conceptualizing and Measuring the Effects of Schools and Schooling." Chicago: Center for Educational Finance and Productivity. Mimeographed. December.

Bielby, William T., Hauser, Robert M., and Featherman, David L.
1977a "Response Errors of Black and Nonblack Males in Models of the Intergenerational Transmission of Socioeconomic Status." *American Journal of Sociology* 82 (May):1242–1288.
1977b "Response Errors of Nonblack Males in Models of the Stratification Process." In *Latent Variables in Socioeconomic Models,* edited by D. J. Aigner and A. S. Goldberger. Amsterdam: North-Holland.

Bijou, S. W.
1971 "Environment and Intelligence: A Behavioral Analysis." In *Intelligence: Genetic and Environmental Influences,* edited by R. Cancro, pp. 221–239. New York: Grune and Stratton.

Birnbaum, Allan.
1968 "Some Latent Trait Models and their Use in Inferring an Examinee's Ability." In *Statistical Theories of Mental Test Scores,* edited by Frederic M. Lord and Melvin R. Novick. Reading, Mass.: Addison-Wesley.

Blalock, Herbert M., Jr.
1971 *Causal Models in the Social Sciences.* Chicago: Aldine-Atherton.
1974 "Beyond Ordinal Measurement: Weak Tests of Stronger Theories. In *Measurement in the Social Sciences,* edited by Herbert M. Blalock, Jr. Chicago: Aldine.

Blau, P., and Duncan, O. D.
1967 *The American Occupational Structure.* New York: Wiley.

Block, H. H., ed.
1971 *Mastery Learning: Theory and Practice.* New York: Holt.

Bloom, Benjamin S.
1963 "Testing Cognitive Ability and Achievement." In *Handbook of Research on Teaching,* edited by N. L. Gage. Chicago: Rand McNally.
1964 *Stability and Change in Human Characteristics.* New York: Wiley.
1971 *Individual Differences in School Achievement: A Vanishing Point?* Bloomington, Ind.: Phi Delta Kappa.
1974 "Time and Learning." *American Psychologist* 29:682–688.
1976 *Human Characteristics and School Learning.* New York: McGraw-Hill.

Boring, Edwin G.
1963 *History, Psychology and Science: Selected Papers.* New York: Wiley.

Bormuth, J. R.
1970 *On the Theory of Achievement Test Items.* Chicago: University of Chicago Press.

Boudon, Raymond
1974 *Education, Opportunity, and Social Inequality: Changing Prospects in Western Society.* New York: Wiley.
1976 "Comment on Hauser's Review of *Education, Opportunity, and Social Inequality.*" *American Journal of Sociology* 81 (March):1175–1186.

Bowles, Samuel S.
1970 "Towards an Educational Production Function." In *Education, Income and Human Capital,* edited by W. Lee Hansen. New York: National Bureau of Economic Research.
1972a "Schooling and Inequality from Generation to Generation." *Journal of Political Economy* 80 (May/June, Part II):S219–S251.
1972b "Unequal Education and the Reproduction of the Social Division of Labor." In *Schooling in a Corporate Society,* edited by Martin Carnoy, pp. 36–64. New York: McKay.
1973 "Understanding Unequal Economic Opportunity." *American Economic Review* 63:346–356.

Bowles, Samuel, and Gintis, Herbert
1976 *Schooling in Capitalist America: Educational Reform and the Contradictions of Economic Life.* New York: Basic Books.

Bowles, Samuel, and Levin, Henry M.
1968a "The Determinants of Scholastic Achievement—An Appraisal of Some Recent Evidence." *Journal of Human Resources* 3 (Winter):2–24.
1968b "More on Multicollinearity and the Effectiveness of Schools." *Journal of Human Resources* 3 (Summer):393–400.

Bowles, Samuel, and Nelson, Valerie.
1974 "The 'Inheritance of IQ' and the Intergenerational Reproduction of Economic Inequality." *Review of Economics and Statistics* 56 (February):39–51.
Brail, Richard K.
1969 "Activity Systems Investigations: Strategy for Model Design." Ph.D. dissertation, University of North Carolina.
Brail, Richard K., and Chapin, F. Stuart, Jr.
1973 "Activity Patterns of Urban Residents." *Environment and Behavior* 5 (June):168–190.
Brown, Byron, and Saks, Daniel H.
1975 "The Production and Distribution of Cognitive Skills within Schools." *Journal of Political Economy* 83:571–593.
Brueckner, L. J., and Distad, H. W.
1924 "The Effect of Summer Vacation on the Reading Ability of First-Grade Children." *Elementary School Journal* 24:698–707.
Bruene, Elizabeth
1928 "Effect of Summer Vacation on the Achievement of Pupils in the Fourth, Fifth, and Sixth Grades." *Journal of Educational Research* 18:309–314.
Burawoy, Michael
1976 "The Organization of Consent: Changing Patterns of Conflict on the Shop Floor, 1945–1975." Ph.D. dissertation, University of Chicago.
Burch, William R., Jr.
1969 "The Social Circles of Leisure: Competing Explanations." *Journal of Leisure Research* 1 (Spring):125–147.
Burkhead, Jesse, Fox, Thomas, and Holland, John W.
1967 *Input and Output in Large City High Schools.* Syracuse, N.Y.: Syracuse University Press.
Bush, R. R., and Mosteller, F.
1955 *Stochastic Models for Learning.* New York: Wiley.
Cain, Glenn G., and Watts, Harold W.
1970 "Problems in Making Policy Inferences from the Coleman Report." *American Sociological Review* 35 (April):228–242.
Calhoun, D.
1973 *The Intelligence of a People.* Princeton, N.J.: Princeton University Press.
Cammarota, Gloria, Stoops, John A., and Johnson, Frank R.
1961 *Extending the School Year.* Washington, D.C.: National Education Association.
Campbell, Donald T.
1971 "Temporal Changes in Treatment-Effect Correlations: A Quasi-Experimental Model for Institutional Records and Longitudinal Studies." *Proceedings of the 1970 Invitational Conference on Testing Problems.* Princeton, N.J.: Educational Testing Service.
Campbell, Donald T., and Erlebacher, A.
1970 "How Regression Artifacts in Quasi-Experimental Evaluations Can Mistakenly Make Compensatory Education Look Harmful." In *Compensatory Education: A National Debate,* vol. 3, *The Disadvantaged Child,* edited by J. Hellmuth, pp. 185–210. New York: Brunner/Mazel.
Campbell, Donald T., and Stanley, Julian C.
1963 "Experimental and Quasi-Experimental Designs for Research on Teaching." In *Handbook of Research on Teaching,* edited by N. L. Gage, pp. 171–246. Chicago: Rand McNally.
Cancro, R.
1971 *Intelligence: Genetic and Environmental Influence.* New York: Grune & Stratton.

Carnoy, Martin, and Levin, Henry M.
1976 *The Limits of Educational Reform.* New York: McKay.
Carroll, John B.
1961 "The Nature of the Data, or How to Choose a Correlation Coefficient." *Psychometrika* 26:347–372.
1963 "A Model for School Learning." *Teachers College Record* 64:723–733.
1973 "Fitting a Model of School Learning to Aptitude and Achievement Data Over Grade Levels." Educational Testing Service *Research Bulletin* 51:1–41.
Carver, Ronald P.
1974 "Two Dimensions of Tests: Psychometric and Edumetric." *American Psychologist* 29:512–518.
1975 "The Coleman Report: Using Inappropriately Designed Achievement Tests." *American Educational Research Journal* 12 (Winter):77–86.
Cattell, R. B.
1971 *Abilities: Their Structure, Growth, and Action.* Boston: Houghton Mifflin.
Chapin, F. Stuart
1971 "Free Time Activities and Quality of Urban Life." *Journal of the American Institute of Planners* 37 (November):411–417.
1974 *Human Activity Patterns in the City.* New York: Wiley.
Charters, W. W., Jr.
1963 "The Social Background of Teaching." In *Handbook of Research on Teaching,* edited by N. L. Gage. Chicago: Rand McNally.
Cicourel, A. V., Jennings, K. H., Jennings, S. H. M., Leiter, K. C. W., Mackay, R., Mehan, H., and Roth, D. R.
1974 *Language Use and School Performance.* New York: Academic Press.
Clark, Kenneth
1965 *Dark Ghetto.* New York: Harper and Row.
Clausen, John A.
1967 *Socialization and Society.* Boston: Little, Brown.
Cleary, Florence D., Allen, Ruth S., and Allen, Edmund E.
1968 *The Effect of a Librarian-Centered Reading Guidance Program on the Reading Skills and Habits of Elememtary School Pupils.* Final Report, Project No. 7-1212. Washington, D.C.: U.S. Office of Education.
Coffman, William E.
1961 "Sex Differences in Response to Items in an Aptitude Test." In *The 18th Yearbook,* edited by Edith M. Huddleston, pp. 117–124. Ames, Iowa: National Council on Measurement in Education.
Cohen, David K., and Lazerson, Marvin
1972 "Education and the Corporate Order." *Socialist Revolution* 2 (March–April): 1002–1019.
Coleman, James S.
1961 *The Adolescent Society: The Social Life of the Teenager and its Impact on Education.* New York: The Free Press.
1966 "Equal Schools or Equal Students?" *The Public Interest* 4 (Summer):73–74.
1968a "The Concept of Equality of Educational Opportunity." *Harvard Educational Review* 38 (Winter):7–22.
1968b "The Mathematical Study of Change." In *Methodology in Social Research,* edited by Herbert M. Blalock and Ann B. Blalock. New York: McGraw-Hill.
1971 *Resources for Social Change.* New York: Wiley-Interscience.
Coleman, James S., Campbell, Ernest Q.; Hobson, Carol J., McPartland, James; Mood,

Alexander M., Weinfeld, Frederic, and York, Robert L.
1966 *Equality of Educational Opportunity.* Washington, D.C.: Office of Education, National Center for Educational Statistics, U.S. Government Printing Office.

Coleman, James S., and Karweit, Nancy L.
1972 *Information Systems and Performance Measures in Schools.* Englewood Cliffs, N.J.: Educational Technology Publications.

Coleman, W., and Cureton, E. E.
1954 "Intelligence and Achievement: The Jangle Fallacy Again." *Educational and Psychological Measurement* 14:347–351.

Coles, Robert
1970– "The Doctor and Newcomers to the Ghetto." *American Scholar* 40 (Winter):
1971 66–80.

Conant, James B.
1961 *Slums and Suburbs.* New York: McGraw-Hill.

Converse, Philip E.
1968 "Time Budgets." *The Encyclopedia of the Social Sciences* 16:42–47.

Cook, R. C.
1942 "Vacation Retention of Fundamentals by Primary Grade Pupils." *Elementary School Journal* 43:214–219.
1952 "Dozen Summer Programs Designed to Promote Retention in Young Children." *Elementary School Journal* 52:412–417.

Coolbaugh, J. A.
1972 "Research on Campers and Improved Self-Concept." *Camping Magazine* (November):12.

Coombs, C. H.
1964 *A Theory of Data.* New York: Wiley.

Coons, John E., and Sugarman, Stephen D.
1978 *Education by Choice: The Case for Family Control.* Berkeley: University of California Press.

Coser, Lewis A., and Howe, Irving
1977 *The New Conservatives: A Critique from the Left.* New York: Meridian.

Cotton, J. W., and Harris, C. W.
1973 "Reliability Coefficients as a Function of Individual Differences Induced by a Learning Process Assuming Identical Organisms." *Journal of Mathematical Psychology* 10:387–420.

Crain, Robert L., and York, Robert L.
1976 "Evaluating a Successful Program: Experimental Method and Academic Bias." *School Review* 84 (February):233–254.

Cremin, Lawrence A.
1961 *The Transformation of the School.* New York: Knopf.

Cronbach, Lee J.
1957 "The Two Disciplines of Scientific Psychology." *American Psychologist* 12:671–684.
1970 *Essentials of Psychological Testing.* 3rd ed. New York: Harper and Row.
1971 "Test Validation." In *Educational Measurement,* 2nd ed., edited by Robert L. Thorndike, pp. 443–507. Washington, D.C.: American Council on Education.

Cronbach, Lee J., and Furby, L.
1970 "How Should We Measure 'Change'—or Should We?" *Psychological Bulletin* 74:68–80.

Cutright, Phillips

1973 *Achievement, Mobility and the Draft: Their Impact on the Earnings of Men.* Washington, D.C.: U.S. Social Security Administration.

David, Jane

1974 *Follow Through Summer Study: A Two-Part Investigation of the Impact of Exposure to Schooling on Achievement Growth.* Ed.D. dissertation, Harvard Graduate School of Education.

Davis, Allison, and Havighurst, R. J.

1946 "Social Class and Color Differences in Child-Rearing." *American Sociological Review* 11:698–710.

Davis, F. B., and Fifer, G.

1959 "The Effect on Test Reliability and Validity of Scoring Aptitude and Achievement Tests with Weights for Every Choice." *Educational and Psychological Measurement* 19:159–170.

de Grazia, Sebastian

1962 *On Time, Work, and Leisure.* New York: Anchor.

DeGroot, A. D.

1948 "The Effects of War Upon the Intelligence of Youth." *Journal of Abnormal and Social Psychology* 43:311–317.

1951 "War and the Intelligence of Youth." *Journal of Abnormal and Social Psychology* 46:596–597.

Dewey, John

1959 "Progressive Education and the Science of Education." In *Dewey on Education,* edited by Martin S. Dworkin. New York: Teachers College Press.

Disch, Robert, ed.

1973 *The Future of Literacy.* Englewood Cliffs, N.J.: Prentice-Hall.

Dreeben, Robert

1968 *On What Is Learned in School.* Reading, Mass.: Addison-Wesley.

Duncan, Beverly

1965 *Family Factors and School Dropout: 1920–1960.* Cooperative Research Project No. 2258, U.S. Office of Education. Ann Arbor: University of Michigan.

1967 "Education and Social Background." *American Journal of Sociology* 72 (January):363–372.

Duncan, Greg

1974 "Educational Attainment." In *Four Thousand American Families,* edited by James N. Morgan *et al.*, pp. 305–327. Ann Arbor, Mich.: Institute for Social Research.

Duncan, Otis Dudley

1961 "A Socioeconomic Index for All Occupations." In *Occupations and Social Status,* edited by Albert J. Reiss, Jr., pp. 109–138. New York: Free Press.

1966 "Path Analysis: Sociological Examples." *American Journal of Sociology* 72 (July):1–16.

1968a "Ability and Achievement." *Eugenics Quarterly* 15 (March):1–11.

1968b "Inheritance of Poverty or Inheritance of Race?" In *On Understanding Poverty,* edited by Daniel Patrick Moynihan. New York: Basic Books.

1970 "Partials, Partitions, and Paths." In *Sociological Methodology: 1970,* edited by E. Borgatta, pp. 38–47. San Francisco: Jossey-Bass.

1975 *Introduction to Structural Equation Models.* New York: Academic Press.

Duncan, Otis Dudley, Featherman, D. L., and Duncan, Beverly.

1972 *Socioeconomic Background and Achievement.* New York: Seminar Press.

Duncanson, J. P.
1964 *Intelligence and the Ability to Learn.* Princeton, N.J.: Educational Testing Service.
Durost, Walter N, Bixler, Harold H., Hildreth, Gertrude H., Lund, Kenneth W., and Wrightstone, J. Wayne
1962 *Manual for Interpreting Metropolitan Achievement Tests.* New York: Harcourt, Brace & World.
Dyer, Henry S.
1971 "The Role of Evaluation in Accountability." In *Proceedings of the Conference on Educational Accountability.* Princeton, N.J.: Educational Testing Service.
Eells, Kenneth, Davis, Allison, Havighurst, Robert J., Herrick, Virgil E., and Tyler, Ralph W.
1951 *Intelligence and Cultural Differences.* Chicago: University of Chicago Press.
Elder, Harry E.
1927 "The Effect of the Summer Vacation on Silent Reading Ability in the Intermediate Grades." *Elementary School Journal* 27:541–546.
Fägerlind, Ingemar
1975 *Formal Education and Adult Earnings.* Stockholm: Almqvist & Wiksell.
Featherman, David L.
1972 "Achievement Orientations and Socioeconomic Career Attainments." *American Sociological Review* 37 (April):131–143.
Fennessey, James
1973 "Using Achievement Growth to Analyze Educational Programs." Center for Social Organization of Schools, report no. 151. Mimeographed, March.
Ferge, Susan
1972 "Social Differentiation in Leisure Activity Choices: An Unfinished Experiment." In *The Uses of Time,* edited by A. Szalai *et al.* The Hague: Mouton.
Finch, F. H.
1946 "Enrollment Increases and Changes in the Mental Level." *Applied Psychological Monographs 10.* Stanford, Calif.: American Psychological Association.
Findley, W. G., ed.
1963 *The Impact and Improvement of School Testing Programs. The 62nd Yearbook of the National Society for the Study of Education.* Chicago: University of Chicago Press.
Fleishman, E. A.
1965 "The Description and Prediction of Perceptual-Motor Skill Learning." In *Training Research and Education,* edited by R. Glaser, pp. 137–175. New York: Wiley.
Fox, D. J.
1967 *Expansion of the More Effective Schools Program.* New York: Center for Urban Education.
Friedenberg, Edgar Z.
1969 "Social Consequences of Educational Measurement." In *Proceedings of the 1969 Invitational Conference on Testing Problems.* Princeton, N.J.: Educational Testing Service, pp. 23–30.
Gagné, Robert M., ed.
1967 *Learning and Individual Differences.* Columbus, Ohio: Merrill.
Galton, Sir Francis
1869 *Hereditary Genius: An Inquiry into Its Laws and Consequences.* London: Macmillan.

Gardner, Eric F.
1947 "Determination of Units of Measurement Which Are Consistent with Inter- and Intra-Grade Differences in Ability." Ph.D. dissertation, Harvard University Graduate School of Education.
1950 "Comments on Selected Scaling Techniques with a Description of a New Type of Scale." *Journal of Clinical Psychology* 6:38–43.

Garfinkle, M. A.
1919 "The Effect of Summer Vacation on Ability in the Fundamentals of Arithmetic." *Journal of Educational Psychology* 10:44–48.

Gaver, Mary Virginia
1963 *Effectiveness of Centralized Library Services in Elementary Schools.* New Brunswick, N.J.: Rutgers University Press.

Gintis, Herbert
1971 "Education, Technology, and the Characteristics of Worker Productivity." *American Economic Review* 61 (May):266–279.

Glass, G. V.; Peckham, P. D.; and Sanders, J. R.
1972 "Consequences of Failure to Meet Assumptions Underlying the Analysis of Variance and Covariance." *Review of Educational Research* 42:237–288.

Gold, Seymour
1972 "Non-Use of Neighborhood Parks." *Journal of the American Institute of Planners* 38 (November):369–378.

Goodman, Paul
1970 *New Reformation: Notes of a Neolithic Conservative.* New York: Random House.

Green, Robert L., Hoffmann, Louis J., Morse, Richard J., Hayes, Marilyn E., and Morgan, Robert F.
1964 "The Educational Status of Children in a District Without Public Schools." Cooperative Research Project 2321. Washington, D.C.: U.S. Office of Education.

Griffin, Larry J.
1976 "Specification Biases in Estimates of Socioeconomic Returns to Schooling." *Sociology of Education* 492 (April):121–138.

Griliches, Zvi
1977 "Estimating the Returns to Schooling: Some Econometric Problems·" *Econometrica* 45:1–22.

Griliches, Zvi, and Mason, William M.
1973 "Education, Income, and Ability." In *Structural Equation Models in the Social Sciences,* edited by Arthur S. Goldberger and Otis Dudley Duncan, pp. 185–316. New York: Seminar Press.

Guilford, Joy Paul
1941 "The Difficulty of a Test and Its Factor Composition." *Psychometrika* 6:67–77.
1956 *Fundamental Statistics in Psychology and Education,* 4th Ed. New York: McGraw-Hill.
1967 *The Nature of Human Intelligence.* New York: McGraw-Hill.

Gulliksen, Harold
1950 *Theory of Mental Tests.* New York: Wiley.

Guthrie, James W.; Kleindorfer, George B.; Levin, Henry M.; and Stout, Robert T.
1971 *Schools and Inequality.* Cambridge, Mass.: MIT Press.

Gutenschwager, Gerald A.
1973 "The Time Budget-Activity Systems Perspective in Urban Research and Planning." *Journal of the American Institute of Planners* 39 (November):378–387.

Hallinan, Maureen, and Sørensen, Aage B.
n.d. "School Effects on Growth in Academic Achievement." Working paper 75–6, Center for Demography and Ecology. Madison: University of Wisconsin–Madison.

Hambleton, R. K., Roberts, P. M., and Traub, R. E.
1970 "A Comparison of the Reliability and Validity of Two Methods for Assessing Partial Knowledge on a Multiple Choice Test." *Journal of Educational Measurement* 7:75–82.

Hamblin, Robert L., Buckholdt, David, Ferritor, Daniel, Kozloff, Martin, and Blackwell, Lois
1971 *The Humanization Processes: A Social, Behavioral Analysis of Children's Problems.* New York: Wiley.

Hanoch, Giora
1974 "An Economic Analysis of Earnings and Schooling." *Journal of Human Resources* 2:309–329.

Hansen, W. Lee, ed.
1970 *Education, Income and Human Capital.* New York: Columbia University Press for the National Bureau of Economic Research.

Hanushek, Eric A.
1970 "The Production of Education, Teacher Quality and Efficiency." In *Do Teachers Make A Difference?*, edited by Alexander M. Mood. Washington, D.C.: U.S. Government Printing Office.

Hanushek, Eric, and Kain, John F.
1972 "On the Value of Equality of Educational Opportunity as a Guide to Public Policy." In *On Equality of Educational Opportunity*, edited by Frederick Mosteller and Daniel P. Moynihan, pp. 116–145. New York: Vintage Books.

Hargens, Lowell L., Reskin, B. F., and Allison, P. D.
1976 "Problems in Estimating Measurement Error from Panel Data." *Sociological Methods and Research* 4 (May):439–458.

Harman, David
1970 "Illiteracy: An Overview." *Harvard Educational Review* 40 (May):226–243.

Harnischfeger, Annagret, and Wiley, David E.
1976 "Exposure to Schooling: Method, Conclusions, Policy." *Educational Researcher* 5 (February):18.

Harvard Educational Review
1973 *Perspectives on Inequality: A Reassessment of the Effect of Family and Schooling in America*. Cambridge, Mass.: Harvard University, February.

Hause, John C.
1971 "Ability and Schooling as Determinants of Lifetime Earnings, or If You're So Smart, Why Ain't You Rich." *American Economic Review* 61 (May):289–298.

Hauser, Robert M.
1968 "Family, School, and Neighborhood Factors in Educational Performance in a Metropolitan School System." Ph.D. dissertation, University of Michigan.
1969 "Schools and the Stratification Process." *American Journal of Sociology* 74 (May):587–611.
1971 *Socioeconomic Background and Educational Performance*. Washington, D.C.: Rose Monograph Series, American Sociological Association.
1973 "Disaggregating a Social-Psychological Model of Educational Attainment." In *Structural Equation Models in the Social Sciences*, edited by Arthur S. Goldberger and Otis Dudley Duncan, pp. 255–284. New York: Seminar Press.

1976 "On Boudon's Model of Social Mobility." *American Journal of Sociology* 81 (January):911–928.

Hauser, R. M., Koffel, J. N., Travis, H. P., and Dickinson, P. J.

1975 "Temporal Change in Occupational Mobility: Evidence for Men in the United States." *American Sociological Review* 40 (June):279–297.

Hauser, R. M., Lutterman, K. G., and Sewell, W. H.

1971 "Socioeconomic Background and the Earnings of High School Graduates." Paper presented at the meeting of the American Sociological Association, September. Denver, Colorado. Mimeographed.

Hauser, Robert M., Sewell, William H., and Alwin, Duane F.

1976 "High School Effects on Achievement." In *Schooling and Achievement in American Society,* edited by W. H. Sewell, R. M. Hauser, and D. L. Featherman, pp. 309–341. New York: Academic Press.

Havighurst, R. J., and Lanke, L. L.

1944 "Relation between Ability and Social Status in a Midwestern Community. I. Ten-Year-Old Children." *Journal of Educational Psychology* 35:357–368.

Hayes, Donald P., and Grether, Judith

1969 "The School Year and Vacations: When Do Students Learn?" Revision of a paper presented at the Eastern Sociological Assocation Convention, New York City, April. Mimeographed.

Hayes, Donald P., and King, John P.

1974 "The Development of Reading Achievement Differentials During the School Year and Vacations." Mimeographed. Ithaca, N.Y.: Cornell University.

Heise, David R.

1969a "Separating Reliability and Stability in Test-Retest Correlation." *American Sociological Review* 34 (February):93–101.

1969b "Problems in Path Analysis and Causal Inference." In *Sociological Methodology, 1969,* edited by Edgar F. Borgatta, pp. 38–73. San Francisoco: Jossey-Bass.

1970 "Causal Inference from Panel Data." In *Sociological Methodology, 1970,* edited by E. F. Borgatta and G. W. Bohrnstedt, pp. 3–24. San Francisco: Jossey-Bass.

Hendrickson, G. F.

1971 "The Effect of Differential Option Weighting on Multiple Choice Objective Tests." *Journal of Educational Measurement* 8:291–296.

Henry, Jules

1965 "White People's Time, Colored People's Time." *Transaction* 2 (April): 31–34.

Herriot, Robert E., and Muse, Donald W.

1973 "Methodological Issues in the Study of School Effects." In *Review of Research in Education,* edited by Fred N. Kerlinger. Itasca, Ill.: Peacock Press.

Herriot, Robert E., and St. John, Nancy H.

1966 *Social Class and the Urban School.* New York: Wiley.

Herzog, Elizabeth, Newcomb, Carol H., and Cisin, Ira H.

1974 "Double Deprivation: The Less They Have, the Less They Learn." In *A Report on Longitudinal Evaluations of Preschool Programs,* edited by Sally Ryan. Washington, D.C.: Department of Health, Education and Welfare.

Heyns, Barbara

1971 "Curriculum Assignment and Tracking Policies in Forty-Eight Urban Public High Schools." Ph.D. dissertation, University of Chicago.

1974 "Social Selection and Stratification within Schools." *American Journal of Sociology* 79 (May):1434–1451.

1976a "Education, Evaluation, and the Metrics of Learning." *Journal for Teaching and Learning* 2 (April):2–16.

1976b *Exposure and the Effects of Schooling.* Final Report, Grant No. 10301. Washington, D.C.: National Institute of Education.

1977 "Measuring the Effects of Education." *Science* 196 (May):763–765.

Hill, Russell, and Stafford, Frank

1974 "Time Inputs to Children." In *Five Thousand American Families, Vol. 2*, edited by James N. Morgan. Ann Arbor, Mich.: Institute for Social Research.

Hirschman, Albert O.

1970 *Exit, Voice, and Loyalty: Responses to Decline in Firms, Organizations, and States.* Cambridge, Mass.: Harvard University Press.

Hoachlander, E. Gareth

1975 "Residential Location Patterns and Availability of Local Public Services." Working paper, Childhood and Government Project. Berkeley: University of California, Berkeley.

Hodge, R. W.

1970 "Social Integration, Psychological Well-Being, and Their Socioeconomic Correlates." *Sociological Inquiry* 40:182–206.

Hodgson, Godfrey

1975 "Do Schools Make a Difference?" In *The "Inequality" Controversy*, edited by D. M. Levine and M. J. Bane. New York: Basic Books.

Hoffmann, Banesh

1962 *The Tyranny of Testing.* New York: Collier.

Holthouse, Norman D.; Stofflet, Frederick P.; and Tokar, Edward B.

1976 *Achievement, Social Class and the Summer Vacation.* Final Report, Project 3-0194, National Institute of Education. Norfolk, Virginia: Norfolk Public Schools.

Honzik, Marjorie P.

1957 "Developmental Studies of Parent-Child Resemblance in Intelligence." *Child Development* 28 (June):215–228.

Horton, John

1967 "Time and Cool People." *Transaction* 4 (April):5–12.

Hunter, Floyd

1953 *Community Power Structure: A Study of Decision Makers.* Chapel Hill: University of North Carolina Press.

Hurn, Christopher J.

1976 "Theory and Ideology in Two Traditions of Thought About Schools." *Social Forces* 54 (June):848–865.

Husén, Torsten

1951 "The Influence of Schooling Upon IQ." *Theoria* 17:61–88.

1972 "Does More Time in School Make a Difference?" *Saturday Review* 29 (April):32–35.

Husén, Torsten, ed.

1967 *International Study of Achievement in Mathematics, Vol. II.* New York: Wiley.

Hyman, Herbert H., and Wright, Charles R.

1971 "Trends in Voluntary Association Memberships of American Adults: Replication Based on Secondary Analysis of National Sample Surveys." *American Sociological Review* 36 (April):191–209.

Hyman, Herbert H.; Wright, Charles R.; and Reed, John Shelton

1975 *The Enduring Effects of Education.* Chicago: University of Chicago Press.

Illich, Ivan

1970 *Deschooling Society*: New York: Harper and Row.

Irmina, Sister M.
1928 "The Effect of Summer Vacation on the Retention of the Elementary School Subjects." *Catholic University Educational Research Bulletin* 3:99.
Jamison, D., Suppes, Patrick, and Wells, S.
1974 "The Effectiveness of Alternative Instructional Media: A Survey." *Review of Educational Research* 44 (Winter):1–68.
Jencks, Christopher S.
1972a "The Coleman Report and the Conventional Wisdom." In *On Equality of Educational Opportunity*, edited by F. Mosteller and D. P. Moynihan, pp. 69–115. New York: Random House.
1972b "The Quality the Data Collected by the *Equality of Educational Opportunity* Survey." In *On Equality of Educational Opportunity*, edited by F. Mosteller and D. P. Moynihan, pp. 437–512. New York: Random House.
Jencks, Christopher, Bartlett, Susan, Corcoran, Mary, Crouse, James, Eaglesfield, David, Jackson, Gregory, McClelland, Kent, Mueser, Peter, Olneck, Michael; Schwartz, Joseph, Ward, Sherry, and Williams, Jill
In press *Who Gets Ahead? A Study of the Determinants of Economic Success in America.* New York: Basic Books.
Jencks, Christopher S., and Brown, Marsha D.
1975 "Effects of High Schools on Their Students." *Harvard Educational Review* 45 (August):273–324.
Jencks, Christopher, Smith, Marshall S., Acland, Henry, Bane, Mary Jo; Cohen, David, Gintis, Herbert, Heyns, Barbara, and Michelson, Stephan
1972 *Inequality: A Reassessment of the Effect of Family and Schooling in America.* New York: Basic Books.
Jenkins, Joseph R., and Deno, Stanley L.
1969 "Effects of Instructional Objectives on Learning." Paper presented at the annual meeting of the American Educational Research Association, February, Los Angeles. Mimeographed.
Jensen, Arthur R.
1966 "Cumulative Deficit in Compensatory Education." *Journal of School Psychology* 4:37–47.
1967 "Estimation of the Limits of Heritability of Traits by Comparison of Monozygotic and Dizygotic Twins." *Proceedings of the National Academy of Science* 58:149–157.
1969 "How Much Can We Boost IQ and Scholastic Achievement?" *Harvard Educational Review* 39 (Winter):1–123.
1974 "Cumulative Deficit: A Testable Hypothesis?" *Developmental Psychology* 10:996–1019.
1977 "Cumulative Deficit in IQ of Blacks in the Rural South." *Developmental Psychology* 13 (May):184–191.
Joreskog, K. G.
1969 "A General Approach to Maximum Likelihood Factor Analysis." *Psychometrika* 34:183–202.
Kadushin, Charles
1964 "Social Class and the Experience of Ill Health." *Sociological Inquiry* 34 (Winter):67–80.
Kalecki, M.
1945 "On the Gibrat Distribution." *Econometrica* 13:161–170.

Kamin, Leon J.
1974 *The Science and Politics of IQ*. New York: Wiley.

Karabel, Jerome, and Astin, Alexander
1975 "Social Class, Academic Ability, and College 'Quality'." *Social Forces* 53 (March):381–398.

Karier, Clarence J., ed.
1975 *Shaping the American Educational State: 1900 to the Present.* New York: The Free Press.

Karweit, Nancy
1973 "Rainy Days and Mondays: An Analysis of Factors Related to Absence from School." Report no. 162, Center for Social Organization of Schools. Baltimore, Md.: Johns Hopkins University. Mimeographed.
1976a "A Reanalysis of the Effect of Quantity of Schooling on Achievement." *Sociology of Education* 49 (July):236–246.
1976b "Social Influences on Student Interaction Patterns." Report no. 220, Center for Social Organization of Schools. Baltimore, Md.: Johns Hopkins University, December. Mimeographed.

Kayser, Brian D., and Summers, Gene F.
1973 "The Adequacy of Student Reports of Parental S.E.S. Characteristics." *Sociological Methods and Research* 1 (February):303–315.

Keats, J. A., and Lord, F. M.
1962 "A Theoretical Distribution for Mental Test Scores." *Psychometrika* 27:59–72.

Keats, J. A.
1964 "Some Generalizations of a Theoretical Distribution of Mental Test Scores." *Psychometrika* 29:215–231.

Keller, Suzanne, and Zavalloni, Marisa
1964 "Ambition and Social Class: A Respecification." *Social Forces* 43:58–70.

Kerckhoff, Alan C.
1971 *Educational, Familial, and Peer Group Influences on Occupational Achievement.* Final report on project No. 8-0053. Washington, D.C.: Office of Education, U.S. Department of Health, Education, and Welfare.
1974 *Ambition and Attainment: A Study of Four Samples of American Boys.* Washington, D.C.: American Sociological Association.
1976 "The Status Attainment Process: Socialization or Allocation?" *Social Forces* 55 (December):368–381.

Kerckhoff, Alan C.; Mason, William M., and Moss, Sharon S.
1973 "On the Accuracy of Children's Reports of Family Social Status." *Sociology of Education* 46 (Spring):219–247.

Kerlinger, F. N.
1964 *Foundations of Behavioral Research.* New York: Holt.
1973 *Review of Research in Education.* Itasca, Ill.: Peacock Press.

Keyfitz, Nathan
1973 "Can Inequality be Cured?" *The Public Interest* 31 (Spring):91–101.

Keys, N., and Lawson, J. V.
1937 "Summer Versus Winter Gains in School Achievement." *School and Society* 46:541–544.

Kirp, David L.
1977 "Law, Politics, and Equal Educational Opportunity: The Limits of Judicial Involvement." *Harvard Educational Review* 47 (May):117–137.

Kleemeier, R. W., ed.
1961 *Aging and Leisure: A Research Perspective into the Meaningful Use of Time.* New York: Oxford University Press.

Kmenta, Jan
1971 *Elements of Econometrics.* New York: Macmillan.

Kohen, Andrew I.
1971 "Determinants of Early Labor Market Success Among Young Men: Ability, Quantity, and Quality of Schooling." Paper presented at the meeting of the American Educational Research Association, New York. Mimeographed.

Kohn, Melvin L.
1963 "Social Class and Parent-Child Relationships: An Interpretation. *American Journal of Sociology* 68 (January):471–480.
1969 *Class and Conformity: A Study in Values.* Homewood, Ill : Dorsey Press.

Kohs, Samuel C.
1923 *Intellectual Measurement.* New York: Macmillan.

Kolberg, O. W.
1934 "A Study of Summer Time Forgetting." *Elementary School Journal* 35:281–287.

Krantz, D. H.; Luce, R. D.; Suppes, P.; and Tversky, A.
1971 *Foundations of Measurement.* New York: Academic Press.

Krathwohl, David R.
1969 "Presidential Address." Paper presented at the annual meeting of the American Educational Research Association, Los Angeles, February. Mimeographed.

Labovitz, Sanford
1967 "Some Observations on Measurement and Statistics." *Social Forces* 46 (December):151–160.
1970 "The Assignment of Numbers to Rank Order Categories." *American Sociological Review* 35 (June):515–525.

Land, Kenneth C.
1969 "Principles of Path Analysis." In *Sociological Methodology, 1969,* edited by E. Borgatta. San Francisco: Jossey-Bass.

Lazarsfeld, Paul F., and Henry, N. W., eds.
1966 *Readings in Mathematical Social Science.* Chicago: Science Research Associates.

Leacock, Eleanor
1969 *Teaching and Learning in City Schools.* New York: Basic Books.

Leibowitz, Arleen
1974 "Home Investments in Children." *Journal of Political Economy* 82 (March–April):S111–S135.

Lennon, Roger T.
1971 "Accountability and Performance Contracting." Paper presented at the annual meeting of the American Educational Research Association, New York, February. Mimeographed.

Lesser, Gerald S.; Fifer, Gordon; and Clark, Donald H.
1965 "Mental Abilities of Children from Different Social Class and Cultural Groups." *Monographs of the Society for Research in Child Development* 30 (No. 4). Chicago: University of Chicago and the Society for Research in Child Development.

Lessinger, Leon
1970 "Engineering Accountability for Results in Public Education." *Phi Delta Kappan* 52:217–225.

Levanto, J.
1973 "The Identification and Analyses of Factors Related to Secondary School Absenteeism." Ph.D. dissertation, University of Connecticut.

Levin, Henry M.
1977 "A Radical Critique of Educational Policy. *Journal of Educational Finance* 3 (Summer):9–31.

Levine, Donald M., and Bane, Mary Jo
1975 *The "Inequality" Controversy: Schooling and Distributive Justice.* New York: Basic Books.

Levine, Murray
1976 "The Academic Achievement Test: Its Historical Context and Social Functions." *American Psychologist* (March):228–238.

Levy, Frank S.; Meltsner, Arnold J.; and Wildavsky, Aaron
1974 *Urban Outcomes: Schools, Streets, and Libraries.* Berkeley: University of California Press.

Lieberman, Myron
1970 "An Overview of Accountability." *Phi Delta Kappan* 52:194–195.

Linder, Staffin B.
1970 *The Harried Leisure Class.* New York: Columbia University Press.

Lindquist, E. F., ed.
1951 *Educational Measurement.* Washington, D.C.: American Council on Education.

Lindquist E. F., and Hieronymus, A. N.
1964 *Manual for Administrators, Supervisors, and Counselors, Iowa Tests of Basic Skills.* Boston: Houghton-Mifflin.

Lord, Frederic M.
1952 "A Theory of Test Scores." *Psychometric Monograph* no. 7. The Psychometric Society, Philadelphia: George E. Ferguson.
1953 "On the Statistical Treatment of Football Numbers." *American Psychologist* 8:750–751.
1958 "Further Problems in the Measurement of Growth." *Educational and Psychological Measurement* 18:437–454.
1960 "An Empirical Study of the Normality and Independence of Errors of Measurement in Test Scores." *Psychometrika* 25 (March):91–104.
1964 "Elementary Models for Measuring Change." In *Problems in Measuring Change,* edited by Chester W. Harris, pp. 21–38. Madison: University of Wisconsin Press.
1965 "A Strong True-Score Theory, with Applications." *Psychometrika* 30:239–270.
1967 "A Paradox in the Interpretation of Group Comparisons." *Psychological Bulletin* 68:304–305.
1969 "Statistical Adjustments When Comparing Pre-Existing Groups." *Psychological Bulletin* 72:336–337.
1974 "Individualized Testing and Item Characteristic Curve Theory." In *Contemporary Developments in Mathematical Psychology,* edited by David H. Kranz. San Francisco: Freeman.
1977 "Practical Application of Item Characteristic Curve Theory." *Journal of Educational Measurement* 14 (Summer):117–138.

Lord, Frederic M., and Novick, Melvin R.
1968 *Statistical Theories of Mental Test Scores.* Reading, Mass.: Addison-Wesley.

Lorge, I.
1945 "Schooling Makes a Difference." *Teachers College Record* 46:483–492.

Lortie, Dan C.
1967 "National Decision-Making: Is It Possible Today?" *The EPIE Forum* 1:1–6.

Lundberg, George A.; Komarovsky, Mirra; and McInerny, Mary A.
1934 *Leisure: A Suburban Study*. New York: Columbia University Press.

Maccoby, Eleanor E.
1951 "Television: Its Impact on School Children." *Public Opinion Quarterly* 15 (Fall):421–444.

Maccoby, Eleanor E.
1966 *The Development of Sex Differences*. Stanford, Calif.: Stanford University Press.

Maccoby, Eleanor, and Jacklin, Carol
1974 *The Psychology of Sex Differences*. Stanford, Calif.: Stanford University Press.

MacDonald, M.; McGuire, C.; and Havighurst, R.
1949 "Leisure Activities and the Socioeconomic Status of Children." *American Journal of Sociology* 54 (May):505–519.

Mager, Robert F.
1962 *Preparing Objectives for Programmed Instruction*. San Francisco: Fearon Press.

Margolis, Julius
1968 "The Demand for Urban Public Services." In *Issues in Urban Economics*, edited by Harvey S. Perloff and Lowdon Wingo, Jr., pp. 527–565. Baltimore, Md.: Johns Hopkins Press.

Marjoribanks, K.
1972a "Environment, Social Class, and Mental Abilities." *Journal of Educational Psychology* 63:103–109.
1972b "Ethnic and Environmental Influences on Mental Abilities." *American Journal of Sociology* 78:3238337.

Marley, A. A. J.
1967 "Abstract One-Parameter Families of Commutative Learning Operators." *Journal of Mathematical Psychology* 4:414–429.

Mason, William M.; Hauser, Robert M.; Kerckhoff, Alan C.; Poss, Sharon S.; and Manton, Kenneth
1976 "Models of Response Error in Student Reports of Parental Socioeconomic Characteristics." In *Schooling and Achievement in American Society*, edited by William H. Sewell, Robert M. Hauser, and David L. Featherman, pp. 443–494. New York: Academic Press.

Mayer, Lawrence S.
1970 "Comment on 'The Assignment of Numbers to Rank Order Categories.' " *American Sociological Review* 35 (August):916–917.
1971 "A Note on Treating Ordinal Data as Interval Data." *American Sociological Review* 35 (June):519–520.

Mayeske, G.; Wisler, C. E.; Beaton, A. E.; Weinfeld, F. D.; Cohen, W. M.; Okada, T.; Prostrek, J. M.; and Tabler, K. A.
1969 *A Study of Our Nation's Schools*. Washington, D.C.: U.S. Office of Education.

Mayersohn, Rolf
1969 "The Sociology of Leisure in the United States: Introduction and Bibliography, 1945–1965." *Journal of Leisure Research* 1 (Winter):53–68.

Maynard, Z. M.
1952 "Summer School with a Difference." *National Educational Association Journal* 124 (March):27–28.

McCall, Robert
1977 "Childhood IQ's as Predictors of Adult Educational and Occupational Status." *Science* 197 (July 29):482–483.

McDill, E. L., Meyers, E. D., and Rigsby, L. C.
1967 "Institutional Effects on the Academic Behavior of High School Students." *Sociology of Education* 40 (Winter):181–199.

McDill, E. L., McDill, M. S., and Sprehe, J. T.
1969 *Strategies for Success in Compensatory Education.* Baltimore, Md.: Johns Hopkins Press.

McGhan, Barry R.
1970 "Accountability as a Negative Reinforcer." *American Teacher* 55:13.

McNemar, Quinn
1942 *The Revision of the Stanford-Binet Scale.* Boston: Houghton-Mifflin.
1958 "On Growth Measurement." *Educational and Psychological Measurement* 18:47–55.

Medrich, Elliott A.
In press "Patterns of Consumption in the Public Sector." In *Public Service and Disadvantaged Populations*, edited by Richard Baird. New York: Praeger.

Meier, Deborah
1973 *Reading Failure and the Tests.* New York: Workshop Center for Open Education.

Meier, Richard L.
1959 "Human Time Allocation: A Basis for Social Accounts." *Journal of the American Institute of Planners* 25:27–33.

Michelson, William
1971 "Some Like It Hot: Social Participation and Environmental Use as Functions of the Season." *American Journal of Sociology* 76 (May):1072–1084.

Miller, Gordon W.
1970 "Factors in School Achievement and Social Class." *Journal of Educational Psychology* 61:260–269.

Miller, LaMar P., and Gordon, Edmund W., eds.
1974 *Equality of Educational Opportunity.* New York: AMS Press.

Miller, Marv
1965 "Scholars in Shirt Sleeves: Summer School Comes of Age." *American School Board Journal* 150 (April):21–22.

Mincer, Jacob
1958 "Investment in Human Capital and Personal Income Distribution." *Journal of Political Economy* 66 (August):281–302.
1974 *Schooling, Experience, and Earnings.* New York: National Bureau of Economic Research.

Mood, Alexander M., ed.
1970 *Do Teachers Make a Difference?* Washington, D.C.: U.S. Office of Education.

Morgan, James
1966 *The Productive Americans.* Ann Arbor, Mich.: Institute for Social Research.

Morgan, James N., Dickinson, Katherine, Dickinson, Jon, Benus, Jacob, and Duncan, Greg
1974 *Five Thousand American Families: Patterns of Economic Progress, Vol. I, An Analysis of the First Five Years of the Panel Study of Income Dynamics.* Ann Arbor, Mich.: Institute for Social Research.

Morgan, L. D.
1929 "How Effective Is Specific Training in Preventing Loss Due to Summer Vacation?" *Journal of Educational Psychology* 20:466–471.

Morrison, J. Cayce
1924 "What Effect Has the Summer Vacation on Children's Learning and Ability to Learn?" *Ohio State University Educational Research Bulletin* 3:245–249.

Mosher, Frederic A.
1976 *Final Report on the Instrumentation Study.* Prepared for the Office of Education, Contract No. 0-74-0394. New York: The Carnegie Corporation, June.

Mosteller, Frederick, and Moynihan, Daniel P., eds.
1972 *On Equality of Educational Opportunity.* New York: Random House.

Moynihan, D. P., ed.
1969 *On Understanding Poverty.* New York: Basic Books.

Murnane, Richard
1974 "The Impact of School Resources on the Learning of Inner City Children." Ph.D. dissertation, Yale University.

Nash, Robert J., and Agne, Russell M.
1972 "The Ethos of Accountability: A Critique." *Teachers College Record* 73 (February):357–370.

National Education Association
1965 *Length of School Day for Teachers and Pupils, 1964–65.* Washington, D.C.: National Education Association, Research Division and American Association of School Administrators, Educational Research Service.
1968a "Summer Enrichment Programs." *NEA Research Bulletin* 46:44–47.
1968b *The Rescheduled School Year. Research Summary 1952–1968.* Washington, D.C.: National Education Association, Research Division.

Neff, W. S.
1938 "Socioeconomic Status and Intelligence: A Critical Survey." *Psychological Bulletin* 35:727–757.

Nelson, M. J.
1929 "Difference in Achievement of Elementary School Pupils Before and After Summer Vacation." *University of Wisconsin, Bureau of Educational Research Bulletin* 10:47–48.

Nichols, Robert C.
1966 "Schools and the Disadvantaged." *Science* 154 (December):3754.

Nolte, M. Chester
1966 "Rapid Growth of Summer Schools." *American School Board Journal* 152 (May):60–61.

Noonan, Margaret E.
1926 "Influence of the Summer Vacation on the Abilities of Fifth and Sixth Grade Children." *Contributions to Education* 204.

Norris, Charles I.
1976 "Introduction." In *Education, Inequality and National Policy*, edited by Nelson F. Ashline, Thomas R. Pezzullo, and Charles I. Norris. Lexington, Mass.: D. C. Heath.

North, R. D.
1955 "Achievement Growth Trends of Independent School Pupils as Reflected by Fall and Spring Results on the Stanford Achievement Test." *Achievement Testing Program in Independent Schools and Supplementary Studies, 1955.* New York: Educational Records Bureau, July.

Osborne, R. T.
1960 "Racial Differences in Mental Growth and School Achievement: A Longitudinal Study." *Psychological Reports* 7:233–239.

Osburn, H. G.
1968 "Item Sampling for Achievement Testing." *Educational and Psychological Measurement* 28:95–104.

Otto, Luther B.
1975 "Extracurricular Activities in the Educational Attainment Process." *Rural Sociology* 40 (Summer):162–176.
1976 "Social Integration and the Status-Attainment Process." *American Journal of Sociology* 81 (May):1360–1383.

Otto, Luther B., and Featherman, David L.
1975 "Social Structural and Psychological Antecedents of Self-Estrangement and Powerlessness." *American Sociological Review* 40 (December):701–719.

Overlan, Frank
1968 "Out of the Mouths of Babes: The Accuracy of Students' Responses to Family and Educational Background Questionnaires." Cambridge, Mass.: Harvard University Graduate School of Education. Mimeographed.

Parsley, K. M., and Powell, M.
1962 "Achievement Gains or Losses During the Academic Year and Over the Summer Vacation." *Genetic Psychology Monographs* 66 (November):286–342.

Patnaik, D., and Traub, R. E.
1973 "Differential Weighting by Judged Degree of Correctness." *Journal of Educational Measurement* 10:281–286.

Patterson, M. V. W., and Rensselaer, A. M.
1925 "The Effect of Summer Vacation on Children's Mental Ability." *Education* 46:222–228.

Patton, Michael Q.
1975 *Alternative Evaluation Research Paradigm.* Bismarck: University of North Dakota Press.

Pearlin, Leonard I., and Kohn, Melvin L.
1966 "Social Class, Occupation, and Parental Values: A Cross-National Study." *American Sociological Review* 31 (August):466–479.

Pennock, J. R., and Chapman, J. W., eds.
1967 *Equality.* New York: Atherton Press.

Perkinson, Henry J.
1968 *The Imperfect Panacea: American Faith in Education, 1865–1965.* New York: Random House.

Perlman, Robert
1973 "Vacations—For Whom?" *Social Policy* (July-August):50–55.

Pettigrew, Thomas; Useem, Elizabeth; Normand, Clarence; and Smith, Marshall S.
1973 "Busing: A Review of 'The Evidence' ". *The Public Interest* 30 (Winter):88–118.

Porter, Andrew C.
1969 "Comments on Some Current Strategies to Evaluate the Effectiveness of Compensatory Education Programs." Paper presented at the annual meeting of the American Psychological Association. Mimeographed.

Porter, James N.
1974 "Race, Socialization, and Mobility in Educational and Early Occupational Attainment." *American Sociological Review* 39 (June):303–316.
1976 "Socialization and Mobility in Educational and Early Occupational Attainment." *Sociology of Education* 49 (January):23–33.

Potthoff, Richard F.
1966 "Statistical Aspects of the Problem of Biases in Psychological Tests." Institute of Statistics Mimeographed Series no. 479, May.

Racine Unified School District No. 1.
1969 "ESEA Title I Evaluation Report, Summer Session 1969." Racine, Wisconsin. Mimeographed.
Rasch, Georg
1960 *Probabilistic Models for Some Intelligence and Attainment Tests.* Copenhagen: Nielsen and Lydiche.
1961 "On General Laws and the Meaning of Measurement in Psychology." In *Proceedings of the Fourth Berkeley Symposium on Mathematical Statistics and Probability,* edited by J. Neyman, pp. 321–324. Berkeley: University of California Press.
1966 "An Item Analysis which Takes Individual Differences into Account." *British Journal of Mathematical and Statistical Psychology* 19:49–57.
Reese, T. W.
1943 "The Application of the Theory of Physical Measurement to the Measurement of Psychological Magnitudes, with Three Experimental Examples." *Psychological Monographs* 55:1–89.
Reilly, R. R., and Jackson, R.
1973 "Effects of Empirical Option Weighting on Reliability and Validity of an Academic Aptitude Test." *Journal of Educational Measurement* 10:185–194.
Reissman, Leonard
1954 "Social Class, Leisure, and Social Participation." *American Sociological Review* 19 (February):76–84.
Restle, Frank
1961a *Psychology of Judgment and Choice.* New York: Wiley.
1961b "Statistical Methods for a Theory of Cue Learning." *Psychometrika* 26:291–306.
Rice, Arthur H.
1970 "Atlanta Schoolman Discusses His Year-Round Program." *Nation's Schools* 86 (December):12.
Rickover, H. G.
1962 *Swiss Schools and Ours: Why Theirs Are Better.* Boston: Little, Brown.
Rivlin, Alice M.
1971 *Systematic Thinking for Social Action.* Washington, D.C.: Brookings Institute.
Rogoff, Natalie
1961 "American Public Schools and Equality of Opportunity." In *Education, Economy and Society,* edited by A. H. Halsey, Jean Floud, and C. Arnold Anderson, pp. 140–141. New York: Free Press.
Rossi, Peter H., and Williams, Walter, eds.
1973 *Evaluating Social Programs: Theory, Practice, and Politics.* New York: Seminar Press.
Rubin, Donald B.
1974 "Estimating Causal Effects of Treatments in Randomized and Nonrandomized Studies." *Journal of Educational Psychology* 66:688–701.
Rubin, Victor
1975 "The Time Budget Research Tradition: Lessons for Planning with Young People." Working paper, Childhood and Government Project. Berkeley: University of California, Berkeley, March. Mimeographed.
Ryan, Alan
1970 *The Philosophy of the Social Sciences.* London: Macmillan.
Ryan, Kevin; Johnston, John; and Newman, K.
1977 "An Interview with Ralph Tyler." *Phi Delta Kappan* 58 (March):544–547.

Sabers, D. L., and White, G. W.
1969 "The Effect of Differential Weighting of Individual Item Responses on the Predictive Validity and Reliability of an Aptitude Test." *Journal of Educational Measurement* 6:93–96.

Sartore, Richard L.
1975 "How Open Schools View Standardized Testing." *The SAANYS Journal* New York: School Administrators Association (March):25–26.

Schiller, Bradley R.
1970 "Stratified Opportunities: The Essence of the 'Vicious Circle'." *American Journal of Sociology* 76 (November):426–442.

Schoenberg, Ronald
1972 "Strategies for Meaningful Comparison." In *Sociological Methodology, 1972*, edited by Herbert L. Costner. San Francisco: Jossey-Bass.

Schrepel, Marie, and Laslett, H. R.
1936 "On the Loss of Knowledge by Junior High School Pupils Over the Summer Vacation." *Journal of Educational Psychology* 27:299–303.

Schultz, Raymond E.
1958 "A Comparison of Negro Pupils Ranking High with Those Ranking Low in Educational Achievement." *Journal of Educational Sociology* 31:265–270.

Schweitzer, Sybil, and Schweitzer, Donald G.
1971 "Comment on the Pearson *r* in Random Number and Precise Functional Scale Transformations." *American Sociological Review* 36 (June):518–519.

Scottish Council for Research in Education
1949 *The Trend of Scottish Intelligence.* London: University of London Press.

Sewell, William H., and Armer, J. Michael
1966 "Neighborhood Context and College Plans." *American Sociological Review* 31 (April):159–168.

Sewell, W. H., Haller, A. O., and Portes, A.
1969 "The Educational and Early Occupational Attainment Process." *American Sociological Review* 34 (February):82–92.

Sewell, W. H., Haller, A. O., and Ohlendorf, G. W.
1970 "The Educational and Early Occupational Attainment Process: Replication and Revision." *American Sociological Review* 35 (December):1014–1027.

Sewell, William H., and Hauser, Robert M.
1975 *Education, Occupation, and Earnings: Achievement in the Early Career.* New York: Academic Press.

Sewell, William H., Hauser, Robert M., and Featherman, David L., eds.
1976 *Schooling and Achievement in American Society.* New York: Academic Press.

Sewell, William H., and Shah, Vimal P.
1968 "Parent's Education and Children's Aspirations and Achievements." *American Sociological Review* 33 (April):191–209.

Sexton, Patricia
1961 *Education and Income.* New York: Viking Press.

Shapiro, M. M., Bresnahan, J. L., and Knopf, I. J.
n.d. "Achievement Test Scores in Children from Different Socioeconomic Levels." Progress report for OEO contract. Atlanta, Georgia: Emory University. Mimeographed.

Shaw, F.
1963 "Educating Culturally Deprived Youth in Urban Centers." *Phi Delta Kappan* 45:91–97.

Shulman, Lee S.
1970 "Reconstruction of Educational Research." *Review of Educational Research* 40 (June):371–396.

Sigel, I. E.
1963 "How Intelligence Tests Limit Understanding of Intelligence." *Merrill-Palmer Quarterly* 9:30–56.

Silberman, Charles E.
1970 *Crisis in the Classroom.* New York: Random House.

Simon, Brian
1973 *Intelligence, Psychology, and Education: A Marxist Critique.* London: Lawrence and Wishart.

Simpson, Richard L.
1962 "Parental Influence, Anticipatory Socialization, and Social Mobility." *American Sociological Review* 27:517–522.

Smith, Marshall
1972 "Equality of Educational Opportunity: The Basic Findings Reconsidered." In *On Equality of Educational Opportunity,* edited by Frederick Mosteller and Daniel P. Moynihan, pp. 230–242. New York: Random House.

Smyth, John A.
1971 "Utility and the Social Order: The Axiological Problem in Sociology." *British Journal of Sociology* 22:381–394.

Snedecor, George W., and Cochran, William G.
1967 *Statistical Methods,* 6th ed. Ames: Iowa State University.

Soar, Robert S., and Soar, Ruth M.
1969 "Pupil Subject Matter Growth During Summer Vacation." *Educational Leadership Research Supplement* 2 (March):577–587.

Solmon, Lewis C., and Taubman, Paul J., eds.
1973 *Does College Matter?* New York: Academic Press.

Sommers, Dixie, and Eck, Alan
1977 "Occupational Mobility in the American Labor Force." *Monthly Labor Review* 100 (January):3–19.

Sontag, L.; Baker, C. T.; and Nelson, Virginia L.
1958 "Mental Growth and Personality Development: A Longitudinal Study." *Monograph of the Society for Research in Child Development* 23 (No. 2). LaFayette, Indiana: Purdue University Child Development Publications.

Sørensen, Aage B., and Hallinan, Maureen T.
1977 "A Reconceptualization of School Effects." *Sociology of Education* 50 (October):273–289.

Spady, William G.
1976 "The Impact of School Resources on Students." In *Schooling and Achievement in American Society,* edited by William S. Sewell, Robert M. Hauser, and David L. Featherman, pp. 185–223. New York: Academic Press.

Spearman, C.
1927 *The Abilities of Man.* London: Macmillan.

St. John, Nancy
1970 "Desegregation and Minority Group Performance." *Review of Educational Research* 40 (February):111–133.

Staehle, Hans
1943 "Ability, Wages, and Income." *Review of Economic Statistics* 25 (February):77–87.

Stallings, Jane A.

1976 "How Instructional Processes Relate to Child Outcomes in a National Study of Follow Through." Menlo Park, California: Stanford Research Institute, February. Mimeograph.

Stake, Robert E.

1961 "Learning Parameters, Attitudes, and Achievements." *Psychometric Monograph 9*. Psychometric Society, np.

Stanley, Julian C.

1966 "Analysis of Variance of Gain Scores When Initial Assignment is Random." *Journal of Educational Measurement* 3:179–182.

1967 "General and Special Formulas for Reliability of Differences." *Journal of Educational Measurement* 4:249–252.

1971 "Reliability. In *Educational Measurement*, 2nd ed., edited by Robert L. Thorndike, pp. 356–442. Washington, D.C.: American Council on Education.

Stanley, Julian C., and Wang, M. D.

1970 "Weighting Test Items and Test-Item Options, an Overview of the Analytic and Empirical Literature." *Educational and Psychological Measurement* 30:21–35.

Stearns, Marian Sherman

1971 "The Effects of Preschool Programs on Children and Their Families." Santa Monica, Calif.: Rand Corporation. Mimeographed.

Steiner, George

1972 "After the Book?" *Visual Language* 6:197–210.

Stendler, Celia Burns

1949 *Children of Brasstown*. Urbana: University of Illinois.

Stephens, J. M.

1967 *The Process of Schooling*. New York: Holt.

Sterrett, M. D., and Davis, R. A.

1954 "The Permanence of School Learning: A Review of Studies." *Educational Administration and Supervision* 40:449–460.

Stevens, Joseph C., and Savin, Harris B.

1962 "On the Form of Learning Curves." *Journal of the Experimental Analysis of Behavior* 5 (January):15–18.

Stevens, S. S.

1951 "Mathematics, Measurements, and Psychophysics." In *Handbook of Experimental Psychology*, edited by S. S. Stevens. New York: Wiley.

1966 "A Metric for the Social Consensus." *Science* 151 (February):530–540.

Stinchcombe, Arthur

1965 *Rebellion in a High School*. Chicago: Quadrangle.

1968 *Constructing Social Theories*. New York: Harcourt.

1969 "Environment: The Cumulation of Effects Is Yet to Be Understood." *Harvard Educational Review* 39:511–522.

1972 "Theoretical Domains in Measurement." *Acta Sociologica* 16 (Fall):3–97.

Stone, Clarence N.

1976 *Economic Growth and Neighborhood Discontent: System Bias in the Urban Renewal Program of Atlanta*. Chapel Hill: University of North Carolina Press.

Summers, Anita A., and Wolfe, Barbara L.

1977 "Do Schools Make a Difference?" *The American Economic Review 67* (September):639–652.

Sundquist, J. L.

1969 *On Fighting Poverty*. New York: Basic Books.

Swidler, Ann
1975 "Organization Without Authority: A Study of Two Alternative Schools." Ph.D. dissertation, University of California, Berkeley.

Szalai, Alexander
1964 "Differential Work and Leisure Time Budgets." *New Hungarian Quarterly* 5:16.
1973 *The Use of Time.* The Hague: Mouton.

Tallmadge, G. Kasten, and Horst, Donald P.
1974 *A Procedural Guide for Validating Achievement Gains in Educational Projects.* RMC Research Corporation Report UR-240, May.

Taubman, Paul, and Wales, Terence
1972 *Mental Ability and Higher Educational Attainment.* New York: McGraw-Hill.
1973 "Higher Education, Mental Ability, and Screening." *Journal of Political Economy* 81 (January/February):28–55.

Thomas, Gail E.
1977 "Race and Sex Effects on Access to College." Center for Social Organization of Schools, Report No. 229. Baltimore, Md.: Johns Hopkins University, May. Mimeographed.

Thorndike, Robert L., ed.
1971 *Educational Measurement.* 2nd ed. Washington, D.C.: American Council on Education.

Thurow, Lester C.
1970 *Investment in Human Capital.* Belmont, Calif.: Wadsworth.

Tiedeman, H. R.
1948 "A Study of Retention of Classroom Learning." *Educational Research* 41:516–531.

Torgerson, W. S.
1958 *Theory and Methods of Scaling.* New York: Wiley.

Torrance, E. Paul
1965 "Different Ways of Learning for Different Kinds of Children." In *Mental Health and Achievement: Increasing Potential and Reducing School Dropout,* edited by E. P. Torrance and R. D. Strom, pp. 253–262. New York: Wiley.

Trow, Martin
1975 "Higher Education and Moral Development." In *Proceedings of the 1974 ETS Invitational Conference - Moral Development.* Princeton, N.J.: Educational Testing Service.

Tukey, John W.
1977 *Exploratory Data Analysis.* Reading, Mass.: Addison-Wesley.

Tyler, R. W., ed.
1969 *Educational Evaluation: New Roles, New Means. The 68th Yearbook of the National Society for the Study of Education,* part II. Chicago: University of Chicago Press.

Tyler, R. W., and Wolf, R. M., eds.
1974 *Crucial Issues in Testing.* Berkeley, Calif.: McCutchan.

U.S. Committee on Education and Labor
1967 *Annual Vacations and Vacation Laws: Recent Developments in the United States and Abroad.* Report prepared for the Select Subcommittee on Labor. 90th Congress, first session, March.

U.S. National Center for Health Statistics, U.S. Public Health Service
1964 *Vital Health Statistics: Medical Care, Health Status and Family Income,* series 10, no. 9. Washington, D.C.: U.S. Government Printing Office.

Vargo, Louis G.
1971 "Comment on 'The Assignment of Numbers to Rank Order Categories.' " *American Sociological Review* 36 (June):5178518.

Wachtel, Paul

1975 "The Effect of School Quality on Achievement, Attainment Levels, and Lifetime Earnings." *Explorations in Economic Research,* 2:502–536.

1976 "The Effect of Earnings of School and College Investment Expenditures." *Review of Economics and Statistics* 63:326–331.

Waller, Willard

1932 *The Sociology of Teaching.* New York: Wiley.

Wang, Marilyn W., and Stanley, Julian C.

1970 "Differential Weighting, A Survey of Methods and Empirical Studies." *Review of Educational Research* 40 (December):663–705.

Wasek, B., and Sibley, S. A.

1969 "An Experimental Summer Kindergarten for Culturally Deprived Children." Durham, N.C.: Duke University. Mimeographed.

Washington Research Project and Children's Defense Fund

1974 *Children Out of School in America: A Report by the Children's Defense Fund.* Washington, D.C.: Children's Defense Fund.

Weisbrod, Burton A.

1962 "Education and Investment in Human Capital." *Journal of Political Economy* 70 (October):S106–S123.

Wellman, B. L.

1940 *Iowa Studies on the Effects of Schooling. National Society for the Study of Education,* 39th Yearbook, part 2, pp. 377–399.

Werts, Charles E., and Linn, Robert L.

1969 "Analyzing School Effects: How to Use the Same Data to Support Different Hypotheses." *American Educational Research Journal* 6 (May):439–447.

Werts, Charles E., Joreskog, Karl G., and Linn, Robert L.

1971 "Comment on 'The Estimation of Measurement Error in Panel Data'." *American Sociological Review* 36 (February):110–113.

Westinghouse Learning Corporation

1969 *The Impact of Head Start: An Evaluation of Head Start on Children's Cognitive and Affective Development.* Springfield, Va.: Customer Service Clearinghouse, U.S. Department of Commerce.

Wheeler, L. R.

1942 "A Comparative Study of the Intelligence of East Tennessee Mountain Children." *Journal of Educational Psychology* 33:321–334.

White, Sheldon H.

1975 "Social Implications of IQ." *Principal* 54 (March–April):4–13.

Whitfield, Raymond P., and Egger, Eugene

1965 "School Attendance of Swiss and American Children." *School and Society* 93 (April):254–256.

Wilensky, Harold L.

1961 "The Uneven Distribution of Leisure: The Impact of Economic Growth on 'Free Time'." *Social Problems* 9 (Summer):32–56.

Wiley, David E.

1976 "Another Hour, Another Day: Quantity of Schooling, a Potent Path for Policy." In *Schooling and Achievement in American Society,* edited by William H. Sewell, Robert N. Hauser, and David L. Featherman, pp. 225–265. New York: Academic Press.

Wiley, David E., and Harnischfeger, Annegret

1974 "Explosion of a Myth: Quantity of Schooling and Exposure to Instruction." Major Educational Vehicles, Studies of Educative Processes Report No. 8, February. Mimeographed.

Wiley, David E., and Wiley, James A.
1970 "The Estimation of Measurement Error in Panel Data." *American Sociological Review* 35 (February):112–117.
Wiley, James A., and Wiley, Mary Glenn
1974 "A Note on Correlated Errors in Repeated Measurements." *Sociological Methods and Research* 3 (November):172–188.
Williams, E. B., and Tannenbaum, R. S.
1967 *Educational Enrichment for Disadvantaged In-School Neighborhood Youth Corps Enrollees During the Summer, 1967.* New York: Center for Urban Education.
Williams, Trevor
1976a "Teacher Prophecies and the Inheritance of Inequality." *Sociology of Education* 49 (July):223–236.
1976b "Abilities and Environments." In *Schooling and Achievement in American Society*, edited by W. H. Sewell, R. M. Hauser, and D. L. Featherman, pp. 61–101. New York. Academic Press.
Wilson, Alan B.
1959 "Residential Segregation of Social Classes and Aspirations of High School Boys." *American Sociological Review* 24 (December):836–845.
1963 "Social Stratification and Academic Achievement." In *Education in Depressed Areas*, edited by A. H. Passow. New York: Teachers College Press.
1969 *The Consequences of Segregation: Academic Achievement in a Northern Community*. Berkeley, Calif.: Glendessary Press.
Wilson, Kenneth L., and Portes, Alejandro
1975 "The Education Attainment Process: Results from a National Sample." *American Journal of Sociology* 81 (September):343–363.
Wilson, Thomas P.
1971 "Critique of Ordinal Variables." *Social Forces* 49:432–444.
Winch, Peter
1958 *The Idea of a Social Science and Its Relation to Philosophy*. New York: Humanities Press.
Winkler, Donald R.
1975 "Time and Learning: An Economic Analysis." Paper presented at the American Educational Research Association, April 3, Washington, D.C. Mimeographed.
Wonnacott, Ronald J., and Wonnacott, Thomas H.
1970 *Econometrics.* New York: Wiley.
Woodrow, H.
1946 "The Ability to Learn." *Psychological Review* 53:147–158.
Wright, Benjamin O.
1977 "Solving Measurement Problems with the Rasch Model." *Journal of Educational Measurement* 14 (Summer):97–116.
Wright, S.
1960 "Path Coefficients and Path Regressions: Alternative or Complementary Concepts?" *Biometrics* 16:423–445.
Zeaman, David, and House, Betty J.
1967 "The Relation of IQ and Learning." In *Learning and Individual Differences*, edited by Robert M. Gagné. Columbus, Ohio: Merrill.
Ziegler, Carl W.
1928 "School Attendance as a Factor in School Progress." *Contributions to Education* 297, Teachers College, Columbia University.
Zusman, J., and Wurster, C. R., eds.
1975 *Program Evaluation: Alcohol, Drug Abuse, and Mental Health Services.* Lexington, Mass.: Heath.

Author Index

Subject Index

A
B
C 8
D 9
E 0
F 1
G 2
H 3
I 4
J 5